PARIS MANHATTAN

PARIS MANHATTAN

Writings on Art

━━━━━◆━━━━━

PETER WOLLEN

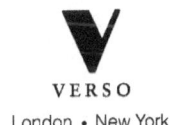

London • New York

First published by Verso 2004
© Peter Wollen 2004
All rights reserved

The moral rights of the author have been asserted

1 3 5 7 9 10 8 6 4 2

Verso
UK: 6 Meard Street, London W1F 0EG
USA: 388 Atlantic Ave, Brooklyn, NY 11217
www.versobooks.com

Verso is the imprint of New Left Books

ISBN 978-1-85984-403-8

British Library Cataloguing in Publication Data
Wollen, Peter, 1938–
  Paris Manhattan: writings on art
  1. Art, Modern – 20th century – History
  I. Title.
  700.9'04

  ISBN 1859844038 (paperback)
  ISBN 1859845800 (hardback)

Library of Congress Cataloging-in-Publication Data
Wollen, Peter.
  Paris Manhattan: writings on art / Peter Wollen.
    p. cm.
  Includes bibliographical references and index.
  ISBN 1–85984–403–8 (pbk.: alk. paper) ISBN 1–85984–580–0 (hardcover: alk. paper) 1. Arts.
  I. Title.

  NX65.W65 2004
  700'.9–dc22
                                          2003025192

Typeset in Garamond
Printed in the United States

CONTENTS

1	Government by Appearances	1
2	Global Conceptualism and North American Conceptual Art	15
3	Tanks	35
4	The Question of Technology	51
5	Museums and Rubbish Theory	61
6	October 18, 1977	75
7	Kitsch	87
8	Salome	101
9	Blue	113
10	Magritte and the Bowler Hat	128
11	Mappings: Situationists and/or Conceptualists	146
12	Art and Fashion: Friends or Enemies?	161
13	The Myth of the West	182
14	The Situationists and Architecture	202
15	Barthes, Hitchcock, Burgin	219
16	Fridamania	235

Select Bibliography	249
Acknowledgements	257
Index	259

I

GOVERNMENT BY APPEARANCES

In the course of his celebrated discussion of Jeremy Bentham's Panopticon, Michel Foucault wondered whether Bentham had got the idea of his ideal prison from Le Vau's octagonal design for Louis XIV's menagerie at Versailles:

> At the centre was an octagonal pavilion which, on the first floor, consisted of only a single room, the king's salon; on every side large windows looked out onto seven cages (the eighth was reserved for the entrance), containing different species of animals. By Bentham's time, this menagerie had disappeared. But one finds in the programme of the Panopticon a similar concern with individuating observation, with characterization and classification, with the analytic arrangement of space. The Panopticon is a royal menagerie; the animal is replaced by man, individual distribution by specific grouping and the king by the machinery of a furtive power.

Like the Panopticon, Louis's menagerie was a kind of observatory, in which from a single central point of view, a series of specimens, both confined and illuminated, could be examined and controlled. Observation was indeed for Louis a form of mastery. As Colbert noted at the opening of a new Observatory in 1671: 'Triumphal Arch for the conquests of the Earth. Observatory for the heavens'.

It is hard not to take another step and wonder whether it was not so much the menagerie, as the Court of Versailles itself that was the virtual prototype of the Panopticon. In the *Mémoires* prepared for his son and heir, Louis came rapidly to this vivid summation, when discussing the work of the King:

> All that is most necessary to this work is at the same time agreeable; for, in a word, my son, it is to have one's eyes open to the whole earth; to learn each hour the news concerning every province and every nation, the secrets of every court, the moods and the weaknesses of every prince and every foreign minister; to be well-informed on an infinite number of matters about which we are supposed to know nothing; to elicit from our subjects what they hide from us with the greatest care; to discover the most remote opinions of our own courtiers and the most hidden interests of those who come to us with quite contrary professions. I do not know of any other pleasure we would not renounce for that, even if it was given to us out of curiosity alone.

In a nutshell, the nobility of France were confined, illuminated (and classified) in the palace of Versailles in order to gratify the solar scopophilia of their all-seeing supervisor, a pleasure in looking which led directly to the sublimated sadism of his pleasure in governing and ordering.

Yet Louis's regime is usually associated not with surveillance so much as with spectacle, with exhibitionism rather than voyeurism, with the fabrication of the king's image as visual spectacle, rather than the pleasure of the king as the furtive power at the centre of a global Panopticon. Foucault begins his book by describing, in grim and gruesome detail, the 'spectacle of the scaffold', a ceremony of annihilation, displaying an absolute lack of power, in contrast to the positive spectacles of the king's totalized surplus of power—the coronation, the entry into a subject city, the submissive ceremonial of the court. Yet, in Foucault's view, this regime of the spectacle was soon to be swept away and reversed by a new regime—that of surveillance, with the Panopticon rather than the public scaffold as its emblematic figure. In the economy of the spectacle, the annihilation or concentration of power were doubled by a spectacular fragmentation or surplus of the body, whereas within that of surveillance, the body is idealized (the observer) or classified and disciplined (the observed), reduced to an abstract order rather than vividly displayed in its concrete carnality.

It is clear that the image of Louis XIV was indeed that of a spectacularly excessive body, enhanced by all the resources of art, ceremonial and ritual. It was a body magnified and designed to be looked at. Courtiers were forbidden to turn their back on it and, in his absence, they were even forbidden to turn their back on his portrait, which hung in his place, and substituted for his presence, a true 'representation'. Perhaps the most directly spectacular display of the king's body was that of the king as dancer. In this role, the king was explicitly a performer, literally centre-stage in the theatrical sense. The king danced over a hundred roles in public and the court ballet was, for a period, the leading art form of the court, in which the royal family and high nobility both participated as performers and formed the admiring audience, attending as both stars and fans.

Louis's father had himself been an accomplished dancer and musician, dancing in court ballets and singing and playing the lute to airs of his own composition. From an early age, Louis was given dancing lessons and he became an adept and enthusiastic pupil. He is said by a contemporary to have had a dancing lesson every day for over 20 years from his dancing master, Charles Beauchamps, and his medical records show evidence of collapse after exhausting dance rehearsals as well as injury incurred by strenuous vaulting. He seems to have had an acute musical sense, being able 'to distinguish among a troop of musicians the one who makes a false note', and as a result he insisted on high musical standards at his court. During his youth, he is reported to have practiced the guitar and discussed dance steps rather than sit through tedious meetings of the royal council. The Venetian ambassador noted censoriously in 1652, when Louis was 14, that 'games, dances and comedies are the king's sole pursuits'. The previous year he had made his debut public appearance on the serious stage as a dancer in the Court Ballet of the Feasts of Bacchus, in which he appeared in a number of roles, culminating in that of Apollo.

Louis continued to dance on stage for almost 20 years. He made his final public appearance in 1670, leaving the stage, of course, once more in the role of Apollo. Thus, dance was not simply a childhood pursuit, to be abandoned with maturity. On the contrary, he continued to dance in public for ten years after his famous seizure of power, following the death of Mazarin and the arrest of Fouquet. Perhaps even more significantly, the first Academy he established was the Royal Academy of Dance. Louis took power on 10 March 1661 and on 31 March he issued the Letters Patent which established the new Academy. As he observed in the Letters,

> The art of dance has always been recognized as one of the most respectable and necessary to train the body and to give it the first and most natural dispositions to every kind of exercise, to that of arms among others; consequently, it is one of the most advantageous and useful to our nobility and to others who have the honour of approaching us, not just in war times, but even in times of peace in the divertissements of our ballets.

The establishment of Academies became a keystone of Louis's regime. First, this fulfilled a mercantilist function, establishing the arts as a form of luxury good, no longer imported at great expense from Italy, but produced under the direction of the state, thus contributing to the abundant wealth and treasure of France. Second, there was also a propaganda function, glorifying the king and celebrating his exploits. The Academies further institutionalized the cultural program favoured by Louis of honouring serious training and serious learning as the armature of courtly accomplishments, thus encouraging the formation of a polished and reasonable court culture rather than a crude and passionate one; more sublimated, less driven. This softening or sweetening of the court was, of course, particularly 'useful', as Louis liked to say, in that it diminished the threat of impulsive noble outbursts, which in previous times had led to disorder and disobedience. The Academies also served a direct political function in limiting and replacing the authority of the old independent craft guilds.

At the same time, lessons in dance were coupled with lessons in arms. Louis himself makes the same linkage in his *Mémoires*, when he remarks that 'if you believe your dancing master and your master-at-arms, and all the others, they will tell you, and it is true, that their art requires a total commitment [l' homme tout entier] and there is always something still to learn'—but, Louis continues, the king has to draw a limit to these pleasurable pursuits, which although they are worthwhile—even politically worthwhile—can become counter-productive in their effects if they are taken to extremes and thus detract from other weightier priorities. He reminds his heir of the bygone king who asked his son why he was not ashamed to perform so well on the lyre. This section, incidentally, was edited in its final form, by Pelisson, soon after Louis's own last on-stage performance.

Louis's establishment of the Academy of Dance was contested, naturally enough, by the musicians' guild, the Brotherhood of Saint-Julian, who argued that dancing should not be separated from music, which was its model. The dancing masters, in response, argued that dance was independent of music. They too stressed the importance of training the body and improving its posture and gait, noting that good dancers had often been able to rise rapidly in a military career. Trained dancers are 'more able to serve their prince in battles and to please him in divertissements'. The violins to which dancers danced were no more necessary, they argued, than the drums and trumpets which encouraged soldiers to fight. The violins did not dictate the movements of the dance any more than the drums dictated the course of the battle. Here, it should be noted, the choreographers were implicitly comparing themselves to officers, in charge of both drill and manoeuvres. Dance, they also argued, improves the mind as well as the body, by polishing the manners of the nation, unlike music, which, by implication, acts only on the passions. Perhaps also they had in mind the character of dance as an emblematic art, much emphasized by other contemporary theorists, especially the Jesuits, who insisted on the allegorical aspect of dance as 'mute poetry'.

Given the support of the king, the dancers were of course vindicated. However, the establishment of an Academy had long-term and, I think, unforeseen repercussions. One of Louis's main motivations seems to have been his wish to improve the standard of dancing at court, which had been disrupted by the effects of the Fronde in the previous decade. In the end, however, the Academy led to a professionalization of dance, from which even the most gifted amateurs found themselves excluded. In this respect, the history of dance in France in the seventeenth century is not unlike the history of sports such as cricket in England in the nineteenth century, as professional 'Players' gradually gained the upper hand over amateur 'Gentlemen'. Gentlemen survived longest as team captains, before this citadel too finally fell to the Players. Even today, however, they still carry weight as team selectors! Much the same trajectory was followed in the dance. Originally, all the dancers were amateurs. Then professionals were added (first male, then female) in supporting roles, until, finally all the performers were professional, even if the patrons remained amateur.

This professionalization of the stage following the establishment of the Academy was also accompanied by the development of Italian perspective stage design and the lavish use of Italian stage machinery. The Italian stage designers and machinists, Torelli and Vigorelli, were imported into Paris to construct machines for special effects, first in a specialized *salle des machines* at the Tuileries palace, then for use in the open-air festivals at Versailles which became a major preoccupation of the king. Unlike the traditional court ballet, which was fundamentally a shrovetide entertainment, incorporating elements of carnival masquerade and grotesquerie, these large-scale productions were financed, not from the Office of Small Pleasures [*menus plaisirs*], but out of Colbert's budget for Buildings. Consequently they were also memorialized by Felibien, the official historian of royal artistic enterprises. Before Louis's seizure of power, Mazarin had tried to import Italian opera into the French court, on the model of the Barberini court in Rome, complete with professional Italian singers, including castrati. But as a result of violent political opposition, this was dropped until the Italian-born Lully proved able to launch a suitably French form of opera, *tragedie lyrique*. An Academy of Opera was established by Louis in June, 1969, a few months before his departure from the stage, and Lully's first opera, *Psyche*, was the command performance which immediately followed the abandonment of court ballet by Louis. Opera, of course, involved fully professional singers and musicians, while still retaining professional dancers for interludes.

Thus the spectacle of the king and nobility as dancers could only last as long as the gap between amateur and professional performance had not widened too visibly. The perspective stage, with its transformation of point-of-view and clear separation of performer and spectator into two distinct spaces, was a precondition of professionalization, as was the capital investment involved in complex stage machinery. As Louis recognized, kings could not allow themselves to be, in effect, professionalized, however great their natural gifts and ambition to excel. The king was forced to choose social dancing rather than show dancing. Court ballet had originally emerged out of informal revels and, soon after Louis's retirement from the stage, the court returned to social dancing, but in a more formal mode, dependent on dancing masters as leaders of fashion, while their professional performances were displaced from court on to the commercial stage.

Thus, in the palace of Versailles, dancing still remained a central feature of court life, alongside card-playing and billiards, but it was no longer spectacular. It had become, once again, simply a pastime. On the other hand, it was a much more ordered and polished pastime than it was in the days of the Valois. One of the main achievements of the Academy was to refine the social dances learned by the nobility. The energetic hopping and cavorting of rustic and exotic dances was smoothed into the acceptable forms of the court versions of the gavotte, courante, minuet and so on. In fact, the minuet began its long reign precisely in 1670, when it was first danced socially at court. In effect, from the point of view of a courtier, the recreational minuet replaced the spectacular court ballet, which abandoned the court for the theatre.

This process of refinement went hand-in-hand with those of notation and standardization. It was in this period that Charles Beauchamps developed, for the Academy, the dance notation of graphs and symbols which, in due course, allowed any aspiring dancer to learn and study social dances at home from a handbook. These books all had a similar structure: first comes a description and notation of the five basic positions of the feet, then the five so-called 'false' positions (used for comic effect), then the basic steps, then their combination into dance routines, then extra details like arm movements. They also contained instruction on the various modes of bowing, curtseying and so on, which framed the dances by constituting and de-constituting the couple. In the more sophisticated books, court etiquette was also described, as an essential part of the framing of the dance, explaining how to relate to the presence of the king. The dancing-master who wrote or used these books pedagogically became a key figure in aristocratic society and, in the end, a much-lampooned target for reformers and revolutionaries, who sought a less 'artificial' and more 'natural' body.

At the same time, the choreography and notation of the professional ballet as a theatrical form was also developed. Indeed, ballet still uses the

French terminology-of-art developed in Beauchamps' Academy. It might almost be said that bureaucracy and ballet were the two great legacies left us by Louis XIV—and perhaps this would neither have surprised nor shocked him! Like the ant and the grasshopper, they formed a linked pair of contraries. Indeed, Louis divided his time between administrative duties in the morning, hunting in the afternoon, dancing and diversion in the evening, and sleep and sex at night. It was in the morning and the evening that he made his most lasting contributions. Both administration and dancing came to require, under his regime, the establishment of accurate records, fixed routines and assiduous practice.

In this sense, we can see in dance itself the seeds of the disciplined social order that Foucault was to write about in *Discipline and Punish*. Indeed, Foucault himself comments on the role played by the institution of military drill in France at the same period. The military provides the third term that links bureaucracy and ballet: both the hierarchical, rule-governed model of organization and the site of bodily discipline and routine, displayed theatrically in the form of the military review. Indeed, the seventeenth-century army shared with seventeenth-century dance not only a fascination with measure and rhythm, but also a certain spirit of geometry: the complex patterns traced on the floor by the dancers and illustrated in the dancing manuals have their counterparts in the patterns made by marching soldiers on the parade ground, or even the plans for fortifications drawn up for Louis XIV by Vauban. Similarly, the regime of confinement which Louis instituted in his army by building barracks paralleled not only his construction of prisons, hospitals and orphanages, but also the enclosure of the nobility in the palace of Versailles, where the dance-floor replaced the drill-hall.

Military activities, like dancing, were also enacted as spectacles for the court, which Louis would take with him in order to observe and applaud a siege, and, in the recreational form of riding and hunting, they were also part of the everyday social life of the king and the courtiers. Indeed, in the spectacular Carrousel or tournament, soldiering and dancing more or less blended together, as intricate equestrian ballet merged with competitive jousting in one choreographed show. It was at the Carrousel of 1662 that Louis first assumed his heraldic device of the Sun as an official emblem. In his *Mémoires*, he dwells on this Carrousel at some length, describing how, originally intended simply as a light amusement, it was expanded into a magnificent allegorical spectacle. He reflects on its double impact on the people at large and on the court in particular. For the multitude, it was simply a spectacle, and, as such, more effective in winning their hearts than tangible rewards or benefits. For the court, however, it was a way of sharing and, so to speak, co-operating in an enjoyable activity with his nobles, so that they were charmed by his courteous familiarity with them. In a word, it was a convivial way of bonding, while at the same time preserving a necessary formality and ceremonial calibration of rank.

Louis explained this in two contexts. On the one hand, he harked back to the excesses and disorders of the Fronde. Louis drew two conclusions from this traumatic period. First, as king, he should centralize power. Second, he should convince the nobility that this was really to their benefit. This was to be done by appealing not simply to their interests, but also to their passions. Immuring his nobility at court both separated them from their local, territorial power bases, but also opened up for them the chance of participating in a novel and splendid way of life, in which the king shared his greatest pleasures with them. Together they would form a glorious company, like the Gods of Olympus or like Charlemagne and his paladins, model courts invoked over and over again in the ballets and other divertissements he organized for them. They would ride with the king, feast with the king, dance with the king, act with the king, identify with the king.

In contrast, on the other hand, Louis drew the picture of the cruel despot who ruled over a servile people by means of fear and terror. Evidently, Louis was willing to resort to cruel means in dealing with rebels or in raising taxes (from which the nobility were mostly immune), but as far as the court was concerned, charm and good feeling were to be the rule of the day. Despots, he pointed out, hid themselves away, so that they were scarcely ever seen. Louis, on the other hand, was happy to hold audiences and to hear public requests and petitions. He willingly mingled with the nobility every day, sharing their lives, while still retaining the necessary formal distance. Thus Louis sat comfortably in his armchair, while the court perched nearby on stools or remained standing, at a slight distance, and he scarcely ever chose to tower over them from an elevated throne—only, in fact, when he joined them in greeting the Ambassadors from Turkey, Persia, Algiers and Siam. Plainly there was an implicit theory of 'Oriental Despotism' here. But the significant point was that Louis routinely granted access to his subjects ('the honour of approaching'), particularly to the nobility, whereas despots hid themselves away like the furtive powers in the Panopticon. Dancing together was an important aspect of this strategy of access and conviviality, meant to underline the fact that the common interests of king and nobility ran deeper than their differences. It symbolically recreated the ambiance of an earlier feudal society, with its ties of personal loyalty and its mythic bodily solidarity of Frankish race and noble blood.

It is clear that the connection between spectacle and surveillance is more complex than the simple transition which Foucault suggests. Indeed, this has already been pointed out in other contexts. For instance, Jonathan Crary, in his book *Techniques of the Observer*, dealing with nineteenth-century theories and techniques of perception, notes that 'Foucault's opposition of surveillance and spectacle seems to overlook how the effects of these two regimes of power can coincide'. 'The organization of mass culture', he continues, as it developed in the nineteenth century, 'was fully embedded within the same transformations Foucault outlines'—namely regulation, codification, fixing the observer and so on. Crary obviously wishes to integrate Foucault's concept of surveillance with Guy Debord's concept of the 'Society of the Spectacle'. Nonetheless, like Foucault, he still sees a crucial break occurring at the beginning of the nineteenth century, with the ever-increasing 'dissociation of touch from sight' occurring 'within a pervasive "separation of the senses" and industrial remapping of the body' that marks the end of absolutism. Thus, in Crary's view, both Foucault and Debord were investigating the different but related social consequences of the abstraction and promotion of the sense of sight—in both surveillance and spectacle—which have characterized the last two centuries.

In support of this view, Crary cites a passage from Debord's book on *The Society of the Spectacle*, which runs, in Crary's own translation, as follows:

> Since the spectacle's job is to cause a world that is no longer directly perceptible [*saisissable*] to be seen via different specialized mediations, it is inevitable that it should elevate the human sense of sight to the special place

once occupied by touch; the most abstract of the senses, and the most easily deceived [*mystifiable*], sight is naturally the most readily adaptable to present-day society's generalized abstraction.

I have two immediate comments to make on this quotation in relation to Louis XIV. First, the sense of sight was already paramount to Louis, who in fact could not be touched, except in the prescribed manner or at his own wish or command. Second, Louis used many different 'specialized mediations' in order to make his own image seen, as detailed most recently, for example, in Peter Burke's *The Fabrication of Louis XIV*.

Essentially, what we are dealing with when we use terms like 'surveillance' and 'spectacle' is the optical register of the administrative and the theatrical mentalities. The former seeks to gather the maximum information and, for this reason, to improve and elaborate the means and techniques of perception, particularly optical perception. As Louis noted, it is a centripetal system. The latter seeks to reach the maximum audience for a performance or an exhibition, and, for this reason, to improve and elaborate the means of optical display. It is a centrifugal system. Louis XIV was committed to both types of system—both gathering information about others and distributing information about himself. In each case he made use of a variety of 'specialized mediations', such as official records and paid informers, on the one hand, and a profusion of medals, paintings, gazettes and so on, on the other. In the court, the two systems began to converge: courtiers were typically both informers and spectators.

In *The Society of the Spectacle*, Guy Debord differentiated between 'concentrated' and 'diffuse' forms of the modern social spectacle. Stalinist Russia and Nazi Germany produced tightly controlled 'concentrated' forms of artistic and media spectacle, monopolizing the field of public display with government-controlled propaganda. In effect, these were 'post-absolutist' societies, which sprang up in the crisis caused by the collapse of the ancien regimes in Russia and Germany, the one based on a monopoly of state ownership beyond Louis's wildest dreams, the other occupying the centre of political power while allowing a regulated, directed and protectionist form of capitalism, on more strictly Ludovican lines. Neither, however, depended on the existence of a Versailles. On the contrary, both Stalin and Hitler functioned much more like the despots from whom Louis differentiated himself. Stalin certainly ruled his Politburo and party barons by terror, and Hitler's bloody disposal of Romm provided the unspoken backdrop to Riefenstahl's spectacular *Triumph of the Will*. The 'diffuse' spectacle, on the other hand, typical of democratic regimes, in which the state can only influence—rather than control—the media, necessarily requires the development of forms of elite bonding.

Like the king of France, the president of the United States seeks through his Office of Communications, to produce and control a constant flow of favourable images. Similarly, he receives a constant flow of sensitive intelligence. The major difference is that, as an elected monarch, he must seek to manipulate public opinion in ways that the god-ordained Louis would have found incredible. The president, like the king, sees himself as potential prey to a host of special interests [*intérêts particuliers*]—lobbies, Congress, press and so on, rather than great magnates, Parliaments or church. Within his court—'inside the Beltway' as it is known—the president actually prefers to use more direct means of contact—handshakes or telephone calls, for instance. But in order to command these rival centres of power, the president acts both by exerting pressure downwards, through his own authority and resources, and also upwards, by influencing the media and manipulating public opinion in order to bring pressure to bear from beneath.

But perhaps the most interesting analogue to the court ballet is the 'Corporate Convention', which, as Judith Barry has pointed out, bears surprising resemblances to the Stuart masque, the English equivalent to the French court ballet. Barry writes that

> this kind of production exists today, not in statecraft per se, but in the central controlling metaphor of life, that of corporate capitalism .... This form of corporate spectacle is a relatively recent phenomenon developed over the last ten years and used increasingly to manage the non-tangible aspects of worker-relations in an increasingly white-collar work-force .... The corporations have identified that these are personnel who need to be continually motivated .... Furthermore, they realize that capitalism is built on intangibles and the deliberate manufacture of specific ideological systems. Consequently, they are looking for ways to foster company loyalty as well as lower absenteeism and boost productivity. In developing the idea

of the corporate spectacle, they have, perhaps inadvertently, returned to the Renaissance model outlined above .... Usually the president and his assistants participate directly in the spectacle as the stars or announcers; the overt message is nearly always masked, using entertainment, story-ideas and humor; and there is the use of elaborate and expensive special-effects to please the audience and add a 'specialness' to the occasion .... It is not unusual for a multi-media presentation to be followed by a kind of variety show, complete with stars, but hosted by the president of the company.

The corporation is a closed group which maintains the hierarchical power structure elaborated within the absolutist bureaucracy. In this sense it is like the army, with its parades and war-games (our tournaments), or the church, with its ornate rituals and theatrical ceremonies. These institutions exist within and alongside the structures of the state, but without involvement in its democratic forms. They are like islands of late feudalism which have survived into the twentieth century from the seventeenth when, indeed, they first took their historic form. For Guy Debord, the court was simply the ornamental feudal finery worn by the proto-bourgeois state bureaucracy which was the essence of Louis's regime. In fact, he was wrong. The court—the alliance of king and landed nobility—was the essence of absolutism. Bureaucracy was the secondary device which it passed on in different forms to its successors—to Western democracy, to fascism and to communism. Bureaucracy was the instrument of power rather than its agent.

In effect, Foucault's book is about the mentality of bureaucracy. Hence its retrospective gaze back to the menagerie at Versailles, a symbol, in its way, of the bureaucratic vision which was first fully developed by Louis XIV. If there is a moment when we can see a point of transition, not from a society of the spectacle to one of surveillance, but from a pre-modern to a modern society, it is at some moment of mutation within Louis's reign. Commentators have chosen many different moments to exemplify this shift of mentality, this victory of the modern over the ancient. I agree with Jean-Marie Apostolidès, who, in his book *Le Roi-machine*, identifies the crucial moment as that when Louis left the stage on the 7 February—shrovetide—1670. By removing his own body from view as centre of the spectacle, he transformed himself into the ghost in the machine, the abstract supervisor of the Panopticon and the subject of media representation rather than performance.

There are probably many reasons why Louis took this decision, not least the recurrent giddy spells from which he was suffering at the time, which his doctor dates and describes in the medical record. But the effect, as we have seen, was to put an end to the ballet as an amateur form and propel the spectacle as a professional form into the market-place, thus establishing the conditions for 'diffuse' rather than 'concentrated' spectacle. In part, of course, this was because Louis, now bent on military conquest, was no longer willing to pay for it out of either personal or state funds. In part, as I have argued above, it was because his favourite musician, Jean-Baptiste Lully (also a dancer) had finally convinced Louis that a French form of opera was viable, and persuaded Louis to give him control over the new Academy entrusted with its presentation. Above all, perhaps, it was because Louis was preparing himself for the great series of disastrous wars which in due course destroyed the reforms and achievements of the sixties.

Apostolidés sees the ensuing Versailles period as a process of gradual petrifaction, whereby life was slowly drained from Louis's body into a dead machine. It is as if the legacy of Apollo himself was split into two—on the one hand, the patron of the arts, who presided over the dance of the Muses, and on the other, the celestial centre-point whose movements were entirely predictable, never halting or deviating for an instant, around whom his courtiers rotated in their prescribed paths. Dance, on the other hand, was to enjoy its own history, tied in the form of ballet to the courts and nobility of Europe right up to the twentieth century, when reform finally came—internally from Diaghilev and his collaborators, externally from the counter-cultural modern dance of Isadora Duncan and her successors. Ballet, the body aesthetic, proved able to regain its energy and originality, to become, once again, an exemplary spectacle, albeit with a new and reformed regime of the body. The monarchical absolute state, on the other hand, the body politic, which nurtured it, finally disappeared. Following Foucault, we might say, more prudently, that the body of the ant mutated into the bureaucratic ant-heap of modern society. No doubt the balletic grasshopper will still have to pay for its bodily pleasure in the end.

2

GLOBAL CONCEPTUALISM AND NORTH AMERICAN CONCEPTUAL ART

Conceptualism, as this exhibition suggests,* was a global movement. However, unlike surrealism, which had important adherents and followers in the Caribbean, Mexico, Japan and the Arab world, it did not simply spread out from a centre in Europe or the United States—from the traditional art capitals of Paris or New York. Conceptualism was a genuinely broad-based trend—Japanese or Latin American conceptualism, for example, each had their own, quite distinct local trajectories with their own unique characteristics. Nonetheless, because of its strategic location at the institutional centre of the global art world and because of its self-conscious militancy, North American conceptual art inevitably came to play a disproportionate role in the emergence of a lasting and much broader conceptualist movement. This broader movement, which still dominates key sectors of the art world, would never have become so widely and lastingly influential, however, if it had not been for the impetus initially given to it by New York-based conceptual artists, whose breakthrough came in the late 1960s. To grasp the spread of conceptualism as a broad global movement, it is essential to understand both that it was multipolar in its origins and that it was the creation of a very small, but very vocal and productive, phalanx of artists, strategically situated in New York and committed to a typically avant-garde strategy, complete with

* 'Global Conceptualism: Points of Origin 1950–1980', Queens Museum of Art, New York, 1999.

manifestos, journals and theoretical statements. Working in an atmosphere of powerful group solidarity riven with contention, these artists set the theoretical parameters which consequently made it possible for conceptual art to transform the landscape of the global art world in a lasting way.

Conceptual art sealed the fate of modernism in the visual arts, but paradoxically it also brought back into currency the avant-garde ideas of Marcel Duchamp and the Russian constructivists, particularly Rodchenko and Tatlin. Moholy-Nagy's telephone paintings played their part too. Without these avant-garde commitments and its base in the Manhattan art world, it would not have been able to play its historic role. Traditionally, avant-gardism had been seen not as an ongoing artistic tendency with a history of its own, but as a series of isolated outbursts each of which was eventually subsumed into the ongoing history of modernism itself. But in the end it was a new avant-garde, imitating the model of the avant-gardes of the past, that finished modernism off, thus revealing how different their respective missions had always really been. These avant-gardes had never been content simply with finding artistic means appropriate to modernity, to the massive changes which transformed our culture and society from the mid-nineteenth century onwards. Rather, they had always sought, as Peter Burger long since established, to expand their frontiers beyond the core of the art world itself—painting, sculpture, visual design—to make forays into the neighbouring arts and into much broader cultural and political regions. Essentially, these avant-gardes proposed a series of new methodologies and ontologies, new theoretical foundations for art, which were subsequently ransacked for useful technical tricks and formal strategies by the mainstream of modernism. Conceptualism comprised many different tendencies in different countries and continents, which were only retroactively herded together to form an '-ism' fit to take its place alongside cubism, expressionism, dadaism, surrealism, popism, minimalism, and so on, all tributaries flowing into the greater stream of modern art history. But, by so doing, critics and historians robbed conceptual art of its paradoxical distinction—that of being the last avant-garde of all, the one which modernism found it impossible to digest, whose impact had to be smoothed out and rationalized by the invention of a new period hold-all, 'post-modernism', somewhat pathetic in its prepositional dependence on its great predecessor.

The time has come, with this exhibition, to look back at the history of conceptual art and try to understand its significance in a new light, one which challenges the everyday assumptions which underlie the historiography of twentieth-century culture. In this essay, I would like to emphasize from the start, I am writing specifically about North American art— about art in New York, most of all, but also in San Francisco, San Diego, Los Angeles, Toronto, Vancouver and elsewhere, each developing, as we shall see, in significantly different ways. The history of conceptual art in other regions of the world was still more diverse, reflecting their very different circumstances, very different antecedents and very different preoccupations, even if the New York terminology (which we owe primarily to critics' efforts to understand the work of Joseph Kosuth and Sol LeWitt) eventually superseded that of *arte povera*, systems art, language art, information art and so on. It was to be the example of North America which cast a long shadow over developments elsewhere, until all were conveniently huddled together under the same elastic rubric: 'conceptualism'. From this totalizing point of view, conceptual art might canonically seem to have begun in New York in 1967 with the opening at the The Museum of Normal Art of an exhibition titled 'Normal Art', organized by Joseph Kosuth, in which he put together work from a number of artists who later became central figures in the history of the movement—Mel Bochner, Hanne Darboven, Dan Graham, Kosuth himself, Christine Kozlov, Sol LeWitt and Lee Lozano—together with others who would more likely be grouped as minimalists or land artists, such as Carl André, Eva Hesse, Donald Judd, Robert Morris, Robert Ryman, Robert Smithson and even Frank Stella.

Or perhaps, purists might more properly argue, New York conceptual art began in 1968, when the 'Xeroxbook' show, organized by Seth Siegelaub and John W. Wendler, featured work only in the form of a xeroxed catalog, with no on-site gallery exhibits at all. The artists included were Carl André, Robert Barry, Douglas Huebler, Joseph Kosuth, Robert Morris and Lawrence Weiner. This show was followed by another, opening in the first week of 1969 when Barry, Huebler, Kosuth and Weiner showed their work in a rented office space on 52nd Street, intended only as an adjunct to the catalogue descriptions. Nineteen sixty-nine was clearly the year when the movement took off, culminating in an exhibition entitled 'Conceptual Art and Conceptual Aspects' in which Barry, Bochner, Kosuth, Kozlov and Weiner were joined by a more cosmopolitan contingent—Art & Language, Iain Baxter, Daniel Buren, Jan Dibbets, Hans Haacke, On Kawara, Adrian Piper, Ian Wilson and others. In this year, too, significant shows took place in North American cities other than New York. In April there was a show at Newport Beach with Michael Asher, John Baldessari, Barry Le Va and Allen Ruppersberg. In July there was 'Conception-Perception' at the Eugenia Butler Gallery in Los Angeles, with Baldessari, Huebler, Kosuth, Le Va and Weiner. The same month, Seth Siegelaub initiated a show organized 'at various locations throughout the world'—five in Europe, three in the United States (Baltimore, Los Angeles and Niagara Falls), two in Mexico (US artists though: Kosuth and Smithson) and one in Canada (N. E. Thing Co. in Vancouver) or two if you count the other side of the Niagara Falls! Then, in February 1970, Tom Marioni founded the Museum of Conceptual Art in San Francisco, which housed not only a vigorous art scene with members and exhibitions, but also an art collection, always a tell-tale sign that a movement has arrived.

The three things that struck me when I studied this chronology were, first, that this period (1967–69) was also a period of unusually intense political militancy and cultural upheaval, ranging across black power, the student movement, solidarity with Third World struggles, the beginnings of feminism, the Summer of Love and organized opposition to the Vietnam War; second, the speed with which a movement crystallized by bringing together artists from many different backgrounds, artists whose turn to conceptualism was given a special organizational impetus from the group around Seth Siegelaub and Joseph Kosuth, functioning something like a traditional avant-garde; third, that Sol LeWitt, except for the 'Xeroxbook' show and representation of his work in 'Information', a big survey exhibition at MoMA in 1970, seems to have pursued a somewhat solitary path, in which his published work in journals was arguably more important than actual exhibitions, although, of course, these continued. His 'Paragraphs on Conceptual Art' appeared in *ArtForum* in June 1967 and, two years later, his 'Sentences On Conceptual Art' were published in New York in *0/9* (April 1969) and in the first issue of *Art-Language* in England, the following month.

In retrospect, we can see that LeWitt's crisply programmatic texts, like Kosuth's more rambling and much longer theoretical articles, were particularly important historically precisely because conceptual art differentiated itself from other movements preceding or paralleling it by its self-reflexive character, its insistence that it required a meta-language if it was to be understood and that meta-language was intrinsic to the work. The extrinsic meta-language of LeWitt's 'Sentences' and 'Paragraph' served to clarify what this intrinsic meta-language was, to provide a rationale for it. Moreover, LeWitt's pronouncements read like philosophical theorems or, at least, lists of binding definitions. Kosuth's essays, in contrast, are much more discursive and, one might say, opinionated, but they also carry an ambitious philosophical weight, arguing for a definition of art as the necessary pre-condition for the making of art. Kosuth went further by actually incorporating definitions into art-works, seeming, at times, to make them identical, effacing the distinction between signifier and signified, in a way reminiscent of Magritte's *This Is Not A Pipe*, but going further, concerned not simply with the nature of visual representation, but with the nature of art itself as a form of discourse. Due to the semantic loop involved, philosophical statements about art could be presented as works of art, functioning at the same time as a kind of manifesto for themselves. In fact, the manifesto, the theoretical proposal and the art-work became three terms of an interlocking system.

This interlocking system tied together many of the threads which marked out avant-garde work from what we might think of as merely modernist work. This particular avant-garde strategy however was strikingly self-contained. It existed within a unique kind of semiotic circuit, knotting together art object, art theory and art manifesto, without leaving any obvious loose ends, rather like the relationship of mathematics and the theory of mathematics, complete with a proof that they were actually the same thing. To understand how this happened we have to look, it seems to me, at the way in which, in respect to minimalism, art already existed in a specific kind of relation both to the theory of art and to the idea of an avant-garde. With hindsight, we can now see that minimalism not only signified the demise of Clement Greenberg's theoretical system, inextricably linked to modernism as an epochal movement, but also a crucial shift towards the ideas of John Cage, Greenberg's main rival as an art theorist, which we can see as a precondition for the eventual triumph of post-modernism. Cage both sought to efface the boundary between art and life, in true avant-garde style, but also introduced the idea that a work of art was simply the end-product of an arbitrary system of rules, which could be arrived at in a number of different ways, ranging along a spectrum from pure chance to complex mathematical algorithms. It must have seemed to Greenberg that an old devil had returned in a new guise, as if dadaism and surrealism, with their found objects and their chance procedures, had somehow mutated into a new form. Many years were to pass, however, before the truly insidious character of Cage's influence was to reveal itself, as it penetrated the very heart of Greenberg's own fortress.

Minimal art was not, in any obvious sense, an organized movement or even tendency. Like most names of art movements, it was a term applied *post hoc* by critics, who saw something in common between a group of artists which included, in the first instance, Carl André, Dan Flavin, Donald Judd, Sol LeWitt and Robert Morris. Insofar as the minimalist artists had something in common, it could be summed up as follows: they produced three-dimensional constructions based on simple, unornamented rectilinear forms. In general, simple units or modules were repeated to form what David Batchelor, author of the best book on the topic, calls 'an overall regular shape', whose underlying logic could be grasped in a moment. Usually, these works stood on the floor. If coloured, they were deliberately inexpressive. As a rule they used industrial materials of a kind, as Batchelor notes, typically 'available from builders' merchants and the like rather than a fine art or craft supplier'. There was little obvious sign either of craft or of the artist's hand, or of any need for self-expression through personal creativity. The works were simple, direct and unpretentious, while giving clear evidence of thought and planning, just as building a wall would require thought and planning. By 1966 LeWitt was producing floor pieces in which the underlying generative concept of the work was no longer immediately visible, so that, in Batchelor's words, 'the viewer has to complete the system in his or her mind,' and 'the completion of the series thus relies on the viewer's recognition of a certain logic'.

Where did minimalism come from? First there was the example of assemblage, which had already called into question the canonical distinction between painting and sculpture. Second, there was Frank Stella's painting, which we might compare and contrast, as Batchelor does, with Warhol's grid paintings. Third was the move towards the structuring of painting by simple stripes and strata of colour, found, for instance, in work by Barnett Newman and Mark Rothko, both of whom also painted in series. Flavin's work was influenced by Morris Louis's stripes and his move away from painting followed the example of the Russian constructivists. Among sculptors, there was the precedent of Brancusi's endless towers. LeWitt made his first modular cube piece in 1965. From early on, he wanted to make works whose structure was plain to the eye, stripping away the 'surface skin' and simply showing the edges of his cubes. He wanted the work to look 'hard and industrial'. The result was what Batchelor calls a kind of 'linearism' which led him logically towards drawing, just as the use of the cube as a repeated module led him to seriality. Before constructing his three-dimensional units, LeWitt produced working drawings, just as later, as a conceptual artist, he produced sets of verbal instruction, preliminary to making drawings. Constructions were drawings in space; drawings were translations of words and numbers.

In some respects, conceptual art can be seen simply as the logical extension of minimalism. In other respects, however, there was a definite break or rupture, a shift on to quite new ground. Like minimalism, conceptual art challenged the canonical boundaries between painting and sculpture, adopted modularity and seriality as working methodologies, envisaged the finished art-work as simply a realization of an initial idea, which could be realized by an anonymous fabricator. But there was also a decisive shift, which took place over a period of time and involved a number of separate issues. With this in mind, we need to tread warily around issues of precedence. I think it is safe to say that we can see the germs of conceptual art emerging within the work of minimalism, serial art, systems art, and so on, from the early 1960s on. It began to crystallize as a separate tendency for Kosuth in 1967 with the 'Statement' he wrote for a show he organized at the Lannis Gallery early that year, 'Non-Anthropomorphic Art by Four Young Artists' (Kosuth, Kozlov, Michael Rinaldi and Ernest Rossi). This is also the year in which Sol LeWitt wrote his 'Paragraphs on Conceptual Art' for *ArtForum*. The first significant statement by Art & Language, 'Remarks On Air-Conditioning', was also published in 1967, in *Arts Magazine*.

In his 'Statement' (later re-titled 'Notes on Conceptual Art and Models') Kosuth made a number of important claims, among which were the following: (1) 'All I make are models. The actual works of art are ideas. Rather than "ideals" the models are a visual approximation of a particular art object I have in mind. It does not matter who actually makes the model, nor where the models end up.' (2) Each 'art object' is atemporal and meaningless in itself, but it does have 'philosophical implications' which Kosuth does not wish to deny or reject. (3) Each art object is 'concerned totally with art in as much as it is concerned with nothing else'. As a consequence, it must have 'an order, a logic of one kind or another', which will distinguish it from other kinds of object. (4) Mathematics is a kind of tool which makes it 'possible for a structure or object to have an order not associated with natural or useful objects'. (5) Mathematics can provide us with a type of order that is true in itself, rather than because it represents reality or because it is useful. (6) Similarly, art has a 'beauty' which depends upon its 'uselessness', its detachment from reality, which is 'tautological for the idea of *pure or total existence*'. What is immediately striking about these claims is their remorseless aestheticism, well within the modernist tradition. As Victor Burgin remarked, looking back 30 years later, in an interview conducted by John Roberts for his book, *The Impossible Document: Photography and Conceptual Art in Britain, 1966–1976*, Kosuth's concern was with 'the whole question of self-reflexivity, which is nothing other than art for art's sake'. The way Burgin saw it, this was because Kosuth 'identified totally with Ad Reinhardt'.

Burgin's view—expressed in 1997, but describing what he thought at the end of the 1960s—implies, it seems to me, that Kosuth's position at that time reflected his wish to provide an art-for-art's-sake theorization of minimalism as the construction of pure objects, analogous to the conceptual objects of pure mathematics, but anonymously fabricated to give them a form in space. It was only a step from this position, of course, to include conceptual elements of the theoretical definition of art within the object itself in textual form, as Kosuth famously did in his 1967 'Titled (Art as Idea as Idea)', with its dictionary definition of 'meaning', photostatted, blown up and incorporated into the art object—in a sense, being the art object. LeWitt's approach in his 'Paragraphs on Conceptual Art' is significantly different from Kosuth's in that he is concerned not with the concept of art as such, but with the conceptual basis for the making of the work, as Cage had long been. 'This kind of art', LeWitt wrote, 'is not theoretical or illustrative of theories; it is intuitive, it is involved with all types of mental processes and it is purposeless.' There is agreement, significantly, on the uselessness or purposelessness of art (though these concepts are slightly different) but, whereas Kosuth came increasingly to think of the work as theoretically self-reflexive, LeWitt was not at all interested in its 'philosophical implications'. Instead, he was interested in its practical implications as a method of work—the artist had an idea, which was then executed in a mechanical kind of way. The idea, in itself, could be intuitive or irrational. It certainly did not need to stand up to theoretical scrutiny. It simply needed to be 'interesting'.

LeWitt's approach, like Kosuth's, was committed to the uselessness of the art object, but not to its aesthetic beauty or to its tautological self-reflexivity. In this sense, LeWitt was less radical than Kosuth, more concerned with pushing back the limits of minimalism by stressing the initial conceptual plan rather than the finished work. LeWitt never got drawn into the post-Duchampian questions about the definition of art which absorbed other conceptual artists. Whereas Kosuth complicated both his theory and his practice as time went by, developing it by introducing new ideas and new procedures, LeWitt soon settled on a relatively simple way of working—producing formulas for potential drawings and then having them executed. In fact, LeWitt sometimes seems like a particularly manic-obsessive version of a Fluxus artist, endlessly having whimsical ideas for drawings, but stripping them both of any 'philosophical implications' and of anything which might suggest caprice or madcap humour. In this sense, he was like Duchamp—he wanted to remain, in his own words, 'emotionally dry' and to eliminate subjectivity.

The concept of 'conceptual art' appears to have entered the discourse of the art world in a substantial way only from 1969 onwards. In that year Germano Celant used the term for his exhibition 'Arte Povera: Earthworks, Impossible Art, Actual Art, Conceptual Art' and Gillo Dorfles reiterated it in the title of an article for *Art International* in which he tried to make a distinction between '*arte concettuale*' and '*arte povera*'. Soon afterwards, an exhibition in Leverkusen (with a catalog introduction by Sol LeWitt) was titled 'Konzeption–Conception'; then Catherine Millet wrote on 'L'Art Conceptual' for *Opus International* in Paris and Harald Szeeman used the word Concepts after the colon in the title of his exhibition in Bern, 'When Attitudes Become Form', linking it with Works, Processes, Situations and Information. By 1970 critical essays on conceptual art were widespread in the US, Europe and Australia. In America, there was an article in *Harpers Bazaar* and a piece on Joseph Kosuth in *Newsweek*. The first US exhibition which referred (indirectly) to 'conceptual art' as such, appears to be Perpetua Butler's show in Los Angeles in July 1969. This was followed in November by the Leverkusen exhibition mentioned above and in the next two years by shows in New York, Turin, Jerusalem, Innsbruck, Milan and Basel (Buenos Aires also had 'El Arte Como Idea in Inglaterra'). However, although these shows used the term 'Concept' or 'Conceptual' or 'Idea' their interpretation of what this might mean was still extremely fuzzy. Conceptual art was gradually becoming a typical art world label, applied with a broad brush to a spectrum of works which seemed to break new ground and go beyond the limits of existing 'isms'.

It would appear that it took about two years for historians, critics and curators to catch up with artists—which seems about right. The story, however, does not end with its beginning. Kosuth, in particular, has himself taken a retrospective look at the history of 'conceptual art' and made his own distinctions. In effect, he has defended the tendency he supports as the 'real' version of 'conceptual art' and discarded the rest as false heroes. In 1971, Kosuth gave a lecture in Salvador Allende's Chile, entitled 'Painting versus Art versus Culture (or, Why you can paint if you want to, but it probably won't matter)'. In this talk, he already took pains to differentiate 'conceptual art' from minimalism, describing the former as 'a competitive paradigm or model of artistic activity' with, as its task, 'the dismantling of the mythic structure of art as posited in present-day cultural institutions'. In effect, Kosuth was now making a claim for conceptual art as an avant-garde tendency, rather than just another art movement. He wanted to draw a clear divide between conceptual art and minimalism, even to mark a moment of rupture from modernism itself.

In the second issue of 'his' journal, *The Fox* (1975), Kosuth distinguished between 'Theoretical Conceptual Art' (TCA) and 'Stylistic Conceptual Art' (SCA). TCA, of course, followed the agenda outlined above and remained oppositional. On the other hand, the 'deterioration of the movement into a popular SCA', Kosuth wrote, 'pointed, at least on the surface, to an ultimate victory by the establishment. The form the victory takes is one of annexation.' TCA, he later explained, in a paper studded with references to Habermas, Marcuse, Jameson, and others, should be a 'critical practice', concerned with the 'demystification' of art and the 'restoration of meaning'; it should be 'political' in the sense that 'our very conceptions of both culture and politics, as part of a discourse which trivializes both, must be critically understood as they are re-made for human use' ('Within The Context: Modernism and Critical Practice', 1977). In a further phase (represented by 'No Exit', in *ArtForum*, March 1988) Kosuth took the final step of re-describing SCA as simply a form of post-minimalism.

From the start, he argued, 'conceptual art' had been defined 'in the language of minimalism' and naturally developed, in the context of the art world, into a movement which 'provided the Modernist agenda with a revitalized "avant-garde" face without letting go of the premise that the repository of central artistic concern was still in the object, if only in its absence. In this regard, post-minimalism's primary concern is with a radicalization of alternative materials rather than alternative meanings'— that is, as I understand it, language and even concepts were treated as the materials of a new kind of 'negative' art object, rather than as instruments for the critical investigation (and subversion) of the underlying premises of art within North American culture. In other words, as Kosuth put it,

> What separates Conceptual art from both [post-minimalism and political message art] is the understanding that artistic practice locates itself directly in the signifying process and that the use of elements in an art proposition (be they objects, quotations, fragments, photographs, contexts, texts or whatever) functions not for aesthetic purposes (although, like anything in the world, a proposition can also be aesthetic), but rather as simply the constructive elements of a test of the cultural code.

'Test' here is further defined as 'simply put, a questioning process'. In other words, the function of art is to question the cultural codes within which it operates, is institutionalized and received, including, of course, the codes which give art its political power and meaning.

As I read Kosuth's polemics, I couldn't help suspecting that his critique of post-minimalism had concealed implications for our judgement of Sol LeWitt. LeWitt, after all, was canonical both for Lucy Lippard, herself almost one of the minimalist group, and for Rosalind Krauss, a founding editor of *October*, who writes about LeWitt as though he were a post-minimalist—both in *Grids* and in *The Originality of the Avant-Garde*—even though she herself deploys a very different set of theoretical arguments, drawn from psycho-analysis, Bataille and post-structuralism. What should we really think of all those elegant wall-drawings, with their densely packed collocation of coloured pencil lines? Could this be the heartland of 'SCA'? My own view is that Kosuth's development from post-minimalism to TCA, to art as cultural critique, represents what actually happened more accurately than the SCA version embraced, according to him, by the art world.

In contrast to Kosuth, LeWitt stayed much closer to his original theory and practice, and consequently had the lesser general influence in the long run. Kosuth, by broadening the borders of the movement, prepared the ground for 'conceptualism', a tendency which both emerged from the crisis of modernism and superseded it. Indeed, there is a sense in which the whole of the art world is now dominated by conceptualism—by work driven by 'art ideas', by installation, by art viewed as a form of cultural criticism. In saying this, I don't want to minimize the importance of LeWitt's early role. Moreover, his theoretical positions on conceptual art are much more rigorous than the mainstream reception of his work would suggest. When asked in 1981 whether he felt he had to endorse every wall drawing which followed his instructions, he replied, 'If someone did a work of mine, unknown to me? I think it's fine. It's not like painting a picture, where each is unique. Much work today can be done by anybody.' LeWitt's view, it seems, is that the actual drawings are analogous to the performance of a score. The artist is like a composer, the draughtsperson or fabricator like a performer. The works go out into the world for multiple performances, some better, some worse.

Rather than the legacy of Duchamp, which influenced Kosuth, we are dealing here with the legacy of Cage, deflected in the direction of Moholy-Nagy's telephone paintings or Rodchenko's call for (fabricated) industrial art. The art-object itself is not completely rejected, but its uniqueness is challenged. At the same time LeWitt's multiples are usually site-specific and frequently (in museum shows, mostly) painted over. His 'sale' of works is really payment for authentication, which is not strictly necessary. In this sense, despite LeWitt's own distance from political art-making, his work inevitably raises political questions about the institutions of the art world. On the other hand, the wall-drawings in themselves are plainly post-minimalist art objects, which are indeed regarded as objects of pure aesthetic contemplation rather than challenges to the ideology of art—its absolute uniqueness, its physical creation by the artist, its assumed hierarchy of artist and 'anybody'.

Conceptual art problematized and decentred—even, at times, erased—the traditional art object, the painting or the sculpture. In the place of the object it substituted a discourse, often modeled on the critical apparatus of the historian or the theorist (written text plus photographic documentation) or the contextualizing practices of the curator and exhibition designer (selecting and arranging a series of items to create significant correlations). As the British-based artist Mary Kelly pointed out, in the course of an interview in 1978, these procedures could be described in terms drawn from the new discipline of semiotics, as codified by Roland Barthes. Conceptual Art shifted the axis of meaning in art from the 'metaphoric' to the 'metonymic', from the semantic to the syntactic, from the message to the code (or, in Joseph Kosuth's terms, also cited by Kelly, from the 'synthetic' to the 'analytic'). Art installations not only made use of verbal language, but themselves became language-like in the way they strung a series of items together to make a significant sequence, as words are combined in a linear fashion to make a sentence. This was not simply a formal shift. It brought with it a new way of referring to the world, through complex forms of narrative, documentation and meta-language, far removed from traditional modes of visual representation. Painting and sculpture were not simply problematized but replaced by text, photography and performance. Art-making was seen as a cultural and political activity, rather than an aspect of personal creativity.

This long-term impact of conceptual art, it seems to me, is still underestimated. It was not simply the successor to colour field painting or minimalism or serial art, for instance, although undoubtedly conceptual art would never have occurred without the influence of Johns or Reinhardt or Morris or André or Judd. It was not simply a new style or a new movement. It was the single greatest shift in art since the Renaissance. It successfully dethroned painting and sculpture from their 'natural' position in the hierarchy of the arts. (In 1970, John Baldessari burned his paintings and put the ashes in an urn as a work of conceptual art.) It challenged the primacy which they had enjoyed, as of right, for centuries and transformed the art world into a field of unprecedented semiotic complexity, whose effects are still with us in the form of installation art—the new genre which emerged from the combination of conceptual art with elements of assemblage, environment, performance, photo-text and video. As has often been recognized, the vision which made this new hybrid possible was provided, in the first instance, by Marcel Duchamp, but it was conceptual art which broke apart the time-honoured structures of the old artworld and decisively undermined the leading role of painting and sculpture.

Looking back on it, we can see that, paradoxically, there was a logic to this break which came from within the tradition of painting itself. Greenberg's call for art to emancipate itself from easel painting led inexorably to a further call for art to emancipate itself from painting of any type. The crucial precedent for this further act of emancipation was found in the rediscovered example of Marcel Duchamp and the Russian experimentalists of the 1920s, among whom Rodchenko can now be seen as the most relevant. But the most important step was the turn to theory—first the theory of art itself, seen still in post-Kantian terms, but soon the theory of art as a social and semiotic phenomenon. In retrospect, we might think that conceptual artists often used the wrong theory—it seems strange that during the heyday of semiology, the rise of Barthes and Lacan, the rediscovery of Peirce and the bitter wars around Chomsky which racked linguistics, artists should have turned to Wittgenstein and A. J. Ayer—but nonetheless, theory it was. It is not so much that one kind of theory is intrinsically better than another, but that some theories offered more possibilities than others—were simply much more useful.

Victor Burgin, for instance, has noted how his interest in semiotics began when he came back from Yale in 1967, where Judd, Morris and Reinhardt were all teaching at the time, and 'stumbled across this little Jonathan Cape translation, Roland Barthes's *Elements Of Semiology*, and it changed my life'.

The explanation Burgin gives is that semiology (or 'semiotics', as it was later re-dubbed) was not only 'a non-anecdotal, non-subjective criticism' but also that 'here was a theory which was able to turn its attention, almost indiscriminately, to advertising, to cinema, to literature. This seemed to me to offer a broad base where you could actually connect with other people and other fields and have a discussion in common. So naturally my fantasy was that art would become reintegrated into the broader field of cultural criticism.' As we have seen, this was exactly the move which Kosuth was later to make, although on the basis of a different kind of theory. Doing so meant acknowledging that a clean break had to be made with the logic of modernism, certainly in its Greenbergian version, which had, so to speak, led to a narrowing down of art to an increasingly reflexive preoccupation with its own ontology and an increasing absence of any substantive relationship with the outside world. The break with modernism meant not simply the downgrading of visuality, although this was extremely significant, but also the opening up of art to extrinsic political and cultural issues, formerly considered irrelevant or inappropriate —a state of affairs which was largely the legacy of McCarthyism and the Cold War.

The turn to cultural theory, however, arose in a very specific context. Conceptual art, as Lucy Lippard has often stressed, appeared at a time of unusual political turbulence and confrontation, which swept through the North American art world as it did through the universities and the ghettos. This political climate had a direct impact on the initial formation of conceptual art and it decisively shaped its development. From very early on, the attack on the traditional art object (especially painting) was seen, in political terms, as an attack on the commodification of the art world. The denigration of vision by conceptual artists also carries a clear echo of the denunciation of the 'Society of the Spectacle' by the situationists, what Martin Jay refers to as their 'iconophobia'. For the situationists, the world of the visual had been more or less entirely colonized by the media and by the culture of the market. New artistic techniques were necessary in order to escape incorporation into the world of the spectacle. Conceptual artists too wanted to create a new kind of relationship between artist, gallery and public, which would challenge not only the commercial nature of the art world but also the whole idea of the viewer as passive consumer of sensations rather than thoughtful interlocutor. Text, photography and found objects were incorporated into art work, not simply because they were interesting new media with which to work, but because they offered specific ways of engaging the interest of the art public and, as Burgin observed, opportunities to reintegrate art into a wider cultural field of discourse, from which modernism had increasingly abstracted it.

At the same time, the New York art world itself was changing. Women and artists from a diverse range of cultural and ethnic backgrounds were demanding access and recognition. Always sidelined during the history of modernism, its crisis gave them new opportunities. Conceptual art, in particular, offered a new arena—one which encouraged artists to ask fundamental questions about both art and the art world, about the politics and sociology of art. Moreover, conceptual work was relatively cheap to produce, portable and lacking in the self-conscious heroism of previous modernist movements. Women quickly became prominent in the world of conceptual art. As we have seen, Christine Kozlov and Lee Lozano had been there since the beginning. Kozlov's tape piece for an inaudible tape and Lozano's pieces, in which she instructed herself as to how to behave socially in the art world and ethically in her personal and political life, were early classics of conceptual art. Adrian Piper, a black woman artist with a training in philosophy, was present very early on within the conceptualist movement. Yoko Ono, like Arakawa Shusaku and On Kawara, provided an important link between Japan and the United States. Beginning as a Fluxus artist, she subsequently made the transition from Fluxus to a broader conceptualism, with an increasingly political dimension. Similarly, Hans Haacke, coming to New York from Europe, quickly perceived the potential conceptual art offered as a means of social criticism and analysis.

Politics and social criticism were to become increasingly important in shaping the history and geography of conceptual art. In Los Angeles, Harry Gamboa, Jr, with Gronk and Willie Herrón, a founder of the

ASCO group of Mexican-American guerrilla artists, signed the Los Angeles Museum of Contemporary Art, as a protest against the exclusion of Mexican-Americans, just as, in New York, Faith Ringgold, an African-American member of Art Workers' Coalition and the Guerrilla Art Action Group, re-named a wing of the Museum of Modern Art as the Martin Luther King Wing, noting the absence of black artists from it—an action vividly recounted by her daughter, Michele Wallace, in her book *Invisibility Blues*. Gamboa also moved into film and video, making his conceptualist series of 'No Movies', films that only existed as ideas in photo-text form, given the lack of resources to complete them as movies. That same year, 1971, Robert Morris organized the Art Strike protest against the Venice Biennale's selection of all male white artists (and the extension of the war into Cambodia). Another group of artists, led by Poppy Johnson and Lucy Lippard, demonstrated against the Whitney Annual to demand 50 percent representation of women. These actions, designed to challenge the covert political role of museums, took place in parallel with the critique of the fetishized modernist art object plainly implicit within conceptual art. Questioning the art object led logically to questioning first the gallery show and then the museum exhibition. Conceptual art inherited the mantle of protest from the early activities of Henry Flynt, a Flux artist who had invented the term 'concept art' back in 1963, in relation to the Fluxus movement, and had also inaugurated the first wave of sixties demonstrations against the policy of New York museums.

The extension of art into formerly social peripheral groups was paralleled by its extension into peripheral media—both still photography, in the work of Dan Graham, Hans Haacke, Martha Rosler and Allan Sekula, and also the time-based photographic media of film and video. The sixties was a period of great vitality for avant-garde film and, at the end of the decade, a new paradigm was created with the emergence of structural film, which itself derived from the combined influence of minimalism, serial art, Marcel Duchamp, Andy Warhol and Fluxus. While conceptual art and structural film are rarely connected by critics or historians it is clear that they were in fact closely related. They can be seen, in effect, as two sides of the same coin. The apparent division between them simply reflects the two different discourses inhabited by historians of art and film, each approaching their own field of expertise without taking the other into account. In fact, like Duchamp, Warhol and the makers of Fluxfilms, many experimental film-makers also made gallery art. The work of Michael Snow and Joyce Wieland, for example, can be seen as positioned within the paradigm of conceptual art as logically as within that of structural film. Hollis Frampton's *Zorns Lemma* brought together influences from the art world, especially from Frank Stella and Carl André, who were both close friends of Frampton, with an interest in language, in serialism, in a mathematically based systematicity and in conceptual photography.

Hollis Frampton's xerograph series, *Reasonable Facsimiles*, was an archetypal conceptual work, a set of authentications, cancellations, lists and propositions on the subject of art. *Zorns Lemma* is based upon an axiom of set theory, which proposes that given a set of sets, there is a further set composed of a representative item from each set. The structuring set of sets in the film consists of 24 repetitions of a 24-letter alphabet. At first each letter is represented by a 'found' photographed word with the appropriate initial letter, presented in alphabetical order. Systematically, each set of words is then replaced by a set of fragments of a filmed scene or activity, according to an underlying protocol, as in a LeWitt floor or wall piece. Another conceptual artist, Robert Huot, a former minimalist who made invisible, and therefore unsaleable works, as a protest against the art market, appears in the film as a painter painting a wall within a fixed time-span. Structural film involved an investigation of the conditions of possibility of film itself, in the same way that conceptual art saw itself as an investigation of the conditions of possibility of visual art. Somewhat later and in another vein, Therese Hak Kyung Cha used language as a crucial component of her video work, in order to investigate her own paradoxical place within American culture.

The original focus on the semiotics of visual representation, central to the development of conceptual art, but also pursued with great depth and seriousness by artists such as Arakawa Shosaku and Agnes Denes, gave way, as we have seen, to a much broader re-definition of art as a social construct. Conceptual art—just as it de-centred the traditional aesthetics and semantics of visual representation—also de-centred New York itself from its hegemonic position in the global art world. Among the early shows, Lucy Lippard's exhibitions in Seattle and Vancouver (and later

Buenos Aires) deliberately set out to shift the art world's centre of gravity. Canadian artists such as Carole Condé and Karl Beveridge, Les Levine, and those involved in collaborative groups such as N. E. Thing Company and General Idea, played an important role in the history of Conceptual art. San Francisco opened its own Museum of Conceptual art and there were centres also in Los Angeles (Michael Asher, John Baldessari) and San Diego (Martha Rosler, Allan Sekula) where conceptual art blended with the political influence of Herbert Marcuse. Conceptual art had a significant impact in challenging the geographical, as well as ethnic and gender, hierarchy of core and periphery in the art world. Decentralization, I believe, was the direct effect of the crisis of modernism which, due to its close links with the art market and museum culture, had traditionally played a strongly centralizing role.

Conceptual art provided a timely vehicle for artists determined to break down the elite world of modernism. As a result of this ongoing process of democratization, the historic role of conceptual art cannot be understood simply by rehearsing the early work of its avant-garde of pioneers. It very rapidly burst its Lower Manhattan bounds and became the site of an extremely complex and dynamic movement, with far-reaching implications geographically, politically and semiologically. It was as if the initial New York cohort created a crack in a dam which eventually broke and released a flood of innovative new art. We are still trying to grasp what happened, to chart its sudden eddies, its deviant surges, its confusing crosscurrents. During the 1960s the flow of information within North America and around the world increased dramatically, as a result of cheaper international air-travel and improved communication networks. As a result, the picture that emerges, taken as an ensemble, is that of a complex movement with very different roots—in Europe, in Japan, in North America—which branched out, in the second generation, in a number of new and exciting directions. 'Pure' conceptualism soon shattered on the jagged rocks of theory and politics, driving Kosuth into a different camp from LeWitt and setting Art & Language, Burgin and Haacke on a different track from both of them. Conceptual art cannot and should not be compressed into a movement with an unproblematic origin and a single master-trajectory. In reality, it quickly broke out of what Mel Bochner, back in 1968, already called its 'solipsism'.

For Claude Gintz's exhibition, 'L'art conceptuel, une perspective', the Los Angeles conceptual artist Michael Asher submitted a text arguing that the exhibition was

> as much a view of conceptual art as it is a perspective of the institutions used for the maintenance and historical reproduction of that practice. What are the forces and conditions driving the historical analysis which are beyond conceptual art practice's own definition of its historical context and production procedures? Historical objectification ought to be accelerated while there is still a collective experience and memory which can assist in the clarity of an analysis, simultaneously opening up a space to ask fundamental questions about history making.

This new exhibition gives us an opportunity both to ask these fundamental questions and to introduce new perspectives. The persistent influence of conceptual art is still far from exhausted. It retains the potential to surprise us. Conceptual art, seen as a historic avant-garde, may now be dead, but global conceptualism, as a broad movement, embracing installation art, video art, film, sound tape, performance and text, continues to flourish. It offers us the possibility of making, and responding to, a form of art which has proved resistant to those powerful forces of homogeneity and domination which come inevitably with economic and cultural globalization.

3

TANKS

The tank, I was surprised to learn, was an English invention. Basically it provided a much-needed countervailing response to the recent development of a wave of new defensive measures: barbed wire, fortified trenches and rapid-fire machine-guns. Armoured against both wire and gunfire, the tank could lurch across trenches and traverse roadless battlefields pitted with shell craters. I was even more surprised to learn that the tank was developed in the first instance not by the army but the navy, which had already armoured its gunships and was open-minded about new inventions, prepared to back them even if they had no naval relevance at all. Patrick Wright's fascinating book *Tank* is basically a cultural rather than a military history of the tank, dwelling on images and impressions of the tank, its impact on the general public, the responses of artists and writers, rather than its evolving strategic role and its transformation of the concept of the battlefield. Nonetheless, the tank was and is primarily a military object and, as a result, military history remains the solid foundation upon which the more fanciful constructions of the cultural historian can be built. The story of the tank is inseparable from the development of highly mechanized and mobile armies, equipped with new technologies that enabled troops to combine the means of defence with the means of attack, armour with artillery.

Ernest Swinton gave his indispensable book of memoirs, *Eyewitness*, the subtitle *Being Personal Reminiscences of Certain Phases of the Great War*,

Including the Genesis of the Tank. Before embarking on its prologue, Swinton's book begins with a series of eight photographs of British tanks from the First World War—fallen into a ditch, resisting a flame-thrower attack, lined up in rows at the Central Workshop and ready for issue, surmounting a parapet before crunching down into a redoubt. The most telling of these images, to me at least, is the one entitled 'Method of releasing a carrier pigeon from a porthole in a Tank'. A human hand is poking out through a hole in a tank sponson, grasping a fluffy pigeon by its tail, like Noah with his dove. It reminds us that tanks still lacked any form of radio contact, that the technology of mechanization was running far ahead of the technology of communication. The story of the tank is one of uneven development, fantastic visions of the future coming to terms with technological lags, sudden leaps forward resulting from some unexpected new invention or surprising new turn of fate. Yet throughout its history, the tank retained one constant set of qualities: it was perceived either as terrifying (theirs), inspiring (ours) or ludicrous (in itself).

Swinton believed that he could trace the exact moment which gave rise to the frame of mind which he called 'a machine gun complex' and which led eventually to the creation of the tank. It was in South Africa, the early morning of 14 June 1900, when Swinton first saw a machine-gun manned in an emplacement, to be used against a commando troop of Boers. In fact, it malfunctioned, but Swinton felt confident that it would become the determining weapon of the future. He followed its use in the Russo-Japanese War, which clearly demonstrated the effectiveness of the machine-gun and the howitzer as defensive weapons. Then, in July 1914, he received an interesting letter from an old Boer War acquaintance, a mining engineer who had recently acquired a 'Holt Caterpillar Tractor' with surprising powers of traveling cross country. As Swinton says, 'This knowledge lay dormant in my mind until ten weeks after the War had broken out. When it did recur to me it was as if a ray of light had struck a sensitized plate.' In September 1914, very soon after the outbreak of war, Swinton was instructed by Lord Kitchener, whom he had known in South Africa, to travel immediately to France as an official 'Eyewitness' and write a series of reports to be sent directly to Kitchener as Secretary of State for War, who, having forbidden normal press coverage of the war, could decide whether to authorize publication or not, just as he saw fit. In any case, he would certainly have read them all himself.

Once in France, Swinton became alarmed by the preponderance of the Germans in artillery.

> If our resourceful, industrious and well-equipped opponents were able to accomplish so much in haste and with improvised means, what might they not do, given time, even with field defences? During the first week of October my mind continually returned to this. And, vaguely, I pictured to myself some form of armoured vehicle immune against bullets, which should be capable of destroying machine guns and of ploughing a way through wire. This picture, though not yet in focus and ill-defined, was the germ of our future Tank.

During the next two weeks, Swinton's vague idea 'crystallized in the form of a power-driven, bullet-proof, armed engine, capable of destroying machine guns, of crossing country and trenches, of breaking through entanglements, and of climbing earthworks'. On 19 October, Swinton suddenly remembered the Holt Caterpillar Tractor: 'Why should it not be modified and adapted to suit our present requirements for war? The key to the problem lay in the caterpillar track!'

Kitchener, however, was quite unimpressed by Swinton's idea, which now seemed doomed to sink from sight. However, the persistence of his friend, Colonel Hankey, eventually led to Swinton's proposal coming to the attention of Winston Churchill, then First Lord of the Admiralty. Thus the future tank became a naval project. It was now January 1915, but Swinton did not learn of this new development until late in May. Meanwhile Churchill had made considerable progress. The new 'Landship Committee' was to be chaired by Tennyson D'Eyncourt, a submarine expert. Its secretary was Albert Stern, a banker in civilian life. By the end of summer there was general agreement that caterpillar tracks were the *sine qua non* without which there would be no tank. The Holt, however, proved unsuitable, but—by a great stroke of good luck—Commander Briggs, a navy man, happened to go into 'one of those foreign bookshops off Leicester Square' from which, so A. J. Smithers tells us in *A New Excalibur*, he came out with a copy of the *Scientific American* for

18 February 1911, 'which contained details of a much longer machine designed for moving heavy loads of an agricultural kind over bad surfaces'. An emissary was sent to Chicago and came back with an enthusiastic report on the Bullock Creeping Grip. Two giant tractors were ordered and shipped to Britain on the *SS Lapland*. When they arrived they were tested on a field rented by one of the Committee, Walter Gordon Wilson, a specialist in gear-boxes and a brilliant mechanical engineer. Whereas Swinton had the initial vision, it was Wilson who finally made it into reality.

In June 1915 Swinton, still unaware of the Landship Committee, wrote a lengthy memorandum entitled *Armoured Machine Gun Destroyers (General Description)* which was promptly rejected as fanciful by everyone he showed it to. It was not until July that Swinton finally learned of the Committee, which 'all still sounded like a fairy-tale' as far as he was concerned. He 'was bewildered by the unnatural and devious course things had taken'. Meanwhile Stern and two other members of the Committee had visited France on an investigatory mission, narrowly failing to meet Swinton and eventually being expelled as interlopers by the army. Meanwhile Swinton himself fruitlessly pursued his own efforts until, on 18 July, his term of duty as Eyewitness came to an end. He returned to his office at around seven o'clock and found that, earlier in the day, he had been summoned three times by the Chief of the General Staff. On reporting to him, Swinton learned to his surprise that the Prime Minister, Mr Asquith, now required his services and that he should report to Downing Street as soon as possible.

It turned out that he had been appointed Secretary to the Dardanelles Committee of the Cabinet, an official position which, in Swinton's words, proved to be 'an "Open Sesame"—a key to every door'. He now learned that there was indeed an Admiralty Landships Committee looking into caterpillars and tanks and that he should talk to its chairman, Tennyson D'Eyncourt. Even better, on 30 June the War Office finally communicated its own specification for a 'machine gun destroyer' to the Landships Committee. That same day, a demonstration of a tracked Killen-Strait tractor crossing entanglements was held at Wembley Stadium for the eyes of Churchill and Lloyd George, which led to a decision to shift responsibility for the Landships Committee from the Admiralty to Lloyd

George's Ministry of Munitions as soon as sufficient progress had been made. Just a few days later, according to Smithers, Swinton finally met Stern. 'Lieutenant Stern, this is the most extraordinary thing that I have ever seen. The Director of Naval Construction appears to be making land battleships for the Army who have never asked for them and are doing nothing to help. You have nothing but naval ratings doing all your work. What on earth are you? Are you a mechanic or a chauffeur?' 'A banker', Stern replied. 'This', said Swinton, 'makes it still more mysterious.' Nonetheless the two men got on well together.

At the end of July the Committee finally asked Wilson to design a machine incorporating the Bullock Creeping Grip, a Daimler 105 hp. tractor engine and an armoured body, weighing around 18 tons, and able to cross a trench four feet wide. Swinton now persuaded Lloyd George to call an Inter-departmental Conference on 28 August and the following day D'Eyncourt wrote to Stern that it had 'distinctly cleared the air and put the whole thing on a sounder footing. I'm glad you had a good talk with Swinton.' At last Swinton, the originator of the concept of the tank, had been integrated with the practical managers and engineers. The design team established themselves in Lincoln at the White Hart and set to work with Foster & Co., Engineers and Boilermakers. After a series of revisions to the plans were made by Wilson, the first armoured box (known affectionately as 'Little Willie') finally waddled round the factory on 6 September. Unfortunately, it failed to meet all of its test conditions and Wilson was sent back to the drawing board to design a new model, much larger and with a series of adjustments made in almost every aspect: shape, size, track, sprocket wheels, transmission.

On 29 September the new tank (HMS *Centipede* in its early stages, 'Mother' later) was finally ready for demonstration, once again at Wembley. The new model had a lozenge-like rhomboidal shape, with tracks now running outside the box. Once a problem with the gun emplacement had been solved, it finally went into production. Back in 1903, for a short story published in *The Strand* magazine, H. G. Wells had conjured up the idea of gigantic machines which he called *'The Land Ironclads'*. At last, they were on the verge of becoming a reality. On 28 December a further conference was convened, this time with the happy task of finding an official name for the new creation. According to Swinton, 'we rejected in turn—"container"—"receptacle"—"reservoir"—"cistern". The monosyllabic "tank" appealed to us as being likely to catch on and be remembered. That night, in the draft report of the conference, the word "tank" was employed in the new sense for the first time.' He was apparently the coiner of the new name.

Towards the end of January, the tank was given its first serious test, on Lord Salisbury's Golf Course in Hatfield Park, used to simulate, after a fashion, the battlefield at Loos. Despite a number of deficiencies, the tank passed its first real test. D'Eyncourt wrote immediately to Lord Kitchener, along with a number of other grandees, inviting him to observe a second trial. Lloyd George was delighted with 'the ungainly monster', but Kitchener retained his scepticism—according to Liddell Hart, the Chief of Staff 'dubbed it a pretty mechanical toy which would be quickly knocked out by the enemy's artillery' and Swinton tells how he himself heard Kitchener say 'that the War would never be won by such machines, which would be knocked out by the enemy's artillery'. Others, however, regarded such a brusque dismissal as just a clever ruse to deflect the interest of enemy powers. In any case, the War Office finally ordered one hundred machines. Nonetheless, it has to be said that 'Mother' still had a great number of faults. It took time and battlefield experience to create a truly successful tank; and it wasn't until the battle of Amiens, at the very end of the war, that the tank finally came into its own. The Mark IV and Mark V models were vastly improved in comfort, mobility, armour and firepower. Ahead lay a host of developments in many other countries, as the tank became the classic twentieth-century land weapon. But for it to succeed, however, a spate of quite new strategic concepts was needed.

For J. F. C. Fuller, 'the War of 1914–1918 was a blind evolution from mass to machine fighting, for whereas mass by multiplying numbers begets defensive power, machines by enhancing mobility beget offensive power'. Fuller had joined the Tank Corps in France, at Bermicourt, on Boxing Day 1916, to take up the post of General Staff Officer. He first encountered the tank, as Patrick Wright recounts, in August 1915, at a demonstration at Yvrench. He was reminded of 'Epsom Downs on a Derby morning. There were scores and scores of cars there and hundreds and hundreds of spectators both English and French. Everyone was talking and chatting, when slowly came into sight the first tank I ever saw. Not a monster, but a very graceful machine, with beautiful lines, lozenge-shaped, but with two clumsy-looking wheels behind it.' (These wheels were soon to be phased out in subsequent models.) Fuller went on to become Britain's most influential tank strategist, a ceaseless advocate of mechanized and mobile warfare. As he once put it, 'war is becoming ever more a struggle between inventors than between soldiers'. He clarified this dictum by defining two equally necessary categories of inventor: those who invent new weapons, whose 'category of inventiveness is related to the imagination' and those who devise new fighting organizations, whose inventiveness 'is related to ratiocination'. Fuller presented himself as a ratiocinator. At heart, however, he was more of a fantasist. He liked to play the role of prophet and iconoclast.

Patrick Wright enjoys describing the weirdness of Fuller's first published book—*The Star In The West* (1907), a study of the sexual and philosophical ideas of Aleister Crowley, the notorious occultist—and notes its sinister relationship to Fuller's later transfer of allegiance from the 'Great Beast' to Sir Oswald Mosley and the British Union of Fascists. Anti-semitic, anti-homosexual, a devotee of the Tannhauser legend and a believer in 'survival of the fittest', Fuller was obsessed with the ideas of decadence and national decline, with the 'intellectual and moral rottenness' he saw wherever he looked. Crowley, Fuller's hero and partner, had 'seized the social harlot and hurled her from her throne; has forced open her jaws, and administered a sharp emetic, a mental purgative, a rouser! Let us hope it will clean her out, and do her good.' The 'social Harlot'—contemporary England—was to be purified by a religion of free love, pure and uncalculating, which would triumph over the teachings of that 'unfortunate fakir', Christ. Fuller and Crowley fought on two fronts, for just 'as the gigantic edifice of the Christian Church was the child of the neuropathic mystagogues of the dark ages of religion, so now the colossal fabric of Scientific Utilitarianism, offspring of a distorted and epileptic steam-mania, has bemerded us with its panting slime, and wound us tight in the arachnoid meshes of its kakodemoniacal web'.

'Mammon', Fuller proclaimed, 'is the God of today, and Modern Christianity is absolute and unadulterated materialism.' To replace Christianity, he dug deep into esoteric occultism, Eastern religions and idealist philosophy in order to create the weird amalgam he proudly dubbed 'Crowleyanity'. With Crowley as his supreme guide, Fuller sought to overthrow the decadent materialism of the day and replace it with 'true patriotism'. It would be easy to dismiss this overblown farrago as unfortunate juvenilia, but Fuller's interest in esoterica persisted and even his military writings are marked by it. In his provocative book, *Fascist and Liberal Visions of War*, Azar Gat points out that the same mix of elitism and/or anti-semitism with an interest in the occult can be found in many of Fuller's contemporaries, Yeats and Eliot among them. In Fuller's case, as he became increasingly preoccupied with military strategy, occultism merged with the influence of Gustave Le Bon's *Psychologie des Foules*, which described how the generic 'crowd' could be tamed and controlled by a superior elite—just as military training could turn a mob of raw recruits into a disciplined combat force. After the Great War had ended, Fuller was still dividing everything up into mystical triads, as in his new book, *The Foundation of the Science of War*, in order to create '*the Threefold Order*' of strategic thought. In 1925, as Wright notes, he published a new book on Yoga and as late as 1937 he returned again to an occultist theme with *The Secret Order of the Qabala*.

The First World War, Fuller argued, had been fought as a war of self-destructive attrition, which brought no benefit to the victors, any more than it did to the losers: it had been a war stuck in the outdated Age of Steam, which must now give way to the incoming Age of Oil, the new epoch of motorization, the time of the tank. Tank war, according to Fuller, in terms very reminiscent of Italian Futurism, would be highly mobile, highly technological, a matter for elite forces who would seek the most rapid route to victory, aiming to demoralize the enemy leadership through surprise, manoeuvre and shock. The watchwords would be 'penetration', 'outflanking', 'envelopment' and then, deep in the rear, the final 'decisive attack'. Democracy, a product of the Age of Steam, was based on the 'frontal' idea of quantity, now an outmoded basis for power: the successful modern army, a kind of techno-feudal aristocracy, would be based on quality. It would exemplify elite values—typically Fascist in tone—such as courage, honour, self-sacrifice and close comradeship. This military elite would ultimately be a spiritual rather than a material force, united by a shared mystical ideal. The tank war that Fuller championed was simply the appropriate form of war for an idealized neo-feudal elite of latter-day armoured knights.

Of course, the military elites of other countries—including both the Germans and the Russians—were quick to recognize the relevance of Fuller's creed, which combined Futurism with elitism in such a fascinating way. Attracted by the combination of modern techno-warfare with a mystical elitism, de Gaulle, Guderian, Tukhachevsky all instilled respect for his strategic concepts in their armies. Sometimes the influence came directly from Fuller, sometimes from his cohort Liddell Hart, Fuller's 'friend, junior partner and rival', as Gat puts it, who was able to present Fuller's thought in 'a simplified and marketable form—largely free from its Fascist overtones—and thus take much of the credit in the process'. The generals who formulated military strategies of 'deep operations' for the coming Second World War had their own elitist and, often enough, mystical ideas. Tukhachevsky's doctrine, laid out in *The Future War* (1928), owed much to the fraternal military exchanges which took place between elites of the Red Army and the *Reichswehr* during the 1920s. The forthcoming war in the East was won by the strategy of a defensive 'deep battle', masterminded by Zhukov, with reserves far to the rear poised to counterattack, and by the Red Army's superiority in mobile tank warfare, the result of extraordinary sacrifice and a labour–capital balance which shifted from labour to capital, from manpower to machine power, rather than the reverse. Mechanization of the Red Army, moreover, was made possible by the labour of the soldiers' own mothers and wives, who understood what was at stake.

Fuller, who is still read today, was criticized recently by Manuel De Landa, in his extraordinary book, *War in the Age of Intelligent Machines*, because he failed to recognize that 'what mattered now was the assembling of armour and air power into an integrated system joined by radio'. In De Landa's terms, Fuller 'remained in the age of the motor, of unsynchronized motorized armies. As in the case of the transition from clockwork'—drill based—'to motorized armies, warriors trying to cross the new threshold ran into institutional barriers. The main obstacle was that the new distributed-network model involved cooperation between the different branches of the military, and this was, as it always had been historically, difficult to achieve.' It was only in Nazi Germany that 'planes were designed from scratch to provide ground forces with air support' and tanks were 'joined together by a wireless nervous system', which made the strategy of *blitzkrieg* possible. Later, as De Landa stresses, the radio network would be supplemented with a cybernetic technology and potentially decentralized computer systems ('pandemonium robots'). Patrick Wright's chapter on 'Digitization in Fort Knox: Cybertanks and the Army after' clearly corroborates De Landa's vision of the future of warfare, a vision of which we got our first real-world glimpse during the Gulf War.

Patrick Wright describes the new concept of strategy in a chapter entitled, 'Jewish Blitzkrieg', which describes Israel's wars of 1967 and 1973 largely through a face-to-face interview in Tel Aviv with Israel Tal, one of Wright's favourite kinds of soldier, the philosophical commander. Tal talks to him about the Israeli reconceptualization of the tank, with the Merkava, as a 'compromise between firepower and mobility' which, if you get the mix right in every detail (engine, tracks, gunnery) will then give you the third desideratum, protection, both for people inside the tank and for the tank itself. At the same time, the Merkava has a modular construction, so that it can easily be changed and, in effect, redesigned. In Tal's own words, the machine 'is always young, like Dorian Gray'. In the Six Day War Israeli air power and tank power were combined strategically with shattering effect on the Egyptian forces, and tank officers were able to act with a surprising degree of local initiative. The Israeli victory, however, led to an escalation of the military stakes. As Saad El Shazly describes, it brought SAM missiles into Egypt to counter Israeli air superiority and thereby lifted conflict to a new level. The next victory 'would go to whoever happened to have the more sophisticated electronic detection, jamming and counter-jamming devices.' Tanks now took second place.

As warfare moves onwards into the Age of Intelligent Machines, Wright's literary tactic is to concentrate on individuals, preferably artists or writers or eccentrics of various kinds whose path through life has somehow led them into close contact with the tank. Among them we find not only Fuller, the Crowleyite and Mosleyite, but also Clough Williams Ellis, one of the group at Bermicourt, now best known for the village of Portmeirion which he designed and assembled—a bizarre bricolage of architectural styles and elements. Another was Wilfred Bion, whose *War Memoirs* are filled with sketch-maps and vivid drawings, such as the series of fascines, huge tightly-packed bundles of brushwood, each a ton and a half, which could be dropped down into trenches or craters to provide a surface for tank tracks. Chinese labourers imported from Hong Kong and the British protectorate of Weihaiwei were employed to manufacture and position the fascines. Bion's war-time experiences seem to have propelled him towards becoming a psycho-analyst after the war, when he developed a concept of the ego as 'container', later refined by Didier Anzieu into a description of the 'skin ego' as a potential 'carapace'. (Wright spends some time discussing Wilhelm Reich's notion of 'character armour', which must be stripped away to permit the right type of orgasm, but this seems more of a stretch to me.)

The 1914–18 War also saw the first 'war artists', who ranged from Sargent to Nevinson. Others, like Solomon Solomon, a Royal Academician turned Lieutenant Colonel, were given 'tons of paint and other materials and a permanent detachment of men to work under him' in the task of camouflaging tanks, first an exercise in pink and grey dazzle, changing to green and brown shades of mud as reality prevailed. Wright is particularly fond of Nevinson, who, although originally a protégé of Sargent, soon developed Futurist ambitions, becoming friendly in Paris with Boccioni and Severini and subsequently drifting into vorticist circles in London, even suggesting the title *Blast* to Wyndham Lewis for his new avant-garde journal, before breaking with Lewis to follow the Italian Futurist, Marinetti. 'True to his Futurist principles', as Richard Ingleby puts it, he was quick to join in the war, as an ambulance driver, after completing a course in motor engineering. As might be expected, Nevinson's painting stresses the mechanical dimension of the war, depicting bodies of troops as mechanical forces. Patrick Wright is full of praise for *A Tank* (1917), a work included in his Leicester Galleries exhibition of 'War Pictures', replacing the censored *Paths of Glory* which had depicted dead soldiers sprawled in the same dismal mud from which the tank majestically heaves itself up.

Wright's interest is also directed towards writers, especially the reportage of Curzio Malaparte, who covered the German–Russian front in *Kaputt* (1943) and *The Volga Rises in Europe* (1944) and subsequently the allied conquest of Italy in *The Skin* (1949). There is no doubt that Malaparte was the most brilliant and most disturbing of all the writers who covered the War. His books have a vividness of observation and a ghoulish irony which fascinate, bemuse, disturb and sicken the reader. His only rival is Ernst Jünger, although Jünger's fascination with the mechanization of war was largely with the infantry rather than the tank corps. The only tanks in *Storms of Steel* are shell-shot English wrecks, 'monsters' which, 'hoping to baffle the aim of our guns, took a tortuous course over the battlefield like gigantic helpless cockchafers'. Even so, it was Jünger who propounded the concept of mechanization as the essence of modern war. War had produced a new breed of men, Fordist supermen, frenzied heroes suited to a machine environment, subject to 'a marching beat which awakens the representation of vast industrial realms, masters of machines, battalions of workers and cool men of power'. In 1930, looking back on the First World War, he wrote of Germany's defeat as a failure to achieve 'total mobilization', to produce 'a new kind of troops, of commerce, of provisions, of the arms industry—the army of work in general'. Jünger's ideas troubled and intrigued Heidegger, who gave seminars on 'The Worker' and 'Total Mobilization', fascinated and contorted by Jünger's vision of the machine-man, pastiching Jünger while trusting that Hitler would reverse the trend towards machinization that Jünger described.

In England, the most memorable tank novel was May Sinclair's 1917 *The Tree of Heaven*, set partly in Futurist and Vorticist circles, in which one character actually designs the first tank—fictionalized, of course. Later, Keith Douglas's *Alamein to Zem Zem* provided a vivid account of a tank officer's life in the desert war, alternating between phases of aggressive mobility and defensive stasis, during which Douglas would pass the time reading *National Velvet*, *Alice in Wonderland*, *Quest for Corvo*, a short *Survey of Surrealism* and a copy of *Also Sprach Zarathustra*—his copy filched from an enemy vehicle, 'the owner of which had pencil-marked in it most of the quotations applicable to Nazi ideas'. It reminded me, paradoxically, of *Sieg Heil!*—the war letters of Tank Gunner Karl Fuchs, sent home from the Russian Front between 1937 and 1941 and published in America by his widow and son, nearly 50 years later. Driving onwards towards Moscow, then towards Leningrad, he wrote home that 'nothing is more stimulating in this monotonous Russia than a good book'. Among his reading was *Walter von Plettenberg*, a fictionalized story of the struggle of the Teutonic Knights against Ivan the Terrible, and a biography of Hermann Goering. Soon afterwards, battle-weary, he is complaining, 'If we only had something to read. We've gone through all the magazines a dozen times. We've solved all the crossword puzzles and we've done it over and over again only to be entertained a little bit.' A few days later, he is begging, 'I need something to read. No works of literature, mind you, just junk, just anything. Something to pass the time.' Not long afterwards he is killed by a marauding group of 'monster' Russian tanks—the German Army's first encounter with the T-34, the most advanced tank in the war, although still at that time lacking a radio, a defect remedied through Lend-Lease, as agreed later that year.

Malaparte had returned from Russia to Italy at the end of September 1941, shortly before Karl Fuchs was killed. He carried the manuscript of the early chapters of *Kaputt* sewn into his sheepskin coat. His next four months were spent under house arrest, because the Germans had claimed that his despatches from the front were 'inopportune'. Eventually he finished his book, distributed chapters among friends, survived a Gestapo search at Tempelhof Airfield and finally re-assembled the complete manuscript. He was in Finland in 1943 but flew back to Italy as soon as he heard the news of Mussolini's fall, writing *The Skin* on his return, as he accompanied the American army from Naples up to Rome. In 1938 he had begun building work on his extraordinary house in Capri, the Villa Malaparte, best-known as the site of Jean-Luc Godard's film, *Le Mépris* [*Contempt*], where Fritz Lang, in a film within a film, is directing a cinematic version of Homer's *Odyssey*. Wright retells the story of the day in 1942 when Rommel visited the house, uninvited, and asked Malaparte whether he had designed it or bought it 'as is', to which Malaparte replied, falsely, that he had bought it, adding, as he gestured towards the Faraglione rocks, the isles of the Sirens and the golden sands of Paestum, that what he had designed was the scenery.

Wright wonders whether this tale was really true. He is aware, of course, that later in the same book Malaparte tells the story of fellow-guests at a grand luncheon party accusing him of making stories up wholesale throughout *Kaputt*, an accusation which he indignantly denied, insisting that the truth is often stranger than the strangest fiction and recounting, to prove his point, how during that very meal he had consumed a human hand, blown off one of the Moroccan servants by an exploding mine that had disturbed the occasion. The unfortunate *goumier's* hand had flown into a great pot of couscous and then, amidst all the confusion, it had accidentally been served up on Malaparte's plate. Politely, he had eaten it. As evidence, he points to the knuckle-bones and finger-nails which lie neatly arranged around his plate. The guests are shocked. 'That'll teach them to question the truth of what you wrote in *Kaputt*', crows his friend Jack as they leave to join the Sherman tanks on the road to Rome, where one of them crushes a man to death.

We might, indeed, doubt whether Rommel actually visited Malaparte's villa at all—whether he was not another *goumier's* hand, so to speak—since, at the supposed time, in mid-May 1942, Rommel was with the tanks of the Afrika Korps. He had been in Rome on 16 February, where he stayed overnight before flying on to meet Hitler, and he returned again in September, when Malaparte was in Finland. One of Rommel's biographers confidently maintains that, while visiting Rome, Rommel had entered the Duce's enormous room in the Palazzo Venezia and spotted the insignia of an Italian order for valour lying on the immense desk. He assumed, of course, that it was meant for him. However, as the discussion grew heated and Rommel rashly disparaged the Italian Navy, Mussolini glared angrily, opened a drawer, swept the decoration into it and locked it up. 'It was a beautiful thing', said Rommel ruefully. 'Why couldn't I have kept my mouth shut for another ten minutes? He couldn't very well have asked me to hand it back.' Be that as it may, one thing certainly seems true: Malaparte's villa has the classic rhomboidal shape of a tank. The line of the theatrical stairway, then that of the terrace roof, the descent down from its prow to the base of the cistern and then the line obliquely downwards back to the base of the stairs, clearly inscribe for us the form of a somewhat blunted lozenge.

The tank, after all, is an image. As Wright points out, it is an image which can serve for purposes of publicity, for instilling fear, for reminding us of David and Goliath as it seeks to intimidate a smaller, weaker foe with its huge bulk and fearsome armament. The classical example cited by Wright is the press photograph of the encounter of a Chinese tank with a single protester on the road into Tienanmien Square. It's a photograph which has become emblematic of good resisting evil, a tiny figure apparently halting a whole column of tanks. On the other hand, tanks have often been used successfully to intimidate protesters. Wright reminds us of the use of tanks to intimidate strikers in Glasgow in 1919, although there were no actual casualties. Conversely, there is the use of tanks by those who wish to project power, such as Yeltsin riding on a tank to suppress parliamentary opposition (or, the inversion of this, Dukakis self-destructing in an attempt to establish military credentials by being photographed as if commanding a tank). At the other end of the scale, Patrick Wright cites Krzysztov Wodicko's *Poliscar*, a fabulous vehicle designed to invoke the Greek *polis* but, not surprisingly, one which reminded others of a tank—'a robot with a tank-shaped body geared to survival in a police state'. For Wright, this discrepancy of views simply proved his point—the tank has always suffered from 'symbolic excess', an availability to interpretation as benign or cruel, awesome or ridiculous. Wodicko told Wright that he had thought of constructing his mobile homeless shelter with caterpillar tracks, so that it could navigate New York's pot-holed streets, symbolically at least. He gave up the idea, Patrick Wright tells us, because tracks 'would have made the Poliscar altogether too much like a tank, pinning it down to a single meaning and reducing the sense of visual ambiguity that he wanted to retain'—the sense, I presume, of an indefinite tankishness rather than a clear tank identity.

Alongside the *Poliscar*, it is worth considering the radio-controlled tank designed by Matt Heckert and constructed by Survival Research Laboratories in San Francisco. The Matt-Machine, as its designer dubbed it, 'would be full of anger and fury and would make awful, absolutely awful noises. And it would continually change its appearance.' This tank is quite small, powered by two electric motors, with stainless steel treads that drive it backwards, forwards or in a circle. It also has a set of arms, each of which can reach out and grab something firmly, as well as a 26-inch spear 'poised to pierce whatever it holds in its hands. The spear strikes with about 1,800lbs of force, powered by compressed air.' Survival Research Labs have made a number of machines, armed with buzz-saws, flame-throwers and the like, and programmed to careen out of control, fire projectiles, detonate bombs and assault the audience at the climax of gladiatorial performances of crazed fury and aggression. According to Mark Pauline, SRL's guiding spirit, the shows are 'parodies of war' in which small machines have just as much chance as bigger ones; although they are much weaker, they are also much less complex and therefore less likely to break down.

Mark Pauline fears his creations—he already has one mutilated hand, the victim of a rogue rocket blast. Yet, when asked whether we will reach the point where a machine will cease to do a human's bidding and become self-willed, he replies: 'You mean take on a life of their own? I think we've proved that at least in a theatrical presentation type of experience—yes, machines can take on a life of their own. They do have a mind of their own.' His ultimate vision is of cybertanks running wild, out of control. Wright's book ends as follows: 'Prophets already foresee a new kind of "fire ant warfare" in which areas will be dominated not by high-tech Behemoths but by hosts of tiny semi-autonomous insect-machines, and surveyed by "long-loiter high altitude drones" and clouds of "surveillance dust" made up of microscopic winged things carrying sensors.' Powered by photosynthesis rather than diesel fuel, these 'hybrid bio-mechanical devices' will open a 'microscopic theatre of combat and, in all likelihood, bring the human bloodstream into battlespace'. As for the old-fashioned tank, it will be lost on a terrain littered with sensors backed by hidden projectiles and tiny robots, 'giving its position away and then moving on to eat their way through the tank's gaskets or fuse its movable parts'. Roll on, the nano-tank fleet! Tiny control-free robotanks destroy the human race!

4

THE QUESTION OF TECHNOLOGY

Martin Heidegger gave his lecture on 'The Question of Technology' in November 1955. It was one of a series on 'The Arts in the Technological Age', organized in Munich by the Bavarian Academy of Fine Arts and presented by a number of different speakers. Heidegger's paper is best known for his much-quoted remarks on the fate of the Rhine, following the construction of a hydro-electric plant, which 'sets the Rhine to supplying its hydraulic pressure, which then sets the turbines turning', thus setting in motion machines that produce an electric current, which is then distributed across the land through a network of cables. 'What the river is now,' Heidegger commented, is a 'water power supplier', an example of the transformation of nature into 'standing reserve', designated 'on call for duty', prepared to fulfil the mission 'ordered' by its masters. 'Let us ponder for a moment', Heidegger invited his audience—'Let us ponder ... the contrast that speaks from the two titles, *The Rhine*, as dammed up into the power station, and *The Rhine* as uttered out of the art work, in Hölderlin's hymn of that name'.

What struck me immediately was the military nature of Heidegger's philosophical terminology—the river was described as a 'reserve', it was 'on call for duty', it was 'completely unautonomous' because its 'standing', like that of a standing army, derived only from 'the ordering of the orderable'. In effect, the Rhine had been conscripted. In fact, Heidegger is soon comparing the Rhine, as conscripted nature, with human beings as conscripts, 'completely unautonomous'. Yet despite the 'enframing' of the world by modern technology, there remains the possibility, even the 'destiny', of a 'revealing' that can set humanity free. This 'revealing' can come, Heidegger asserts, through 'art'—not in the sense we might think, but in a different sense. 'The arts [in Ancient Greece] were not derived from the artistic. Art works were not enjoyed aesthetically. Art was not a sector of cultural activity.' On the contrary, art was the mode by which 'being' was revealed. It was through pondering the essence of art that the essence of technology could be revealed, if we were resolute enough in our questioning of it.

I must admit that when I first read all this I was completely baffled. It all seemed even more obscure and baffling than the various other writings by Heidegger that I had read and attempted to understand, a task made more difficult, I must confess, by my extreme dislike both for Heidegger's general view of the world and for his particular presentation of the essence of philosophy. I remain an unrepentant follower of the Enlightenment. However, my curiosity was piqued by his suggestion that there was some kind of essential relationship between art and technology, particularly after reading Patrick Wright's fascinating book on the history and cultural impact of the tank. The origin of the tank was marked by many curious coincidences and odd twists of fate. The tank both directly changed the course and even the outcome of the First World War and indirectly influenced the war's cultural side-effects. It became a kind of mythic creature whose status as a symbol of armed power persisted right down to Tiananmien Square and, as I write, the Israeli-Palestinian conflict, in which tanks have been widely deployed.

I also began to reflect on the one-sidedness of the commonplace view of the 1914–18 war, the assumption that the war had created, in England and elsewhere, a national mood of disenchantment and even lamentation, despite the military victory. On the contrary, not only did the role played by tanks in the Allied victory lead to a new fascination with the tank as a crucially successful war-machine but also to a whole new school of strategic thought, inspired by the work of J. C. R. Fuller and his interpreter, Liddell Hart, military theorists whose ideas about the role of tanks in warfare were given practical expression in the Second World War in the two pivotal campaigns fought against German *panzer* divisions both in North Africa and, of course, in the Soviet Union. Together with the plane and, arguably, the use of poison gas, the tank was *the* crucial military innovation of the Great War. Moreover, the conclusion I have slowly worked my way towards is that the war—and its crucial ingredients, such as the tank, had a lasting impact, not only on military thinking, but also on the arts—especially on literature and on the visual arts.

Thus, while Paul Fussell's well-known book *The Great War and Modern Memory* (1975) remains a pathbreaking work, its insistence on the prevalence of disenchantment as a reaction to the war, its emphatic endorsement of the Siegfried Sassoon–Wilfred Owen view of the war, needs to be counter-balanced by an acknowledgement that, to many, the war presented the outline image of a future brave new world. The writer who most obviously adopted this countervailing view was also the writer who had the most influence on Heidegger, a determining influence, in fact— that is to say, it was Ernst Jünger. Jünger had enlisted in the German army when he was just 19 and was in the trenches by December 1914. Wounded fourteen times, he escaped death by a series of miraculous lucky breaks. He ended the war, in the 1918 Ludendorff offensive, by fighting as one of the elite shock troops, whose task was to break through Allied lines in small groups rather than within an extended mass assault. Four years later, after demobilization, he published his book, *Storms of Steel*. It concludes as follows:

> We—by which I mean those of the youth of this land who are capable of enthusiasm for an ideal—will not shrink from [future battles]. We stand in memory of the dead who are holy to us, and we believe ourselves entrusted with the true and spiritual welfare of our people. We stand for what will be and for what has been. Though force without and barbarity within conglomerate in sombre clouds, yet so long as the blade of a sword will strike a spark in the night may it be said: Germany lives and Germany shall never go under.

Jünger was to become a close friend of Heidegger. The book which counted for the most in this friendship was Jünger's *The Worker*, published in 1932. Elliot Neaman, in his study of Jünger, *A Dubious Past*, summarizes this work as follows: 'Junger's analysis was an almost optimistic affirmation of the death of nineteenth-century liberalism and the establishment of an authoritarian soldier-worker state, ruled by [a young and ruthless leadership] who would build an autotelic society of steel-nerved automatons.' After the book came out, Heidegger, also aware of Jünger's 1930 article on 'Total Mobilization', 'discussed these writings in a small circle and tried to show how they express a fundamental understanding of Nietzsche's metaphysics, insofar as the history and present of the Western world are seen and foreseen in the horizon of this metaphysics'.

In 1939/40 (at the onset of the Second World War) Heidegger once again discussed Jünger's book 'with a circle of colleagues'. He now interpreted Jünger's work, still so strange and off-putting even to those in Heidegger's own circle, as indeed borne out by 'the facts' in its conceptualization of the worker and its vision of the future, by its assertion of the 'universal rule of will to power within history'. Although Heidegger had strong reservations about Jünger's generally uncritical attitude towards technology, he nonetheless endorsed Jünger's fascination with 'the will to power within history', as thought through in the light of the power and gestalt of the worker. This will to power was read by Heidegger within an explicitly German and Nietzschean context. Later, as power began to shift away from Germany and towards the Soviet Union, particularly after the failed assault on Stalingrad, and the United States had entered the war after Pearl Harbor, Heidegger began to retreat from a position which flew in the face of reality.

Both Heidegger and Jünger nonetheless found an admiring audience for their work, not only before but also following the Second World War, especially in France. Jünger, in particular, was perceived not simply as a political thinker of value but also as an outstanding writer, in the literary sense of the term. In 1973 he was shortlisted for the Nobel Prize for Literature and in the next decade he won both the Schiller and Goethe prizes in his native Germany, as well as many other literary honours. In fact, Jünger succeeded in re-inventing himself as a traditional conservative, even an Aesopian critic of Nazism, largely on the basis of his weirdly allegorical novel, *On The Marble Cliffs*, translated into English by a well-known left-wing personality, Stuart Hood, an escapee from a Fascist prison camp who had himself fought with the Italian resistance. Jünger, it should be said, was never himself a member of the National Socialist party, unlike Heidegger of course. In fact, in his most activist political phase, Jünger defined himself as a 'National-Bolshevik', a phrase which signified both an affinity to National Socialism and a separation from it, reflecting his view that a regime of the right should be based on mobilization of the workers: a political creed which radicalized the 'Third Way' or 'Plannist' ideologies of a De Man, a Doriot or indeed a Le Corbusier, whose 'engineer's aesthetic' required a top-down leadership to re-shape mass industrial society.

The reactionary modernism of Ernst Jünger, driven by his experience of the 1914–18 war, found many counterparts throughout Europe. In the first place, there were those strands of thought which developed out of Italian Futurism—itself, of course, a movement with a strongly aggressive component, obsessed with speed and noise and violence, all strongly marked characteristics of modern warfare. The Futurists were also explicitly, even stridently, pro-Fascist from the very beginning. Their famous founding manifesto, published in *Le Figaro* in 1909, began with the invocation of 'furious speed ... formidable sound ... the love of danger ... the practice of energy and boldness ... aggressive movement ... the life-risking leap ... [the] roaring automobile, which seems to operate like a machine-gun', before advancing towards a triumphant conclusion with such statements as 'we wish to glorify war—the world's only hygienics—militarism, patriotism', concluding, predictably enough, with 'contempt for women' and a celebration of arsenals.

The Futurists rallied to the war effort from the start. Marinetti looked forward confidently to a war that would last ten years, eventually becoming global. He welcomed the 'new, war-like, plastic dynamism' to be revealed in art and urged his followers to 'try and live the war pictorially and to study all of its marvellous mechanical forms'. In 1915 Boccioni, Marinetti, Sironi and Sant'Elia all enlisted—with a degree of bathos—in the Volunteer Battalion of Cyclists, while evoking in their artwork the shapes and sounds of planes, howitzers and machine guns. The painter Carra noted that 'war is proving to be the best ally of our futurist movement ... The war is creating in man a truly new love for machinism and metallism, which inspire an entire new art in formation.' Severini, in his painting *The War* (1914–15) included the words 'ORDRE DE MOBILISATION GENERALE' amid imagery of guns, planes, wheels and machine parts. Nor was the influence of Futurism contained within Italy and France. It spread to Russia, to England (as Vorticism) and, most significantly of all, to Germany. In all these countries, Futurism expressed itself through the familiar triad of negation of the past, a cult of new technologies and radical nationalism. Negatively, Futurism was anti-bourgeois, anti-passéist, anti-classical, anti-religious, anti-feminist and anti-idealist. Professors, of course, were to be implacably opposed, together with tourist guides and souvenir-peddlers.

In Germany, between 1912 and 1916, Futurist ideas found support in Herwarth Walden's *Der Sturm* and Franz Pfemfert's *Die Aktion*, avant-garde journals now thought of as 'Expressionist' in their allegiance. In fact, Italian Futurism left a powerful imprint on German Expressionism, as Peter Demetz has shown. Walden had studied art in Italy and welcomed Marinetti's support in his own struggle against tradition, publishing Futurist writing and organizing exhibitions of Futurist painting in Berlin, supported by Alfred Döblin, August Stramm and Franz Marc. *Aktion* published the work of Marinetti, whose impact was thus felt by Hugo Ball, the founder of Zurich dadaism. As late as 1934, an exhibition of Futurist *Aeropittura* ('Aero-painting') was held in Berlin (at a time when Goebbels was protecting the radical wing of 'Nordic Expressionism'). Both Goebbels and Goering (who had an interest in aviation) attended the dinner in honour of the exhibition. Surprisingly, perhaps, Schwitters and Moholy-Nagy were also among the diners.

Marinetti's anti-syntactic poetry was also welcomed in Germany. Among those who read Marinetti's work were Stramm, Döblin and Johannes Becher, later Minister of Culture in the DDR [Communist East Germany]. Becher even wrote an introduction to the German translation of an Italian officer's war diary, found in the trenches after the Italian retreat, invoking the motorization and modernity of war. Döblin, best known as author of *Berlin Alexanderplatz*, published a futuristic poem of his own in 1915—*The Battle, The Battle*, in which, as Demetz notes, 'he used the techniques of [words-in-liberation] selectively in order to suggest the chaos of the Western Front and its staging zones (which he knew well from working in the field hospitals [of Alsace])'. Demetz also cites Marinetti's description, in his strange novel, *Mafarka*, of Gazurmah, the African Icarus, who is constructed from wires, flesh, metal and muscles, 'born not from woman but from the constructing will of his father, an airplane as human being, a human being as airplane which/who surges through the universe to Mars.' Later, Günter Grass was to write that he could not speak about his own work without mentioning the Futurist element in that of his mentor, Döblin. Marinetti himself, I might add, enlisted in the Second World War to fight in the Soviet Union, on the outskirts of Stalingrad, only to die eventually in the endgame as he defiantly defended the Duce's short-lived Fascist Republic of Saló.

In England, Futurism mutated into Vorticism, under the leadership of Wyndham Lewis, both writer and painter. As in other countries, it was Marinetti's own visit to London that created the context for a local movement to develop. Lewis wrote about the decisive period in his memoir, *Blasting and Bombardiering*, published in 1937 and covering the period from 1914 through to 1926. 'As chef de bande of the Vorticists,' he wrote, 'I cut a figure in London not unlike that of Degrelle today in Brussels. There were no politics then. There was no Rexist Party or suchlike. Instead there was the Vorticist group. I might have been at the head of a social revolution, instead of merely being the prophet of a new fashion in art.' Degrelle's Rexists, as we might expect, were a nationalist and quasi-Fascist party. For Lewis, the machine was a repeated motif, in paintings and novels. 'Machinery', he wrote in 1919, 'should be regarded as a new resource .... A machinery for making the parts of a 6 inch Mark 19 gun should be regarded apart from its function. Absorbed into the aesthetic consciousness its function would change and through its agency emotions would be manufactured.' However, just as he viewed the artist's studio as an engineering workshop, he also saw himself as a tool of war. 'Who in fact was it', he asked, 'who was proposing to kill or maim me? ... I saw clearly that it was not my German opposite number. He, like myself, was an instrument.'

In his book, *The Mechanic Muse*, Hugh Kenner traces the way Vorticism was taken up by others—by Ezra Pound, for instance. As Kenner notes, Pound (a future Fascist) played a crucial role in the making of the celebrated film, *Ballet Mécanique*, by introducing the composer George Antheil, who had composed a piece of machine music (for player piano and other machine sound sources) which he wanted to perform, accompanied by a film projection (since film was also a mechanical art).

It was Ezra Pound who steered Antheil to the artist Fernand Léger, who was himself fascinated by modern machinery. Kenner also notes Pound's own interest in machines: he had compared the working poet to the designer of a machine in his 1914 Imagist Manifesto and, in 1925, he went on to declare that 'the good forms are in the parts of the machine where energy is concentrated' (like the dynamos in Heidegger's power station, one wonders?).

Kenner also linked the fascination with crowds that he finds in the work of Eliot, Joyce and others to the development of mass public transport—especially the bus and the underground railway. In his famous lines in *The Waste Land*, it might be added, Eliot also links the crowd of commuters flowing over London Bridge to the timetable and the schedule through his invocation of 'the dead sound on the final stroke of nine', as struck by a church clock: 'a crowd-life conducted in clock-bound synchrony', as Kenner put it. At the other end of the political spectrum, Walter Benjamin was also struck by the historical significance of the clock. In his notes for the *Arcades* project, he cited Marx copiously on the subject—Marx's comment that 'the clock was the first automatic device applied to practical purposes' and, along with the mill, provided one of 'the two material bases on which the preparations for machine-operated industry proceeded'. In effect, the clock, as Kenner describes, regulates not only the machine but also the worker, including the city clerk, as became abundantly clear with the development of Taylorism in the United States.

Taylorism also swept through the Soviet Union, together with the cult of the engineer. The impact on the arts was considerable—Meyerhold's theory of 'bio-mechanics' drew on the work of Gastev, the Soviet poet and theorist of the organization of labour. Eisenstein's theory of 'montage' drew on his background as an engineer and his work with pontoon bridges for the Red army. In the early 1930s a team of engineers from Detroit was invited to the Soviet Union, led by Moritz Kahn, brother of the Ford Motor Company's favoured architect, Albert Kahn. In two years the brothers built over 500 factories and trained over 1,000 engineers and apprentices. This trend in Soviet policy did not escape Heidegger's attention. He was quite clear in his view that the main threats to European culture, with German culture at its centre, came from Russia and America, powers that he perceived as 'Roman' rather than 'Greek' in nature. During the Battle of Stalingrad itself, Heidegger noted that 'Who has ears to hear ... can already for two decades hear the word of Lenin: *Bolshevism is Soviet power + electrification*. This means: Bolshevism is the "organic", i.e. calculatively organized ... thrusting together of the unconditioned power of the party with fully realized technologization.'

For Heidegger, the Soviet Union and United States alike embodied specific historical trajectories, which his own work as a philosopher was designed to distinguish from those of Germany and *continental* Europe, for England too was a 'Roman' (i.e. 'imperial') and 'cosmopolitan' power, *imperium* rather than *reich*, a coupling which echoes that of 'civilization' as opposed to 'culture'. Domenico Losurdo persuasively argued that Heidegger revised his previous interpretation of Nietzsche's concept of 'will to power' when technological superiority seemed to have left Germany for its adversaries. He now described it as showing a 'Roman' rather than a 'Greco-German' character and consequently interpreted it as 'negative' rather than 'positive'. At the same time, Heidegger's overall evaluation of the role of technology also changed in the same kind of way. What he failed to foresee, of course, were the massive changes that would take place in the nature of technology itself, rather than in its political and geographical habitat.

As mentioned in the preceding chapter, Ernest Swinton's book, *Eyewitness*, contains a photograph entitled 'Method of releasing a carrier pigeon from a porthole in a Tank.' A hand sticks out through a small hole in the armour of a tank, clutching a pigeon and, presumably, about to release its grip so that the bird can flutter off back to base. By the time of the Second World War, at least in the German *blitzkrieg*, tanks were able to communicate with each other and with spotter planes by radio. As Manuel De Landa put it, in his fascinating book, *War in The Age of Intelligent Machines*, there had been a key transition from a 'motorized' war to a 'distributed network' model of war. In the Second World War, cybernetic technology was applied to artillery targeting. Today, digital and other novel technologies dominate the discussion of new military trends: sensors, lidar, ultrared and infrared detectors or seekers, nightvision devices, thermal imagers. In the future, we are told, Matchbox toy-size wheeled vehicles will carry sensors around the battlefield. Other toy-like small wheeled vehicles could carry complete laboratories. Communications will be routed through GPS locator, digital radio and computer systems.

Mark Pauline's robotic machines, armed with their own weaponry, are able, in his own words, 'to take on a life of their own.' Pauline's vision of cybertanks running wild, out of control, is the final apocalyptic endgame of the history of the tank from the First World War, through the era of massed battles, to the electronic warfare of tomorrow. Perhaps, after all, there is an unexpected conclusion that can be drawn from this. In effect, Pauline's machines, though man-made, can develop their own autonomous will-to-power. Rather than residing in some form of state or government, the will-to-power is transferred to the machine itself, as its computer systems render it autotelic in its own right. Technology thus becomes, not an entity which is enframed, as Heidegger saw it, but one which might transform itself. In this context, Ernst Jünger, in an interview published on his ninetieth birthday, imagined that scientists—'the great incarnations of the figure of Dr Worker'—might find ways to render military conflict pointless and absurd. He might have wondered, perhaps, whether it was not the autonomous machines themselves, rather than the scientists, who would finally put an end to war. Perhaps, as art came to encounter technology, as in Mark Pauline's pointless experimental machines, the will-to-control of human beings would eventually be defused. Rather than 'masters' of technology, human beings would seek to become its partners.

5

MUSEUMS AND RUBBISH THEORY

Museums are relatively recent public institutions which evolved into their current form around the beginning of the nineteenth century. Indeed, it is generally held that it was the transformation of the Louvre from royal palace to national museum after the French Revolution, and then its systematic consolidation under Napoleon and his chosen director, Denon, which marked the beginning of the modern epoch of the art museum. Denon amassed paintings and sculptures from Napoleon's conquests and then inventoried and displayed them in a scholarly manner, following a chronological scheme, while grouping work together in distinct national schools: Italian, French, Northern (Flemish, Dutch, German) and Spanish. Though the cream of the work was repatriated after Napoleon's defeat at Waterloo, the Louvre continued as a model art museum. Denon's institution was basically a national and, indeed, imperial project, and this was directly reflected in the organization of the display: the various national schools were all parts of Napoleon's (and France's) Empire. Hence the absence of a British school (and, perhaps, the enduring French myth that the British have no visual culture). The chronological scheme was designed to culminate with the unity of European art to be achieved under the new Empire.

Napoleon's vision was both national and universal, reflecting the two self-supporting faces of imperialism. There was naturally a tension between these two concepts of the museum's role which persists up to the present day. At the heart of the matter is the problem of which or, put another way, *whose* past the museum represents and displays. Museums are collections of material objects or artefacts from the past, preserved and displayed in a ceremonial way in order to be looked at. They must be accumulated, authenticated, inventoried, evaluated, selected, positioned and interpreted. These artefacts are usually felt to represent the past origins of the shared culture of a community. They are the 'heritage' of this community and are defended as such when other communities lay claim to them. Evidently this aspect of the museum's purpose (implicit or explicit) arises with the historic growth of nationalism, chauvinism and, in due course, other kinds of particularism and identity politics, to use the current term. Heritage, it should be noted, is both the internal construction of a community 'for itself', and the construction of an external image 'for others', for visitors or tourists. (Though it should be noted that, usually, the great majority of museum-goers are themselves 'national', internal tourists.)

The concept of 'heritage' has different meanings in different places. It may be 'universal' (to varying degrees), 'national', 'regional' or 'local', as well as the heritage of different minority groups. Moreover, it is important to remember that these nations, groups and communities do not necessarily exist *a priori*, but often come into historical existence precisely through their construction of a heritage for themselves. If we look at the development of nationalism, we typically find the mobilization of a national language, a national literature, a national geography and landscape, a national history anchored around great events and heroes, and so on. Museums institutionalize and codify an important part of this process. They help to define what the 'heritage' is. In this respect, they take note of the programmatic views of 'official nationalism' as well as the more complex mix of popular sentiment and the highly focused ideas of their colleagues and peers. The museum is a terrain for struggles over the social control of value and meaning. The elaboration of its collection and display policy inevitably involves controversial and even explosive issues as it defines the ethical and aesthetic limits of a heritage and a culture, as well as its centre, its rank order and its internal articulation. Of course, museums strive to contain the danger and to prevent controversy from breaking out of the museum itself. When it does break out it can rouse considerable passion, as we know from the *Sensation* show.

The question of 'which community'—in relation to the social control of value and meaning—has risen most spectacularly, and not surprisingly, in debates about the future of the ethnographic museum. Ethnographic museums were originally modelled on schemas drawn from natural history. Artefacts were classified according to type, eventually within a developmental framework derived loosely from nineteenth-century Darwinism. Some old-fashioned museums of this kind still exist. All the pipes or musical instruments or baskets from around the world are grouped together, sometimes higgledy-piggledy, sometimes to illustrate a supposed evolution in their formal or functional complexity. It was the anthropologist and curator Franz Boas who overthrew this whimsical system and insisted that the various artefacts of a particular people be grouped together coherently to represent their 'culture'. This led Boas to construct stage-like settings with panoramic back-drops and to use posed mannequins to demonstrate artefacts, as it were, in actual 'use'. This method of display had two effects: it presented artefacts as specimens, representative objects from everyday life, seen as constitutive of a 'culture', rather than objects of unique and exceptional value, like artworks, and it de-chronologized the museum, so that it was organized around synchronic 'chunks', set-pieces from an abstract 'past' (presumed to be 'disappearing' or even 'lost'), rather than a still ongoing history.

The most obvious long-term result of Boas's efforts, which were intended to show the richness and diversity of the many cultures which ethnographers studied, was to problematize the role of the ethnographers themselves, and the museums with whom they worked, in 'appropriating' the very cultures which they were aiming to preserve and draw sympathetic attention to. It is important to note that this happened, paradoxically enough, against the grain of Boas's display methods and philosophy. Precisely because artefacts were exhibited in famous museums, unique and exceptional status was conferred upon them, as the most treasured artefacts of a culture, and precisely because they were seen as the representatives of 'times ancestral' in a generic sense, they stimulated 'roots revivalist' demands for their restitution and re-insertion into the narrative space of a still ongoing cultural history. The underlying issue here is that of 'contextualization'. Once Boas had made the step of positioning artefacts within the context of the everyday life of a specific culture, however theatrical or schematic, it followed inevitably that the demand would come to re-position them in the ongoing context of that culture itself, their actual place of origin. Evidently this would be even more 'authentic'.

The question of 'authenticity' is a complex one and I shall return to it later. But there is a sense in which the concept of 'context' is linked to that of 'authenticity' through that of 'origin'. An authentic artefact is one that can be directly and demonstrably linked to a historic place of origin. 'Context' is then construed as the totality of that historic place and circumstance, its original cultural setting. Art museums do not have the same concern with context as ethnography museums, and, though there are evidently arguments that they should, there are also reasons why they should not. Whereas a carved or painted mask may plainly be designed for use in a ceremony, the same is not true of a great many paintings. They were produced precisely as decorative works, art-works, to be valued and displayed autonomously. The whole concept of the autonomy of art is itself a characteristic feature at least of Western culture, developed over many centuries. Few people today would prefer to see religious paintings, which did have a ceremonial function, exhibited in simulated chapels (perhaps visible, like many paintings once were, only on Easter Sunday). Second, a work of art such as a painting has been selected for museum display not because it played a representative part in the everyday life of its community of origin, but because it has been assigned an exceptional status as an aesthetic object in its own right. Indeed, it is more often perceived as giving value *to* a culture, rather than receiving value *from* it. Works of art tend to make 'contextualizing' materials look trivial and clichéd.

Above all, it is not always clear who art 'belongs to' culturally. Who has the best claim to a Picasso museum, for instance: Malaga, Barcelona, Céret or Paris? Fortunately, Picasso was prolific enough for all four to exist. What about the many artists attached to dynastic courts or other sources of patronage far from their place of birth? What is so important about place of birth, in any case, compared with the other places in which an artist may have lived and worked? What about the cultural role of the patron? What about art movements which were themselves explicitly opposed to the culture of their own nations, such as the surrealists? The fact of the matter is that Western art acquired an autonomy before museums and nations, in the modern sense, came into being. Artists learned to see themselves in complex relation to the culture (or set of cultures) within which they were working. They might see themselves (and be seen) as central, as mainstream, as marginal, as in opposition, as in isolation. The more I think about the concept of 'national culture', the more problematic, obscure and potentially reductive it seems.

In questioning the concept of 'culture' and stressing the 'exceptional' and 'relatively autonomous' status of art-works, I am not, of course, overlooking the problems associated with this. The idea that art-works are 'exceptional' evidently presupposes that there is some kind of ordering of value involved, an implicit or explicit hierarchy. I accept this. Indeed, I believe that the denial of an open and explicit hierarchy of value simply leads to the creation of an implicit, unspoken and covert hierarchy. Museums necessarily select artefacts for preservation and for exhibition and any kind of selection already presupposes some kind of priority-setting, although they are often reluctant to make explicit and, so to speak, display the values and assumptions underlying their system of priority-setting. Why is it more important to spend money (or effort) on acquiring the work of one artist rather than another? What exactly is meant by the concept of a 'gap' in a museum collection? Why are works exhibited in a particular sequence? What are the underlying concepts of history and value which are articulated, consciously or unconsciously, in the exhibition policy of a museum? These are crucial questions. They address the problem of the social formation of taste, the construction of a canon, and the relationship between internal museum priorities and external cultural, political and economic forces.

In 1979 Michael Thompson published his wonderfully weird and provocative book, *Rubbish Theory: The Construction and Destruction of Value*. Thompson argued that there were two principal types of object: the durable and the transient. *Durable* objects maintain or even increase in value over time and have (ideally) infinite life-spans. They are treasures, and are often seen as having some transcendent status in relation both to time and to use. They are then removed from circulation and given a special, ceremonial value. In sharp contrast, there are *transient* objects which decrease in value over time and have finite life-spans. Eventually, these transient objects are considered to have lost any value and may be discarded as worthless. They then become 'rubbish'. These are, of course, ideal types. Between the two poles of durability and transience there is what Thompson called a 'flexible' region, where values may rise and fall for a period. But, it seems, there is an implicit threshold beyond which objects become considered as 'transcendent' in one direction or as 'rubbish' in the other. The principal battles over the social control of value take place along the borders of this 'flexible region'. Basically, as Thompson points out, the rich and powerful, who naturally tend to own and control large numbers of highly-valued, durable objects will try to maintain the status of their possessions. Other groups will then try to promote other types of object in a challenge to dominant values.

The relevance of this to museums is intuitively clear. Museums maintain the value of the class of objects owned by rich and powerful collectors, not just by removing them from circulation (scarcity value), but also by conferring a ceremonial status on them and guaranteeing (or appearing to guarantee) their durability. As we all know, a complex negotiation of value is continuously going on between museums, patrons and dealers. Over time, we can perceive large-scale historic shifts, of the kind chronicled in Reitlinger's classic book, *The Economics of Taste*. At one time, for instance, American museums and millionaires valued, acquired and exhibited British eighteenth-century painters: Reynolds, Romney, Gainsborough, etc. In due course, though the work of these painters was still appreciated, their blue-chip status was lost and eventually the nineteenth-century French impressionist and post-impressionist painters came to replace them. Walter Annenberg, a wire-service and media millionaire, collected different works from, say, Huntington, a railroad millionaire. Within the saga of one single family, the Rockefellers, we can see clear generational differences in multi-millionaire taste reflected quite explicitly in museum acquisition policy. Today's museums face new challenges to official taste.

Evidently, the construction of changes in taste is a complex affair. I am not talking about a simple conspiracy. On the contrary, most of the actors involved are more or less unaware of their role in the drama. It is only with the benefit of hindsight that we can begin to speculate on why Vermeer or El Greco made such a rapid rise in the nineteenth century.

We might be struck by the role of enthusiastic critics (Thoré in the case of Vermeer) or contemporary artists (Mary Cassatt in the case of El Greco). Changes of taste in small artworld groups of painters and writers may eventually, or even quite rapidly, feed upstream to patrons—once they have been registered, for instance, by the antennae of dealers. Evidently curators have their part to play as well, mediating and intervening in the name of the disinterested and 'transcendent' values which all (or most) profess to revere. It is easy to see, for example, how Alfred H. Barr acted as a 'transmission belt' of taste, at the Museum of Modern Art, between insider 'artworld' circles and a powerful group of patrons and donors. What has not been sufficiently researched or even considered is the complex of reasons why he found the work of some artists easier to advance than that of others, the nature of the resistances which he undoubtedly encountered to some of his 'educational' efforts, or the areas where it proved comparatively easy to make converts.

Thompson, however, suggests a second scheme for the understanding of value-shifts. As well as conflict and negotiation in the 'flexible region' there is also the surprising and rapid promotion upwards of artefacts from the very bottom end of the scale and even from rubbish. He charts in detail cases of a steady decline to worthlessness followed, in due course, by a spectacularly steep climb back into esteem. A vivid example is the deterioration of used cars into wrecks, and then suddenly, following the ministrations of mechanics and dealers, their startling reappearance as vintage models, even (within their own world) their transformation into museum pieces. 'We are all familiar with the way despised Victorian objects have become sought-after antiques; with bakelite ashtrays that have become collectors' items; with old bangers transformed into vintage motor-cars. So we know the changes take place, but how?' A specific example recounted by Thompson is the history of the evaluation of the Stevengraph. This was a Victorian invention, a woven silk picture manufactured mechanically on a Jacquard loom. Examples were first exhibited by the inventor Thomas Stevens at the York Exhibition in England in 1879.

Stevengraphs were sold at York for 1s (now 5 pence, or 8 cents, but then, of course, worth very much more). Over the years, in accord with consumer taste, the Stevens company changed the subjects of their pictures. Thus, 'Dick Turpin's ride to York on his bonnie Black Bess' exhibited at the York exhibition (presumably because of the local reference) was discontinued two years later. Very soon afterwards this particular picture became commercially worthless. Nor, of course, did it receive any critical acclaim. In 1940, however, the Stevengraph factory in Coventry was destroyed by German bombs. This was an important pre-condition for the subsequent re-evaluation of the artefacts made there. However, throughout the 1950s the Stevengraph remained worthless. It was not till the 1960s that it suddenly began to climb in value, reaching £100 (then $180) by the end of the decade. The second pre-condition for this rise, after the destruction of the factory, was the development of a critical literature. A pioneering scholarly article had been published as early as 1933, in 'Antiques Magazine', but the first full-length book, 'The Silk Pictures of Thomas Stevens' came in 1957, shortly before the climb began, and a second book, 'Thomas Stevens and his Silk Ribbon Pictures', appeared in 1959. It is worth noting, I think, that both these books carried the name of Thomas Stevens, as though he was an artist rather than a manufacturer. We could characterize the process we are discussing as exhibitions, followed by articles, and finally by scholarly tomes.

Another crucial pre-condition of this process was the development of private collections by enthusiastic amateurs. The taste of these collectors, beginning in the 1930s, was at the time frankly 'eccentric', as Thompson rightly notes. Later, however, they could be characterized as 'quiet' and 'discerning' collectors, people who gained an 'innocent enjoyment' from Stevengraphs, which was later proved to reveal great foresight. Finally, there was a fourth and crucial further pre-condition. At the end of the 1950s, Henry James Stevens, last of the Stevens family, died. It turned out that on the night of the fateful bombing, he had taken home one of the two Stevengraph pattern-books from the factory. The other was destroyed in the raid. After his death, this one surviving pattern-book was offered to the Coventry City Museum, which accepted it for its collection. As a result, it was, of course, removed from circulation, but, perhaps more important, it was guaranteed preservation and thus assigned the status of a time-resisting and durable object. It had crossed the threshold. This acceptance into the museum precipitated, in turn, the commercial boom in Stevengraphs which followed. As Thompson notes, the valuation of Stevengraphs was thus transferred from the hands of women (who had created the first collections and written the first critical articles) to the hands of men. Stevengraphs were no longer rubbish, hoarded by eccentric women (the author's grandmother among them), but museum-pieces valued by acquisitive and status-conscious men.

As Thompson observes, 'Things may drift into obscurity, but they leap into prominence.' Years of obsolescence, dilapidation and changing fashion were undone in a trice. In a flash of revaluation, yesterday's kitsch was today's heritage, even today's masterpiece. The underlying idea of 'rubbish theory', then, runs as follows. Artefacts, in general, tend to decline in value. Some of them, however, begin to rise and, after a period of conflict or negotiation, cross a certain threshold to become recognized as time-resistant. Museums are important gate-keepers at this threshold. Those that do not make it may float about in the 'flexible region' but are more likely to join the others in a steady decline. In the end, many of them will cross another threshold and be discarded as rubbish. Critics and taste-makers may help give them a contemptuous push across this threshold. But given the right conditions, some artefacts may leap miraculously from being abject rubbish to being regarded as transcendent, quasi-sacred objects, without having to re-traverse the 'flexible region' of everyday currency. In Bataille's terms, there is a short-circuit in the 'general economy', whereby artefacts are transferred from the extremes of ignominy, of waste, the excremental, the lowest of the low, to the peaks of the sacred, the highest of the high, without re-entering the 'restricted economy' of use-value and commercial circulation.

This second alternative is determined, however, by more complex factors than Thompson realizes. His view derives specifically from a close observation of the chronological sequence of events in relation to Stevengraphs. But, if we step back and take a more general view, we become aware that the Stevengraph phenomenon may be symptomatic of a much deeper change in taste, akin to what Kuhn, theorizing changes in scientific thought, has called a 'paradigm-shift'. Can we divorce the steep climb of the Stevengraph from the simultaneous reappraisal of Victorian photographs? Are we not dealing with a profound change in the evaluation of a whole class of artefacts, images technologically and multiply produced? Shouldn't we also note that Walter Benjamin's now sanctified essay on 'The Work of Art in the Age of Mechanical Reproduction' was first translated into English in the 1960s (in 'Studies on the Left', by an enthusiast, following what seemed an eccentric interest at the time, but one which later proved to be discerning). If we look at it this way, we can see how significant it was that the Stevens pattern-book was presented to an obscure local museum, the Coventry City Museum, rather than a major and much more prestigious museum—the Victoria and Albert Museum's photography collection or the Tate Gallery of British Art—representing a distinction between Stevengraphs and photographs. In fact, it seems there is a series of thresholds which have to be crossed, as a work passes from eccentric enthusiasm to final acclaim. Even durable, time-resisting objects are positioned within a world in which the social control of value has its own distinct pattern of rise and fall, order and hierarchy.

Perhaps we should remember that Alfred Barr's fall from power at the Museum of Modern Art, in the art metropolis of New York, was precipitated by his decision to exhibit a hand-painted shoeshine stand in the museum lobby, at Christmas 1942. Even Barr's strategic calculation of associating the shoeshine stand with Christmas festivity did not save him. 'It was really beautiful and touching', Barr later recalled—'done with love and enthusiasm by a Sicilian bootblack [Joe Milone]—perhaps wishing to create out of New York jetsam the equivalent of a Sicilian painted cart.' Two things stand out here: the first is the melancholy appeal to the prestige of 'Europe', to the echoes of Sicily, in order to validate Milone's work. Barr was mobilizing Europe, as he mobilized Christmas, in an attempt to get the bootblack stand across the threshold, if only as far as the lobby. The second is the word 'jetsam', with its clear connotation of 'rubbish'. The whole incident is like a little fable pointing to the problems of making the leap from low to high, from outsider to insider, from rubbish to art. Finally, I think it is worth mentioning that Milone's work was called to Barr's attention by the sculptor, Louise Nevelson. Once again, we see how the museum mediates between the artist (female, eccentric) and the patron (male, established).

In the world of high art, low art can be dismissed en bloc as 'rubbish'. The technical term is 'kitsch'. Rubbish is only permitted entry when it is validated by or as high art—by Schwitters in his Merz collages, for instance, or by Man Ray in his surrealist objects (although it was some time before 'found objects' found their way into major museums). It is worth noting that Barr did succeed in introducing the 'low art' forms of design and film into the Museum of Modern Art, following the modernist interest in these arts during the 1920s, at the Bauhaus or in the Soviet Union. However, not only were criteria of excellence necessarily applied, on the model of the fine arts, but these other forms were segregated from the paintings in separate specialized departments. Thus a Bauhaus teapot or a De Stijl chair was more likely to be found alongside another teapot or another chair than in the company of a Bauhaus or De Stijl painting. A hierarchy of genres was tacitly established. If 'lower' forms were admitted together with paintings, this was to illustrate a point about paintings or to provide a 'period' context for them. This too was a way of protecting values from destabilization, through constructing a system of graduated and ordered entry into the inner sanctum.

Perhaps I can turn for a moment to my own experience with museums as a curator of temporary exhibitions, all of which were designed to challenge the canon in various ways. The most instructive of these was the exhibition of Frida Kahlo and Tina Modotti which I curated with Laura Mulvey, opening in London at the Whitechapel Gallery in 1980 and travelling in Europe, before ending its journey in New York and, finally, Mexico City. This exhibition had truly startling effects, particularly in its impact on the reputation of Frida Kahlo and the ensuing tidal wave of Fridamania, but also, to a surprising extent, on that of Tina Modotti. Not only did it make a lot of rich collectors much richer, but it also helped unleash a fantastic wave of popular interest in Kahlo's work, reaching the point of adulation. I can hardly bear to look at those eyebrows now. It is interesting to speculate about the reasons why Kahlo was so rapidly promoted from virtual unknown to art star. I think there were four principal preconditions for this. First, although previously considered a kind of 'Sunday painter', she had close connections with the art world from the beginning. Not only was she Diego Rivera's partner, and thus a major figure within the Mexican Renaissance, but she was also assimilated into the surrealist movement and received André Breton's direct endorsement in the 1930s. Like the Douanier Rousseau, another rare example of a

'Sunday painter' who was promoted into the canon, she knew and was admired by famous fellow artists.

Second, she was a woman artist and obviously benefited from the strength of feminist pressures for change within the art world. She fell into the general category of a neglected woman painter, 'hidden from history', obscured, it seemed, during her lifetime, by the greater fame and more assertive and monumental output of Diego. In fact, by a strange twist of fate, it may be that Diego's own future rehabilitation may prove easier because of the acceptance now given to Frida Kahlo. Third, and most importantly, the exhibition occurred around the same time as Hayden Herrera's massive, pioneering biography of Frida Kahlo was published. This was not simply a coincidence—both exhibition and book came from a collateral interest in feminism and in Mexico. However, the conjunction of the two—the possibility of both seeing the paintings themselves and then reading about the melodramatic and tragic life of the painter—obviously contributed to Kahlo's climb, both in specialist circles and, less directly but perhaps even more powerfully, with a broad popular audience.

Fourth, the work was supported by the story of Frida's life in a very specific way. Kahlo's often harrowing paintings were seen to fit in with a particular pattern, almost a kind of bio-mythology, for which an audience had already developed—the representation of the female artist as damaged, the fatal trajectory of tragic accident or premature death, the tremors of narcissistic disturbance, the fearless commitment to self-exposure. In this respect, Frida Kahlo is comparable to Virginia Woolf or Sylvia Plath (or indeed Diana Spencer). In all these instances biography provided a crucial way of interpreting the work and contextualizing it in terms of a legendary life and death. These factors are not specific to the art world, but they helped introduce Kahlo to a wider public and this, in turn, fed back into the art world's own judgment.

The example of Frida Kahlo has interesting points of similarity and difference with that of another Mexican artist, José Guadalupe Posada, of whose work I organized a touring exhibition in 1989. Posada is a particularly significant case of an artist whose work was literally discarded as rubbish, thrown down into the streets where it had been sold by itinerant hawkers of penny prints. In his case too, other artists were responsible for sustaining and reviving Posada's memory and reputation: first Dr Atl, then Jean Charlot, Diego Rivera, Manuel Alvarez Bravo and the groups around *Forma* and *Mexican Folkways*. Later Leopoldo Mendes and other print-makers were inspired by Posada's example to found the Taller de Arte y Grafica Popular. Exactly as with the Stevengraphs, a bound volume containing originals of Posada's work survived in the hands of the family of his printer, Vanegas Arroyo, and this provided a source for further photo-reproductions. Posada also signed much of his work and, even when he did not, it could be authenticated through the printer's records. Thus, unlike the artists of the *lubki* which influenced Goncharova and Larionov, or the glass painters who influenced Kandinsky and Munzer, his prints did not remain anonymous and could thus be isolated and validated as a specific, personal body of work for collectors and museums. Nonetheless, Posada remains marginal in museum terms and his most obvious contemporary successors, the Linares family, who make *papier-maché* monsters and tableaux, have still not been accepted. Instead, there have been lively polemics as to whether they belong in the folk museum or the art museum.

In the end, taste, values and museums do change, although, often enough, in content rather than basic form. The Pompier paintings, Victoriana, the Bougereaus, the Landseers and the Rosa Bonheurs all disappeared from the museum walls (if only into the cellars). They were gradually replaced by the art favoured by a new 'modernist' generation and emergent new taste-makers within the art world. But the general contours of museum art have remained surprisingly stable. Museums have weathered the great storms of modernism and post-modernism with amazing equanimity. Paintings still line the walls in rectangular frames, grouped in schools and movements, ordered in chronological sequence, just as they were in Napoleon's Louvre. The sculptures, it is true, have been demoted, at least in relation to the paintings, and moved out of the main halls and rooms—but only to be re-positioned in the nearby garden.

In the not too distant future, I would like to predict, another wave of change will sweep through the museum halls—one which challenges the boundaries of art itself. Perhaps, when the Rothkos and Francises and Newmans have followed the Landseers and the Bougereaus into the cellar (and eventually, I suppose, into new retro museums of their own, like the Musée d'Orsay in Paris) they will be replaced by today's rubbish—today's kitsch, today's Stevengraphs. Norman Rockwell is already poised at the portal of the Guggenheim, along with Armani and motorcycles. Blockbuster exhibitions will be housed in museums which are themselves architectural showpieces, on the model of the Bilbao Guggenheim or the Getty Center in Los Angeles, mausoleums designed to monopolize the eye and reduce the works they contain to midget status, whose only competition could come from art on the scale of Christo and Jeanne-Claude's wrapping of the Reichstag. Another obvious trend is the elevation of the exhibition designer, whether an ambitious curator or a moonlighting architect, who conceptualizes a whole show as a single visual ensemble. We can at least hope for a countervailing mix of little museums—obsessively specialist museums, community museums, site-specific museums, hopelessly old-fashioned museums. My own favourite museums in California are the Museum of Modern Mythology in San Francisco, the Max Factor Museum in Hollywood, the Unknown Museum in Mill Valley, the Museum of Jurassic Technology in Los Angeles, the bizarre museum in a dinosaur on the road out to Palm Springs, full of what even I feel is irretrievable rubbish. The museums I miss most from England are those which truly belong in a museum of museums—the Soane Museum and the Pitt-Rivers, with its dusty glass cases full of weird souvenirs brought back by generations of imperial travellers.

Finally, a brief post-script on the inevitable subject of the digital museum. This is not a new idea. It derives from André Malraux's concept of the 'Imaginary Museum' contained in art-books and magazines, made possible by the success of specialized art publishers, Phaidon, Skira or Abrams—books I was brought up to browse through, just as you might browse through them on a museum website. Not a great difference, although this triumph of spectacle, of the optical, may bring with it a reversion to the tactile—to museums of texture and touch rather than visual display, museums round which visitors feel their way with connoisseurs' fingertips. Why not? Why should touch remain forever the poor relation of the senses?

6

OCTOBER 18, 1977

In June 1995, the Museum of Modern Art in New York announced that it had acquired a series of 15 paintings by the German artist, Gerhard Richter, collectively titled *October 18, 1977*. The date was a significant one. At 11.00 p.m. on 17 October, the prison officer in charge of the four prisoners on the seventh floor of the high security wing of Stammheim prison, Stuttgart, noted in his night duty report, '23.00 hours. Baader and Raspe given medicaments. Otherwise no incidents.' In the morning, at 7.41 a.m. on 18 October—breakfast time—guards discovered Andreas Baader and Gudrun Ensslin dead in their cells. Jan-Carl Raspe was badly wounded but still alive. He was rushed to the hospital and died soon afterwards. Irmgard Möller, who was also taken to the hospital, survived. She had stabbed herself with a knife, whereas Baader and Raspe were shot in the head and Ensslin was found hanged. There are those who believe that the dead and wounded prisoners on the seventh floor were murdered, but that is not my opinion.

The trial of the prisoners on murder charges had begun on 21 May 1975, in a fortified courtroom specially built for the occasion and further protected by a barbed-wire fence, a detachment of mounted police on constant patrol and canted steel-netting installed above the roof, as a defence against a possible rocket attack. Everyone who entered the courtroom was searched, excepting the judges but including the lawyers. Trouser pockets were emptied and their contents placed in plastic bags.

The prisoners had been arrested in 1971 (Baader, Raspe) and 1972 (Ensslin, Möller, as well as Meinhóf, who was found hanged from a window grating in her cell on 9 May 1976, over a year before the others). After Meinhof's death the defence lawyers, including one court-appointed lawyer, proposed a motion which read,

> A person wholly deprived of freedom makes use of the most mysterious and deepest human freedom there is, the taking of her own life. That should be grounds for deferring the schedule and sending outside witnesses home, so that this state of affairs can be worked out. Something akin to reverence in criminal procedure should make it impossible for the trial to continue while the mortal remains of such a person have not yet been laid to rest.

The judges, however, rejected the motion.

The 15 paintings in Gerhard Richter's series are based on images drawn from Richter's own extensive collection of photo-clippings, a collection which had previously been systematically organized and exhibited under the name of 'Atlas'. The works in the series begin with a painting based on a portrait of Ulrike Meinhof from 1970, when she was 35 years old, probably taken at a press conference. This image is followed by two paintings of the arrest of Holger Meins in 1972, images taken from a news video shot for German television. Meins had died earlier in Stammheim, in November 1974, as the result of a hunger strike. Three images of Ensslin were taken shortly after her arrest, apparently during an identification parade. The series also includes an image of Ensslin's hanged body in her cell; an image of Baader's cell, dominated by its crowded bookcase; an image of the record-player in which Baader is thought to have secreted the gun which killed him; two images of Baader dead and three of Ulrike Meinhof's head and shoulders, resting on the cell floor after her body had been found. These were all prison photographs, whose originals were located in the Stuttgart prosecutors' office. The final image, taken from film footage, shows three coffins being carried through the crowd at the prisoners' funeral.

Much of this information is contained in *October 18, 1997*, which was published by the Museum of Modern Art to accompany their first exhibition of the Richter series in 2000, supplemented, of course, by other sources, principally by Stefan Aust's indispensable *The Baader-Meinhof Group: The Inside Story of a Phenomenon* (1985). The Museum chose to commission and publish their own book, it seems, for two principal reasons. First, because it underlined the importance the Museum gave to their acquisition and, second, to aid and shape public understanding of Richter's cycle of paintings and thus validate the Museum's decision to acquire the work despite its controversial subject matter. For many years, of course, Picasso's *Guernica* had been exhibited in the Museum, but Picasso's painting, though plainly political, was plainly anti-fascist too. Richter's painting, on the other hand, was open to the charge of being a hagiographic work, honouring the memory of terrorists, exhibited and validated in the city which had undergone the World Trade Center bombing and at a time when Americans were particularly concerned with the danger of terrorism, both international and domestic, as with the Oklahoma City bombing.

The museum was right, I am sure, to defend Richter against the charge of hagiography and, although the charge of exploitation might be stronger, I am not convinced by that either. On the other hand, Richter had taken great care not to express any detailed opinion of his own about the events which culminated in Stammheim in October 1977 or about the way in which the work might best be interpreted in the context of its subject matter, preferring to leave his own intentions opaque and thereby, in a certain way, encouraging speculation while disarming direct criticism. I am happy to speculate. First, it is surely important to look at the form of Richter's work, as well as its content. For many years Gerhard Richter has painted from photographs, as, of course, have many other artists, whether by silk-screening them directly onto canvas, like Rauschenberg or Warhol, by underpainting or overpainting them, or by projecting them onto the canvas with a slide projector, or by collaging them, or simply by using them as source material, as with work by Francis Bacon or Richard Hamilton. Photography has long been used by artists as a substitute for drawing or as an iconic intermediary between reality and representation.

Richter makes use of photographs in a way which is both extremely personal, even idiosyncratic, and extremely pointed, even polemical. For many years now, since the early 1960s, he has been painting photographs in such a way as to obscure the original image—an image drawn directly from the real world—and to overlay it with a painterly veil or screen which can only be described as verging on the abstract, like Bacon's work in some respects, but much more extreme in its trajectory towards the abstract. Moreover, in his use of paint, Richter has long favoured monochrome, although there are a few exceptions. In the case of the paintings that make up *October 18, 1977*, his palette is limited entirely to the grey scale, and the original subjects—or rather the photographic images of the subjects—are viewed through an obscuring fog of grey, modulating at times into black. There are no clear outlines. Everything looks as if it has been smudged or shaken. As many critics have pointed out, Richter creates an effect quite counter to the advice that any good photographer would naturally give—his images are blurred as if the focus was wrong, the camera had shuddered or the subject had slipped away into an evanescent haze. These effects, however, are created deliberately, with paint.

Gerhard Richter was born and brought up in Dresden, at that time in Communist East Germany. He studied painting at the Dresden Fine Art Academy but, in 1961, he went to the West, where he became a student again, this time at Dusseldorf's Academy of Fine Arts, the home-base of Joseph Beuys. The following year, 1962, he produced an early painting in oil based upon a photograph he had found in the style magazine *Domus*. This painting was titled *Tisch* ('Table'). It is painted entirely on the grey scale, with no hue but with some variations in brightness. It is not an easy painting to read, even when you know its title and its origin. It seems to fall somewhere between allusion and abstraction. For Richter, photography suggested a way forward for painting which would enable it to incorporate the lessons of abstraction, minimalism and the *informel*, while working with photographic sources rather than directly from life. As Richard Hamilton had observed, at that time 'somehow it didn't seem necessary to hold on to the older tradition of contact with the world. Magazines, or any visual intermediary could as well provide a stimulus.'

At the end of the 1960s Richter began using photographs which he himself had taken and, in 1969, he began to make landscape paintings, featuring waves and clouds and phenomena which, even in nature, had no clear outlines. Then, in the 1970s, he began to paint abstract works, entirely within the grey scale. At first they were just called *Grey*, but in due course they were given titles such as *Tourist (Grey)* and *Tourist (with 2 lions)* or, more minimally, *Tourist (with 1 lion)*. In a letter dating from 1975 Richter observed that, at first, he had produced grey paintings out of misery at his own state of uncertainty, but that subsequently he was able to surmount his personal misery as he came to understand that grey was essentially impersonal, 'the epitome of non-statement'. He became attracted, even committed, to grey because it was 'suitable for illustrating "nothing"'; because it was 'the welcome and only possible equivalent for indifference'; because grey, 'just like shapelessness, etc., can only notionally be real'; because each picture 'is then a mixture of grey as fiction and grey as a visible, proportioned colour surface'. In other words, grey is simultaneously both real and unreal, committed and uncommitted. In the grey photo-based work the real is given a 'transcendental side', each object is given its own particular mysteriousness, becoming a metaphor as it melts away into an 'incomprehensible reality'.

The relevance of Richter's understanding of grey to the grey overpainting which we see in the *October 18, 1977* series is correspondingly both clear and unclear. These images are not abstract. They represent realities, people and objects which really existed, events which really took place. At the same time, they are given a veil of mysteriousness or even incomprehensibility, a conceptual blurring which Richter achieves through his use of the grey over-painting. We feel, simultaneously, both the reality of the grim events of October 1977 and their unreality, the difficulty we have in comprehending or evaluating them. Partly this is because the actual course of the events themselves is still far from clear, on one level, while absolutely clear on another. We know unambiguously who or what these images of people or objects or scenes represent—we can recognize them and relate them to events which we know occurred in the real world—but at the same time they have a 'transcendental side', they melt away into uncertainty and unreality. In one sense, this corresponds to the historical uncertainty which surrounds the events themselves, to our lingering uncertainty as to whether these deaths were suicides or, in some sense, murders.

For a number of reasons, I am convinced the deaths were suicides, although the prison regime played its role. First, because the prisoners had already undertaken a hunger strike, in 1972, which had led to the death of Holger Meins, and because, from then onwards, the resort to hunger strikes as a means of protest had become a basic option for the group. Moreover, because Andreas Baader had always insisted that protests should be undertaken as group rather than individual actions, it makes much more sense that the concluding action of the group—multiple suicide—should indeed be a deliberately collective act, even though the means of death chosen varied from prisoner to prisoner. In fact, this variation was itself an unlikely outcome in the event of a killing by outsiders, particularly since one of the group actually survived. Nonetheless, no explanatory notes or statements were left behind and the three deaths still remain mysterious in respect to many matters of detail. It is also worth observing that the deaths of the Baader–Ensslin–Raspe generation of the Red Army Faction, far from spelling the end of the Faction's activities, actually cleared the path for a 'Second Generation', as the group now became known, and eventually for a 'Third Generation', which continued functioning right through into the 1990s.

Perhaps the closest we can come to understanding the reasoning of the group is by trying to think through the implications of their strange fascination with Herman Melville's novel, *Moby Dick*, the story of a suicidal mission directed against a formidable leviathan. In 1972 Meinhof was already recommending *Moby Dick* to her children and Gudrun Ensslin, always practically minded, used it to provide cover names for the Stammheim group to use in their clandestine communications—Baader was dubbed Ahab; Holger Meins was Starbuck; the group's lawyer, Horst Mahler, was Bildad; and Ensslin was the ship's cook, Fleece in the book but Smutje in the private code. In Melville's book the whale was finally killed, but so too, of course, were all the crew, from captain down to cook, with the single exception of the book's narrator, known as Ishmael, to whom the closest surviving equivalent would perhaps be Astrid Proll, the author and editor of *Baader Meinhof/Pictures On The Run, 67–77* (1998), a historical compilation of around 100 images which includes most of the images used by Richter, simply reproducing the photographs rather than transfiguring them into paintings. Proll began to assemble the images in 1985, when Stefan Aust commissioned her to find photographs as illustrations for his book, but her own book provides a much fuller visual documentation, including, for example, the extraordinary press photograph of one of Rudi Dutschke's shoes, left in the street in front of the SDS centre in Berlin, after he was shot by a right-wing extremist.

Dutschke's shoe is right in the foreground of the photograph. Its status as the sign of an event is extremely clear, even though—or rather precisely because—it has been detached from the missing body of its owner. The *October 18, 1977* cycle, in contrast, is deliberately opaque. As Gertrud Koch puts it in her essay, 'The Open Secret', 'what characterizes these paintings is their reference to the temporality of our imaginations, the haziness of our memory, its vagueness, the sinking into amnesia, the disappearance and blurring'. Koch's essay, published in Paris in 1985, stresses the clouding which overtakes any historical event as it loses definition in our memories and begins to blur. Of course, from a German point of view, like that of Koch, such clouded images must seem all the more 'death-bearing', because through their very cloudiness the viewer must also experience her own ageing, the growing gap between the event and the memory of it.

In another context, the murkiness we might feel reflects our own uncertainty back to us, our doubts in regard to the long-term meaning of the Baader–Meinhoff group's actions, how their fateful trajectory should best be interpreted today, from a considerable distance in time, as opposed to what they might have meant to us 30 years or more ago, when they first took place. Does the passage of time make interpretation more difficult, as Richter seems to suggest and as Koch claims quite explicitly, when she talks of 'the haziness of memory' and of our 'sinking into amnesia'. Without Richter's paintings, I must confess, I doubt that I would now be thinking much about the Red Army Faction and the fate which befell its protagonists in Stammheim. Surveying Richter's cycle of paintings, however, forces us to travel back in time and try to bring our thoughts about the Red Army Faction back into focus, so to speak—to restore some clarity to what would otherwise remain, at best, as dim and fading memories, aware that any clear and distinct ideas that might come into our minds today would be very different from what we thought, or might have thought, over 20 years ago.

Meanwhile, the Red Army Faction recently re-entered the newspapers, even in the United States. On 15 January 2001, the *New York Times* ran a long story about Joschka Fischer, under the headline, 'Germany's Foreign Minister Is Pursued By His Early Firebrand Self', following the arrest of Fischer's former friend Hans-Joachim Klein and his trial on charges related to the terrorist attack on an OPEC meeting in Vienna in 1975, in which three people were killed. According to the *New York Times*, the sudden resurrection of the Foreign Minister's past was largely due to 'the unrelenting vendetta against Mr. Fischer carried out by the daughter of Ulrike Meinhof, the Red Army Faction terrorist who committed suicide —or was killed—in prison in 1976' and 'the discovery by Ms. Meinhof's daughter, a 38-year-old journalist, of the photographs of Mr. Fischer hitting Mr. Marx [a policeman] from behind and then kicking him on the ground'. There was also the fury of a retired policeman, Horst Breunig, in regard to Mr. Fischer's actions in another demonstration, provoked by the death of Ulrike Meinhof in Stammheim prison. Thus the fading images began to come back into focus, as old scores were settled and old memories re-awakened, reprinted in the newspapers, reappearing with an uncanny clarity.

I was particularly intrigued by the role played in the Joschka Fischer story by his erstwhile friend, Hans-Joachim Klein, and by Klein's connection with Jean-Paul Sartre. In February 1973, Sartre had told *Der Spiegel* that he was 'very much interested in the Baader-Meinhof group. I believe it is a real revolutionary group, but I have the feeling it has started a little too soon.' The following year, *Les Temps Modernes* published an article on the 'torture by sensory deprivation' which had been inflicted on Baader–Meinhof prisoners, and in October 1974 Ulrike Meinhof wrote a letter to Sartre inviting him to come and interview Baader in the prison, while warning him that the police 'intend to murder Andreas'. She explained that 'It's not a necessary condition of the interview for you to agree with us on all points; what we're asking is that you'll give us the protection of your name and your gifts as a Marxist, philosopher, journalist and moralist in the interview.' In November, Holger Meins died in Stammheim after a long hunger strike. In December, Sartre finally agreed to visit Baader in order to show solidarity with him as a prisoner, even though he disapproved of the group's use of violence. It was Hans-Joachim Klein who drove the car which took Sartre to Stammheim.

However, as Ronald Hayman has pointed out, 'As Sartre realized, his efforts were ineffectual or possibly counter-productive. It was useless to explain that he was not condoning what Baader had done, only protesting against the conditions of his imprisonment.' Nothing ever came of Sartre's intervention. There was never any chance that the prisoners' conditions would be changed. In some respects, however, the harsh regime imposed in Stammheim could actually prove surprisingly lax. As Aust notes, the record-player featured in one of Richter's photo-paintings was used to play records from a collection of 76 LPs which Baader had accumulated in his cell, together with speakers, an amplifier, an Olivetti typewriter, a mouth-organ, two fur coats, two pairs of sun-glasses and, of course, guns. The guns, it is reasonable to assume, were smuggled in by the defence lawyers. Baader, according to Aust, had for some time had a 7.65 FEG pistol secreted in a hiding place in his cell wall, which he transferred to a hiding place in his record player, sometime after 11.00 p.m. on the 16 October, the time when the prison officers made their last visit, handing out medicaments as usual.

Raspe also had a gun, hidden behind a skirting-board. During the night the prisoners were able to communicate through the electrical circuits which connected their cells, having adapted elements of their stereo equipment in order to create an intercom system. Previously, they had succeeded in setting up an internal radio system, known as 'Stammheim III', which had been detected and dismantled, yet somehow the intercom escaped detection until after the suicides had taken place, when it was finally uncovered by a visiting Federal Mails engineer. Stammheim's own prison electrician acknowledged that he had been quite unaware that the power supply could be utilized to convey messages. Aust concludes that, after a suicide pact was agreed over the intercom, the two guns were removed from their hiding places by Baader and Raspe, while Ensslin cut a stretch of loudspeaker cable with her scissors and tied it to the window grating. Isolated from any kind of normal contact with the world outside, a condition exaggerated still further by a regime of isolation, strict surveillance and sensory deprivation, it is hardly surprising that the group should seek a way to end everything. Suicide was consistent both with their sense of despair and their sense of purpose. It was also a goal that they could achieve.

The prisoners had threatened to commit suicide on a number of occasions. On 8 October, for example, Baader had told Alfred Klaus, head of the Special Commission on Terrorism, that they would soon reach an 'irreversible decision' if prison conditions were not improved, words that Klaus had interpreted as a suicide threat. The following day Ensslin also asked to see Klaus. She told him that, unless their conditions of imprisonment were changed, the group would 'take the decision out of [Chancellor] Schmidt's hands by deciding for ourselves, in the way still open to us'. Klaus interpreted this statement also as a suicide threat, recalling that in a letter intercepted three years previously Ensslin had explicitly suggested that the prisoners should consider committing suicide as a group, one at a time over a period of weeks. On 27 September Raspe had also explained that failure to change their situation would inevitably lead to 'dead prisoners', which would be a 'political catastrophe', presumably for the government. On 9 October Raspe, when asked directly by Klaus whether he was planning suicide, responded that it was possible. 'A living dog is better than a dead lion', Klaus observed. 'That's from *Ecclesiastes*.'

While the suicides may have been intended as a means of turning public opinion against the government, they were also brought about under psychological pressure from within the dynamics of terrorism as such. In fact, the Stammheim suicides were the most effective action undertaken by the Baader–Meinhof group. It is difficult to pick out anything else very positive that the group achieved. They proved adept at robbing banks, stealing cars (especially BMWs but once an Alfa-Romeo), shooting cops, setting fire to a department store, exploding bombs, corrupting lawyers, baiting judges, hiding from the police, throwing Molotov cocktails, negotiating ransoms, killing soldiers, considering sending their children to Palestinian orphanages, quarreling with each other, taking uppers and downers, imposing on other people's well-meaning hospitality, organizing hijackings, taking hostages, forging passports, and putting on disguises—but none of these activities had the same effect as their suicides. A sad record, when one considers the beliefs and hopes that first drove them into their campaign of violence, their vision of a society without NATO or nuclear weapons, without capitalism or consumerism, without psychiatric repression or emergency powers. Armoured against doubt, driven by fear of what might happen if their certainties were abandoned, desperately struggling to maintain their sense of self, afraid of each other's contempt, they staggered from idealism to self-destruction down a tragic, narcissistic and at times atrocious road.

The Stammheim suicides, unlike other actions, produced an enormous cultural response. The following year the film *Germany in Autumn* was produced, with contributions from, among others, Rainer Werner Fassbinder, Alexander Kluge, Edgar Reitz and Volker Schlondorff working together with Heinrich Boll. The Schlondorff–Boll episode showed a panel of television programmers rejecting a production of Sophocles' *Antigone* because it showed Antigone's suicide after Creon refused to permit her to bury her brother, a rebel against the state. The film begins with the public funeral and official mourning of Hanns Martin Schleyer, president of both the German Employers' Association and the Federation of German Industry, held hostage and then executed by the Red Army Faction in response to the deaths of the prisoners in Stammheim. It ends with the public funeral and unofficial mourning of the prisoners. It is a *trauerarbeit*, both a demonstration and an enactment of grief. It reminds us that the suicides, at least, attracted sympathy to the Red Army Faction and conveys a sense that something had been lost, something was amiss.

Fassbinder's section of *Germany In Autumn* shows both his panic when a homeless stranger comes to his apartment and, even more intensely, his fear that the police are at the door. In an interview, Fassbinder described the suicides as the result of a 'witch-hunt' whose aim was 'to destroy individual utopias', a witch-hunt he felt as personally threatening. In Yvonne Rainer's film *Journeys from Berlin/1971*, made in 1980, two characters discuss the Stammheim deaths. One compares the Red Army Faction to the 'Russian Amazons' who 'went to the people', noting that 'my point is that the Baader–Meinhof people preferred robbing banks and kidnapping to going to work in factories'. She agrees that Meinhof's writing 'sounds like hysterical rhetoric' but notes that 'she must have suffered horribly in prison', comparing the isolated, sound-proofed cell in Stammheim with Rosa Luxemburg's access, while imprisoned, to a garden where she could grow flowers and listen to the birds singing. In Fassbinder's subsequent film, *The Third Generation*, prompted by the Red Army Faction's trajectory after Stammheim, the terrorists are portrayed as creating a pretext for the security and surveillance industries to prosper. As Anton Kaes notes, 'Utopia no longer appears as even a vague possibility'.

For Gerhard Richter, I think, the uncertainty has never quite gone away. In his notebook he wrote, 'I'm not sure whether the pictures "ask" anything; they provoke contradiction through their hopelessness and desolation, their lack of partisanship.' His original motivation, he noted, was '"purely human" (dismay, pity, grief)', without any ideological content—and yet, for Richter,

> the pictures are also a leave-taking in several respects. Factually: these specific persons are dead; as a general statement, death is leave-taking. And then ideologically: a leave-taking from a specific doctrine of salvation and, beyond that, from the illusion that unacceptable circumstances of life can be changed by this conventional expedient of violent struggle.

What, if anything, is to replace it? I believe that Richter feels that it can only be grief. Ideas, he writes, have 'a terrifying power' which was demonstrated in Stammheim, but which should be regarded not in terms of the horror we feel when we see the photographs, but in terms of the grief (or 'something more like grief') which we feel when we see the paintings, a grief we feel in response to the loss both of the individuals and of their illusions.

7

KITSCH

The hero of Celeste Olalquiaga's book* is a hermit crab encased within a glass globe which she has chosen to christen 'Rodney'. She first encountered Rodney, as she recounts, in a San Francisco bed-and-breakfast, a Victorian mansion in which every room had been named after a supposed nineteenth-century guest—Isadora Duncan, Enrico Caruso, Luisa Tetrazzini—each decorated in an appropriate style. The author climbed laboriously up to a small 'chamber' in one of the mansion's towers—it was the Jack London room—where among a plethora of nautical bric-a-brac she found, on the bedside table, her crustacean muse. Rodney, of course, was long dead but, ensconced in the mollusc shell that served as his hermitage, he had been encased in his glass sphere by the Iminac company of Lake Jackson, Texas, and thus preserved against decay. In effect, Rodney had become—simultaneously—mummy, exhibit and bibelot, a quintessentially kitsch object which entranced its fascinated discoverer, fond admirer and future theorist. Rodney provoked in her reveries of an underwater world full of sunken treasure and forgotten shipwrecks. As the light failed and darkness loomed, she writes, 'Squinting, I stretch out my arm to grab Rodney. Unwilling to let go of the reverie, I press my face against the transparent bubble that holds him, hoping this gesture will bring him a little closer for a few more seconds. But I have returned from my musing and the spell is broken.'

* *The Artificial Kingdom: A Treasury of the Kitsch Experience* (Pantheon, 1998).

Rodney, she insists, is kitsch and her book, as it develops, is both a historical enquiry into the intertwining histories of the glass-encased bibelot, the cabinet of curiosities, the cluttered drawing-room, the fake mermaid, the subaqueous realm of Captain Nemo and other such dreamscapes and, at the same time, a theoretical enquiry into the nature of kitsch and a defence of it—or certain aspects of it—against the opprobrium under which it usually falls. Drawing on Walter Benjamin, her mentor in such matters, she sketches out a distinction between two contrasting types of kitsch—the nostalgic, which is bad, and the melancholic, which is good. The first of these, the nostalgic, is characterized by a fantasy of keeping the past alive in our imagination, while the second, the melancholic, recognizes the loss that has occurred and mourns it, with no pretence that there can be any restitution, imaginary or otherwise. Thus the author mourns Rodney, irrevocably dead as he is, rather than allowing herself to be carried away by his image into the vision of a utopian past, a golden age when Rodney was still happily at home upon the ocean floor. The experience of melancholic kitsch, she argues, is that of an intense and timeless loss that emerges within the realm of unconscious memory, irrevocably distanced from us, while nostalgic kitsch depends on our sense of a continuous time, of a lost moment which can be reconstructed and restored for us as a fantasy of what might have been.

Thus, when she writes that 'Rodney is kitsch'—melancholic kitsch—Olalquiaga attributes the fascination she feels to the fact that he is present to her gaze as if in a kind of time capsule which has unexpectedly brought him before her from some completely unknown, strangely other dimension of time, speaking 'for those who want to listen, about the hopelessness of attempting to detain life, the vanity of hanging on to what is gone, the beauty of the marks of time'. Thus there is no sense of loss, of regret, of a past world to which Rodney truly belongs and which we can recover—only a kind of dream image, abstracted from our own sense of time past and suspended now purely in the present, like a dream image whose connection to us has been irrecuperably lost. The infrastructure for this theory of kitsch is provided by the author's reading of Walter Benjamin who, while he never wrote about kitsch as such, distinguished between two types of memory—the melancholic and the nostalgic—in his writings on Baudelaire and Proust. Benjamin was also fascinated by bibelots and bric-a-brac, the commodified clutter of the arcade, the department store and the Victorian interior which provided such a fertile environment for the growth and, some might say, final triumph of kitsch.

Benjamin provides the author not only with a typology which she can apply to kitsch but also a model of passionate involvement with the lost and dusty detritus of culture which characterizes the realm of kitsch. She finds in Benjamin an ally, seeing him as that rare creature, the modernist who is attracted to kitsch, whose writings she can use to construct a defence of kitsch in the face of the attacks mounted upon it by Herman Broch, Gillo Dorfles and Clement Greenberg in their caustic anathematization of kitsch as enemy of true modernity. The distinction she makes, extrapolating from Benjamin, between 'nostalgic' and 'melancholic' kitsch, enables her to defend at least the melancholic segment of what elsewhere she has called 'the dark side of modernity's moon'. At the same time, she is well aware that this entails defending commodity culture itself, because it is not the absence or presence of commodification which distinguishes good from bad in the field of kitsch, but the nature of the object commodified. Citing Benjamin again, she argues that commodities are 'dream images' or 'wish images', representing utopian desires. Going even further than this, she also argues that commodities as fetishes (memories turned into souvenirs) can gain a new life of their own, as Rodney has, thus becoming 'an endearing creature whom my friends even say hello to when they visit'.

There is, however, a problem with this line of argument. It dismisses much too rapidly the standard arguments against kitsch, as if Rodney's charm and her attachment to him could somehow, in themselves, override volumes of closely argued condemnation of kitsch by other authors, exempting Rodney on the basis of a few telling citations from Benjamin. She is right, I think, to see kitsch as the other, hidden face of modernity and to wonder why modern art should be praised while Rodney is condemned, but the arguments against kitsch are by no means trivial. In his thoughtful book *Kitsch and Art*, published in 1996, Thomas Kulka proposed three defining conditions of kitsch:

> Condition 1. Kitsch depicts objects or themes that are highly charged with stock emotions.

Condition 2. The objects or themes depicted by kitsch are instantly and effortlessly identifiable.

Condition 3. Kitsch does not substantially enrich our associations relating to the depicted objects or themes.

Given these conditions, Kulka argued, kitsch must inevitably be seen as spoon-feeding its subjects with stereotypes, confirming viewers in attitudes and sentiments which are already deeply engrained, playing to the predictable kind of response aroused by pictures of 'puppies and kittens of various sorts, children in tears, mothers with babies, long-legged women with sensuous lips and alluring eyes, beaches with palms and colourful sunsets, pastoral Swiss villages framed in mountain panorama, cheerful beggars, sad clowns, sad faithful old dogs ...' Olalquiaga might argue, of course, that hermit crabs fall into a completely different kind of category, but I am not sure that such a disavowal could really convince us, nor how certain we can be that the emotional triggers of melancholy and nostalgia are as distinct from each other as she claims. Is a hermit crab immured in a glass globe as a 'Nature Gem' really all that different from an 'Atlantis' reconstructed on a Bahaman beach or the fake ruins of Hubert Robert, both of which she gives as examples of kitsch, just because one is real, the others fake, one melancholic, the others nostalgic? Both categories of object seem to me to trade on the viewer's engrained sentiments and predictable responses.

In this context, it is hardly surprising that kitsch, whether nostalgic or melancholic, should be denounced by those who argue for novelty, difficulty and complexity—that is to say, by modernists such as Clement Greenberg, the New York critic who formulated and led the assault on kitsch in the 1940s and 1950s, an anti-kitsch campaign which, as he saw it, was necessary if the meaning and value of artistic modernism were to be recognized in America and, subsequently, the value of the new American avant-garde recognized world-wide. This was especially important because, in contrast to Europe, America was understandably regarded as the homeland of kitsch. Greenberg published his classic text, *Avant-Garde and Kitsch*, as early as 1939, in *Partisan Review*, re-printing a version of it the following year in the British magazine, *Horizon*, and then authorizing its reprinting in a series of influential collections—*The Partisan Review Reader* (1944), *Mass Culture—The Popular Arts in America* (1957), *Kitsch—The World of Bad Taste* (1969), *Pollock and After: The Critical Debate* (1985), as well as *Clement Greenberg: The Collected Essays and Criticism* (1986). In effect, Greenberg's onslaught has dominated the field of kitsch studies, so to speak, for the past 60 years. Olalquiaga herself describes Greenberg's essay as 'fundamental' to the anti-kitsch position that she herself attempts to challenge in *The Artificial Kingdom*, writing now from a vantage-point that follows the closure of the modernist era, from a new and post-modern perspective.

Greenberg began his essay with an invocation of three examples of kitsch, each drawn from a different artistic field: a Tin Pan Alley song, a Saturday Evening Post cover (presumably by Norman Rockwell) and a poem by Eddie Guest (a now-forgotten poetaster). Over 30 years later, in 1971, speaking at a seminar at Bennington College, Greenberg came up with much the same list, its scope now broadened to include the media, 'bad movies, dime novels, bad TV, Tin Pan Alley music and so on, where all that is involved is a matter of ingenuity, not inspiration, and above all, no risk on the part of the artist and also no risk for the spectator.' In 1939, however, Greenberg was still writing from a point prior to the triumph of American modernism. He was attempting to justify modernism by recalling the avant-garde's origin in the secession of artists from the nineteenth-century French bourgeoisie, first into bohemia and then into the de-politicized embrace of 'art for art's sake' and 'pure poetry'. Artists became engaged in the search for an absolute, eventually realized through abstraction, not for the sake of abstraction in itself, but because abstraction was the only logical conclusion, once the imitation of nature had given way to formal exploration as the primary subject-matter of art.

'Abstraction' was used by Greenberg in a broad sense, to include not only Mondrian or Kandinsky, but also Picasso, Braque and 'even Klee, Matisse and Cezanne', each of whom he saw as deriving 'their chief inspiration from the medium they work in'. Kitsch, in contrast, was the rear-guard which had arisen simultaneously alongside the avant-garde: 'popular, commercial art and literature with their chromotypes, magazine covers, illustrations, ads, slick and pulp fiction, comics, Tin Pan Alley music, tap dancing, Hollywood movies, etc, etc.' Kitsch, for Greenberg, operated mechanically by formulas, provided vicarious experiences and faked sensations, which changed according to style while always remaining essentially the same. Kitsch demanded 'nothing of its customers except their money—not even their time.' Kitsch, in other words, was commercial art, debased, predictable, spurious and facile. In both America and the Soviet Union, it thrived because it 'heightened reality and made it dramatic', because it could be enjoyed without effort, because it found a ready market or because it flattered the masses.

For Greenberg, capitalism and communism were at one in their preference for kitsch as the dominant form of artistic production. In the Soviet Union, artists were compelled to produce kitsch by the state. In the United States, the avant-garde were forced to labour in obscurity, appealing only to a handful of *cognoscenti*, while the masses revelled in their *Saturday Evening Post* covers, Hollywood movies, dime novels and Tin Pan Alley songs. Greenberg's argument, in fact, was unashamedly elitist in its assumptions. The need for an elite—albeit an elite of outcasts, isolated and abused—was justified by the fact that it represented, however desperately, a kind of alternative not only to capitalism and commercialism, but also to Stalinism and fascism, all of them culturally homogenizing forms of mass society. It represented, in fact, difference and resistance, stubbornly maintained. Paradoxically, this avant-garde of outcasts eventually became the foundation for American cultural hegemony, creating an artistic movement which could be presented as daring, pure, idealistic, innovative, unstained by commercialism, free from the taint of either state or commercial control. It is as if Pollock's triumph had relieved America of any responsibility for its own ever-burgeoning production of kitsch.

The problem, however, which Greenberg confronted—or failed to confront—was twofold. First, there was the way in which works long considered masterpieces could somehow be turned into kitsch by the passage of time—the *Mona Lisa*, for instance, or, more alarmingly, Van Gogh's *Sunflowers* or Monet's *Nymphéas*. Paintings which were considered difficult or innovative in their own day could easily be normalized by time—becoming both instantly recognizable and hence, in Olalquiaga's terms, opportunities for nostalgia, both for the tragic life of Van Gogh and for the sunflowers drenched in gold. Kitsch, it seems to me, is the inevitable companion of great art. In the 1970s, Greenberg was still harping on the theme of Norman Rockwell and his *Saturday Evening Post* covers, but also expressing his puzzlement at Pop Art, not quite dismissing it but obviously troubled by its vulgarity and its ready availability to populist responses. Soon afterwards he was frankly hostile to conceptual art, which could be seen as a deliberate rejection of a painterly tradition which had become irrevocably complicit with kitsch.

Was post-modernism now to be seen as the redemption of art from the modernist kitsch of '60s Colour Field painting? Or would post-modernism inevitably bring a new sequence of kitsch in its own wake? Perhaps the arrival of 'far-out art' as Greenberg contemptuously called it, blaming everything on Duchamp, would finally purge the art world of the old, outmoded painterly form of kitsch while opening the door to a new post-painterly variant, Mike Kelley's stuffed toys, for example, battered and bedraggled for sure, but all the more gripping for that, like the proverbial clown with a tear. How could the spectre of kitsch ever be exorcized? Or would the world of art always be forced to suffer an inevitable return of the repressed? Fortunately for him, Greenberg never lived to see the rehabilitation of Norman Rockwell, currently well under way and stage-managed by the new American art world's most beloved critic, the Las Vegas-based Liberace-loving Dave Hickey. Hickey first began his rehabilitation of Rockwell in *Shining Hours/Forgiving Rhyme* (*Art Issues*, 1995), a text which was unashamedly nostalgic in its appreciation of Rockwell, harking back to the writer's own happy childhood memories of *Saturday Evening Post* covers while confidently affirming Rockwell as the great celebrator of American normality, the bard of 'a general state of social and physical equanimity that is unparalleled in the history of humans', lauding the 'kindness, comedy and forgiving tristesse' to which Rockwell was devoted, all those 'little victories' which, Hickey reminds us, pave the way towards a fully realized democracy.

More recently, Hickey returned to the fray again with an article in *Vanity Fair* (November 1999) in praise of Rockwell's *After The Prom* (1957), a painting which shows a teenage girl and boy, in formal dress, sitting sweetly at the bar on their tall stools as the soda jerk sniffs the perfume of the gardenia which the girl has proudly proffered to him, while this sentimental moment is savoured by a third customer, leather-jacketed, smiling, perched on another stool. As if sensing that his own enthusiasm for the everyday utopia of American small-town life, once upon a time, might not carry the day completely unaided, Hickey first invokes the work of Chardin and Fragonard and then manages to make good use of Michael Fried's *Absorption and Theatricality: Painting and Beholder in the Age of Diderot*, which he uses to explicate the meaning of the painting's four looks—five if you include our own nostalgic look at what has now become '*our* gardenia', a look which situates us 'in the same relationship to that white blossom of tactile paint as the soda jerk' who savours the perfume while we 'inhale the atmosphere'. 'When I was eight years old, Johnny Mercer was teaching me how to listen, and Norman Rockwell was teaching me how to see', writes Hickey, and now, more than 40 years on down the long road of life, the debt can be repaid, complete with an an iconographic *explication* whose premises are taken from none other than the heir to Greenberg's very own mantle.

Hickey's insistent enthusiasm for Norman Rockwell needs to be placed within its very specific art-world context. In effect, his articles function as curtain-raisers for next year's appearance of a vast Rockwell Retrospective at the Guggenheim Museum in New York, as the culmination and crowning moment of a national exhibition tour of major American museums. Ranged alongside Hickey as propagandist for the Guggenheim's Rockwell revival we also find the *New York Times* art critic, Michael Kimmelman, who explains that Rockwell's "simple sentimentality 'defied the fundamental credo of modernism that good art should be difficult if not (better yet) discomforting'. Kimmelman bravely nails his colours to the flagstaff of 'narrative transparency' and 'escapism in a sugary old-fogey mode', as he (rather unfairly, I think) characterizes Rockwell's work, taking care to dissociate himself (as Hickey does also) from that part of the *oeuvre* which was explicitly dedicated to the struggle of the 1960s Civil Rights movement, now dismissed as didactic and moralist. Hickey has even asserted that Rockwell could feel no 'instinctive identification' with the young black girl whom he painted for *Look* in 1964, as she was escorted into a newly desegregated school, and blames his friends Erik Erikson and Robert Coles for brainwashing him into an interest in poverty programs and civil rights.

In the very same issue of the *New York Times* there is also a long feature on the work of Thomas Kinkade, whom I first heard of as the only painter quoted on the Nasdaq stock index, where he has posted $125 million in revenues for this fiscal year. Kinkade sells reproductions of scenes like the snow-covered cottage, the waterfall in the forest, which range through 'basic paper prints, canvas lithographs in numbered editions, "Renaissance Editions" enhanced by "master highlighters", and at the top, "semi-originals" highlighted by Mr. Kinkade himself.' In a strange way, Kinkade descends from Warhol, the art world's pioneer of the enhancement of mass-produced images, but he is a descendant whose project is even more blatantly market-driven, more welcoming of the market values which opponents of kitsch, from Adorno to Greenberg, have always distrusted.

Not surprisingly, Hickey's book also offers us a defence of the art market, of art as something which a dealer sells to people who genuinely love it, rather than art as something to be exhibited in museums by curators or financed by bureaucrats at the Arts Council or the National Endowment for the Arts. Hickey was once a dealer himself and he dwells lovingly on his days running a gallery—a 'Mom and Pop store', as he likes to think of it—just a store in which the paper-boy who drops in on his round can come to appreciate the work of Ellsworth Kelly and Ed Ruscha. It all sounds very like a Norman Rockwell painting to me. There they are: Dave and Mary Jane, his wife, with the paper-boy and the mailman, a Christian Scientist who 'had no problems with text or abstraction', standing and looking at a push-pinned drawing or a piece of neon or just a pile of debris on the floor—their very own gardenia—all of them in a happy trance of well-intentioned American normality, a world in which money is not really the point, just 'a piece of green paper with a picture on it', something you might use to buy 'the occasional bowl of Wheaties'. As for the late Leo Castelli, he was just a dealer too, but one who took a much greater risk, because the reputation of his gallery was so much greater, and hence there was much more to lose if he showed paintings that nobody liked or even esteemed. The main point, Hickey thinks, is that showing in a famous gallery will get you plenty of attention and so 'even though it may appear to you that nearly everyone hates Jeff Koons's work, the critical point is that people take time and effort to hate it, publicly and at length, and this investment of attention effectively endows Koons's work with more importance than the work of those artists whose work we like, but not enough to get excited about.'

Hickey's critical rehabilitation of kitsch takes place in the context of his endorsement of the market and the very commercialism which Greenberg so much abhorred, and which has enabled a successful post-modernist like Jeff Koons (or Kinkade) to buy a virtually endless supply of bowls of Wheaties, should he so wish, instead of investing it in the stock market, which I suppose, from Hickey's point of view, is just another, very inflated kind of Mom and Pop store in which people can follow their instincts and tastes and predilections in the normal American way over the Internet. Koons and Kincade are the appropriate heroes for Hickey, I think, even if he and his friends don't like Koons's work enough to get excited about it. After all, Koons's father actually owned an interior decorator's store in which, in true Mom and Pop style, he sold his son's early work, beginning with an oil 'in the manner of Watteau'. In Anthony Haden-Guest's fascinating book on the inner workings of the art world, Koons is quoted as saying, 'My father started selling my work for hundreds of dollars when I was nine years old. These horrendous paintings. This gave me a tremendous amount of confidence'—enough confidence, indeed, to head off to art school and New York, where he quit painting and began to work with inflatables and household appliances. It was not long before Mary Boone scheduled a show for him and, ever the indulgent Mom, installed his rug shampooer piece in her office. Koons planned to put a revolving Mercedes on a turntable in Mary Boone's gallery, but she unexpectedly cancelled the show, thereby propelling the unfortunate artist into selling mutual funds for a living.

Every cloud, however, has a silver lining and, after a show of his vacuum cleaner pieces had worked out rather disappointingly, Koons was offered a job by Merrill Lynch which he turned down after getting an even better offer from Smith Barney. With the money that he earned from them he was able to get another show off the ground, and although the work sold, it still didn't make a profit, considering what it had cost to cast a life-raft in bronze, for example. Still, as Hickey noted, it did get him talked about, and his next show was financed by a dealer. Koons was moving out of the Mom and Pop world by now, towards international celebrity. Then, in 1988, he created what may still be his most celebrated work, a life-size ceramic tableau depicting Michael Jackson playing with his pet chimp, Bubbles, the centrepiece of a breakthrough exhibition (titled *Banality*) which sold out, according to Haden Guest, earning $12 million, split four ways between the artist and three separate dealers, who I like to imagine chatting excitedly to the mailman when he dropped by. Recently, I stumbled unexpectedly upon Michael Jackson and Bubbles in the Eli Broad Foundation's contemporary art warehouse in Santa Monica, a work which, I must admit, is almost majestic in its loathsome kitsch grandeur. It certainly split the critics, whose response ranged from contempt for 'objects that carry the love of kitsch to a new level of atrocious taste' to heart-felt praise for Koons's 'aesthetic perfect pitch'.

Koons is significant to any discussion of kitsch, not only because of his role in launching a new wave of kitsch iconography but because of his own shameless enjoyment of commodity culture and triumphant recycling of media-driven imagery, ranging from the mawkish to the pornographic. The purity of his shamelessness shines through so strongly that it is virtually bound to produce extreme reactions from both ends of the critical spectrum, pro- and anti-kitsch, the delighted and the disgusted. Koons himself denies any cynicism in his choice of material, simply affirming his interest in communicating clearly with the mass audience and his belief that 'the market is the best critic'. Of course, it is this last contention which is both the most symptomatic and also the most dubious. Dave Hickey may not like Koons's work all that much but he seems committed to a shared faith in the beneficence of the market and, as such, finds himself tied, whether he likes it or not, to the same aesthetic presuppositions. Hickey, it seems, wants to have his market cake and eat it too, letting us know that nearly everyone in his corner of the art world hates Koons's work, while applauding the market for bestowing its rewards on Rockwell, and Koons (and Kinkade) alike, without seeing any need to ask how monetary value can be disconnected from artistic value, or even whether it matters that it can.

Kitsch, of course, is not purely and simply an artefact of the market. It fulfils an artistic function of its own and it brings genuine pleasure to its devotees. There are few of us who could claim that they have remained rigorously untouched by any aspect of kitsch. It is because we are all involved with kitsch, in one way or another, that Olalquiaga seems justified strategically in trying to make a distinction between bad 'nostalgic' kitsch and good 'melancholic' kitsch, even if her specific criteria and preferences are open to question. 'Melancholic' kitsch, the kitsch she favours and celebrates, could be re-interpreted, it seems to me, as a taste for a form of 'magic realism', a tendency in the art of the 1940s which Greenberg saw, at that time, as a debased version of surrealism, rigorously rejecting it as another anti-aesthetic vulgarization of modernism which was 'nostalgic and day-dreamy', attempting to 'depress' modern art to a popular level, instead of 'raising the level of popularity itself'. In his book, *Magic Realism Rediscovered, 1918–81*, Seymour Menton argues that a group of artists whose work Greenberg summarily dismissed as kitsch— Grant Wood, Peter Blume and Andrew Wyeth, for instance—should be seen in a line of descent from the Douanier Rousseau and De Chirico, artists Greenberg at least took seriously. Menton was struck by the sharp focus of magic realist paintings, their creation of a toylike world, and their vivid representation of a world which strikes us as fantastic and uncanny, yet still convincingly possible. Greenberg wavered in his judgement of magic realism, and such allied movements as precisionism and photo-realism, finding it difficult to square his admiration for a photographer like Walker Evans with his distrust of any movement away from abstraction in painting.

Hyper-realism returned to the art-world in a much more popular form, however, in the form of installation art. I am thinking, for instance, of Damien Hirst's notorious shark, suspended in formaldehyde, which could well be considered a kind of gigantic and over-blown version of Rodney the hermit crab preserved and encased in his miniature glass sphere. Hirst's shark is a kind of exaggerated 'Nature Gem', a hyperbolic example of high kitsch. In her chapter on 'Rodney and Death', Olalquiaga describes Rodney as caught in a state of suspended death, like an insect caught in resin, as if in a trance or cataleptic stupor, stuck in 'an infinite nightmare that knows no end and no beginning'. The work is thus both a representation of death and, at the same time, a meditation upon it, 'thanatopsis incarnate'. Damien Hirst's shark, it is worth remembering, is actually titled, *The Physical Impossibility of Death in the Mind of Someone Living*. Olalquiaga's insistence that Rodney 'exists in a deadlock between two states of being, unable to fully launch into the lively fluctuations of the sea at night, or the solemn silence of a universe that has surrendered all claims to sensation', seems to me to indicate that her own book is itself a meditation on the physical impossibility of death in the mind of someone living—in this instance, the ingenious, fascinating and melancholic mind of Celeste Olalquiaga. The effect of Damien Hirst's shark on the viewer has also been likened, by art critics, to the effect of a Natural History Museum diorama, which is yet another subject discussed in *The Artificial Kingdom*. In her chapter on *The Copy*, Olalquiaga claims the diorama for melancholic kitsch, just so long as it remains un-narrativized. If the diorama appears to represent a dramatic scene taking place in time, however, it falls back into the category of nostalgic kitsch, a fate spared Hirst's shark as it was spared Rodney.

In the last analysis, however, I think that the subtle distinctions that Olalquiaga tries to make between different categories of kitsch are doomed to failure if they are treated as hard and fast aesthetic or ethical distinctions, fences separating the good sheep (or sharks) from the bad. While it is suggestive to propose that we can make clear distinctions between art and kitsch or between good (melancholic) kitsch and bad (nostalgic) kitsch, the truth is that kitsch and art and good and bad are always inextricably intertwined. They are not clear-cut and separate categories but contending impulses whose co-existence is central to the whole process of art-making as such. At the extremes there are works which are clearly kitsch or clearly not kitsch, while in between there are a whole series of works which cannot be categorized so clearly and so confidently. There is a potential for kitsch, as I have argued, in any work of art, not simply in black velvet paintings of *Dogs Playing Pool* or a Tretchikoff *Chinese Girl* bought off a barrow (like mine was) or Jim Shaw's wondrous collection of *Paintings found in Thrift Stores*. Kitsch, like the repressed, will always return, worming its way suggestively even into the work of a Rothko or a Pollock (*Lavender Mist, Shimmering Substance* ...). Why, after all, as Susan Sontag once asked, 'must a work of art restrict sentimental intervention and emotional participation, which are functions of closeness, in order to be just that—a work of art?' We can have our doubts about the modernist critics' indiscriminate exorcism of kitsch without going to the opposite extreme and endorsing it altogether.

Kitsch has its virtues when it expresses unacknowledged longings and speaks to desires of which we were previously unconscious, capturing us—not through obviousness and calculation—but rather through stealth and happenstance. In this sense, Olalquiaga is right to sing its surreptitious virtues, to see a place where kitsch begins to merge into art, surprising us, catching us unawares, happened upon as a found object which can cut across our preconceived notions with a touching shock of recognition. Even the most extreme work of the avant-garde, the most ironic, might still benefit from just a little glint of Rodney.

8

SALOME

The cult of Salome, in turn-of-the-century iconography, first began in painting. From painting it moved to literature, and from literature it then moved back to painting and the visual arts. In its final stage, it conquered the world of dance and the performing arts. These were not, of course, perfectly smooth transitions. There were overlaps and anomalies, which coincide, in broad terms, with the overlaps and anomalies that mark the transitions between French symbolism, *fin de siècle* decadence, and early modernism. The important point I want to stress, however, is that the image of Salome was not restricted to any one art, but itself served as a point of connection between the arts, functioning somewhat differently in each one, while also contributing towards the creation of a lasting strand of what we might call 'alternative modernism', whose effects we can still feel today.

The image of Salome first becomes historically salient in the extraordinary work of Gustave Moreau. From around 1870 to 1875 Moreau spent his time re-thinking his entire role as an artist and, above all, the foundations of his style and technique of painting. He was deeply shaken by the criticisms which were leveled against his Prometheus, even by formerly friendly critics, when it was exhibited at the 1869 Paris salon. He did not exhibit at the salon again until, seven years later, he showed his *Salome Dancing Before Herod* there in 1876. For some years beforehand he had concentrated on a series of studies for the painting that illustrate in detail the way in which he re-formulated his art, transposing it from the old register of romanticism, albeit with disturbing symbolist overtones, into a fully-fledged and original new style which pointed forward towards the Decadence. Careful drawing and hatching gave way to rich impasto, mysterious lighting and theatrical effects. Salome remains his masterpiece, the work which had the greatest initial impact and with which he is still most identified today.

During this period, Moreau's art was already moving towards performance. It seems that he actually constructed a small clay-coated marionette for the figure of Salome which he could manipulate in a theatrical space as a guide to his painting. He dressed this figure in costume and suspended it from strings. It is clear too that the atmosphere of Moreau's painting had greater affinities with the work of Gautier's *Une Nuit de Cléopatre* or Flaubert's *Salammbo* than it did with any previous painting. (Henri Regnault had exhibited a highly-praised Salom, at the very same 1869 salon where Moreau's Prometheus had been so harshly criticized, but Moreau's own Salom breaks entirely new ground rather than drawing on Regnault.) Essentially Moreau sought to dramatize his subject matter by making it more mysterious, splendid and uncanny, along lines pioneered by contemporary writers, and by introducing a more complex set of characters, placing them in a theatrical setting and deploying what we now think of as stage lighting, as though anticipating the innovations of Wagner and Appia.

Moreau's painting might have remained an isolated event, linked perhaps to Flaubert's *Hérodias*, written within months of the 1876 salon, if it had not been for J.-K. Huysmans's use of it in *A Rebours*, published eight years later in 1884. *A Rebours* was to become the breviary of the Decadents and in it Huysmans supposed that his hero, Des Esseintes, had himself acquired Moreau's Salom, and the accompanying water-colour, *L'Apparition* (which shows John the Baptist's head floating before Salome), for his personal delectation. Des Esseintes was portrayed as an aesthete dedicated, in a world rotted by materialism, to a heroic and solitary quest for useless and refined pleasure. Huysmans was clearly captivated by the hieratic setting of the dance, its overtones of a cathedral or a temple. He noted the glints of light reflected from festoons of jewels and imagined a scene heavy with perfume and a dance which, though openly erotic in its bodily movements, was mainly characterized by the effects of light shimmering and glinting from bracelets, rings, necklaces, pearl embroidery, gold and silver cloth, which moved with the dancer as she danced. Huysmans' Salome was a depraved temple dancer, richly yet ambiguously Phoenician, Egyptian, Indian and Byzantine in appearance and costume, whose lascivious sexuality was displayed principally in glints of light.

It is the lack of precise detail and outline, combined with the lack of clear archaeological or ethnographic reference, which allowed Des Esseintes to meditate on the wealth of profuse connotations which the image of Salome provoked, rather than her singular denotation, her role in the brief and threadbare story recounted in the Bible. In his mind, he turned her into a 'symbolic deity', evoking a capitalized Luxury, Hysteria, and Beauty, marked by catalepsy, monstrosity and indifference. She was both exultantly disquieting as a dancer and magnificently exquisite as a murderess, accursed yet indestructible, immortal. It was the hallucinating combination of animal, goddess, artist, dandy, priestess, killer, seductress and hysteric which gave the image of Salome its uncanny power. Among these many dimensions of Salome, it is worth noting that Charcot had first isolated and demonstrated 'modern' hysteria only a few years before. At stake here was the connection between femininity, sexuality, pathology and degeneracy, a connection soon to be elucidated by Sigmund Freud.

Huysmans' consecration of Salome led in due course to Oscar Wilde's play, *Salome*, written in French (rather than his native English) in 1891. Wilde's Dorian Gray (in *The Picture of Dorian Gray*, first published the previous year) had been inspired to become a Decadent, as we would now recognize him, by his reading of an un-named novel which Wilde later characterized as 'partly suggested by Huysmans's *A Rebours* .... It is a fantastic variation on Huysmans's over-realistic study of the artistic temperament in our inartistic age.' Dorian Gray, Wilde said, was 'what I would like to be' and Salome is undoubtedly the Wilde text which comes closest to that which Dorian Gray might have written.

Wilde came into direct contact with the French Decadence in Paris as early as 1883, when he was introduced to Maurice Rollinat by Sarah Bernhardt. Rollinat, a protégé of Bernhardt, had just published his second collection of Decadent verse, *Les Nevroses*, and gave poetry readings at the infamous Montmartre café concert, *Le Chat Noir*, complete with piano accompaniment. He regaled Wilde with Decadent maxims which survive because Wilde noted them down afterwards, including, significantly, 'I don't believe in progress, but I do believe in the stagnation of human perversity.' Wilde was already aware of Flaubert's version of the Salome story, *Hérodias*, which was lent to him by his mentor, Walter Pater, while he was still a student at Oxford, as well as Stéphane Mallarmé's ongoing *Hérodiade*, a poem nurtured since 1864, but not completed until after Wilde's own Salome had appeared.

More directly important to Wilde, however, were his researches into the iconography of Salome within the history of painting. Wilde was aware of the new emphasis placed on the visual impact of theatre by his friend, and Whistler's close collaborator, E. W. Godwin, whose design for E. W. Wills's now forgotten play, *Claudian* (1883), Wilde had praised in a review for 'its marvellous loveliness' which 'showed us the life of Byzantium in the fourth century, not by a dreary lecture and a set of grimy casts, not by a novel which requires a glossary to explain it, but by the visible presentation before us of all the glory of that great town'. He studied, and criticized, among others, the Salomes of Rubens, Leonardo, Durer, Ghirlandaio and Regnault, which he dismissed briskly as the portrait of a 'gypsy'. He wanted desperately to visit the Prado to see Titian's version but, above all, it was Moreau who impressed him and left a lasting mark on Wilde's own Salome, both directly and through Huysmans. It was with Moreau in mind that Wilde would walk down the Rue de la Paix studying the jewels in the shop windows. In Paris, Wilde absorbed the Decadent influences which he later fused with the Byzantinism of Moreau to create a spectacle of perverse opulence.

Wilde's Salome carried pictorial and literary Decadence directly into the theatre. The themes remained the same—the somnambulism of Salome, her absorption in a dream, which Moreau remarked on in his notebooks, as well as the open-ended matrix of cruelty, indifference, eroticism and hysteria delineated by Huysmans—but the image of Salome was now explicitly embodied, insofar as Wilde's text was intended for performance. In fact, no lesser actress than Sarah Bernhardt herself was in rehearsal as Salome when the play was banned in Britain. It was not till 1896 that the play was first performed—in Paris, at Lugne-Poe's Theatre de l'Oeuvre, with Lina Munte in the title role and a program designed by Toulouse-Lautrec—by which time, tragically, Wilde was already in Reading Gaol, serving a sentence for sodomy. After his release, Wilde wrote of Salome as his greatest achievement, the only one of his plays to enlarge the 'artistic horizons' of the theatre.

Because of the problems of censorship Wilde's play was first known, not in its theatrical form, but as a published book (1894) illustrated by Aubrey Beardsley, whose black-and-white drawings struck many as even more scandalous than Wilde's play and attracted as much attention. Wilde's play was published in Paris a year previously and Beardsley was inspired by this to make a drawing on the theme of 'J'ai Baisé Ta Bouche Iokanaan' ('I have kissed thy mouth, Jokanaan') which, in the words of one historian, 'aroused more horror and indignation than any graphic work produced in England', when it was published in the inaugural issue of *The Studio*, in April 1893. The scene Beardsley chose is that in which Salome, staring fanatically into the sightless eyes of the severed head of John the Baptist, prepares to kiss him. She is floating above the ground as if suspended in space, her hair twisting up from her head like the tentacles of an octopus, while blood pours from his throat, forming a pool below, out of which grows a lily, emblematic flower of virginity.

Thus Beardsley effected the transition from symbolism to Decadence, mediated by Huysmans and Wilde. At the same time, Beardsley again shifted the emphasis of the visual iconography of Salome. He deflected attention from the dance towards the severed head and, although in *The Apparition* Moreau had used the motif, he gave it a scandalous carnality and a further dimension of symbolic complexity. Beardsley also displaced the image from its traditional orientalist setting. His Salome illustrations are in what he called a 'Japonesque' style, drawing on Japanese wood-block artists, such as Utamaro, and French poster-artists such as Chéret and Toulouse-Lautrec. This was a crucial deviation because it 'modernized' the visual impact of Salome—Beardsley's drawings removed their subject from its Biblical setting, encrusted with echoes of antiquity, and placed it in a topical and contemporary context. Hence, to a great extent, the scandal which erupted.

The Japanese wood-block prints, French posters and English caricatures from which Beardsley drew all suggested a vernacular rather than a hieratic context. Beardsley corroborated this by setting many of his illustrations for the book of Salome in quite anachronistic periods. For example, his *The Toilet of Salome*, as published, shows a contemporary woman of fashion on whose Japanese-style dressing-table are placed a stack of scandalous books, including the Marquis De Sade and Zola's *Nana*. (An earlier version of the same drawing showed Baudelaire's *Les Fleurs Du Mal*, alongside Zola and Ibsen.) In this way Beardsley secularized the story of Salome by transposing it from the New Testament to the milieu of the Decadence, the time of Wilde's play itself. He both avoided the representation of biblical characters—the pretext given for banning Wilde's play—and placed scenes of perverse eroticism plainly within modernity.

In 1898 Oscar Wilde, in exile in Paris, wrote to Leonard Smithers, the publisher of *The Ballad of Reading Gaol*, Wilde's great poem describing his life in prison, as well as Beardsley's publisher, in which he asked, 'Have you a copy of Aubrey's drawing of Mlle de Maupin? There is a young Russian here, who is a great amateur of Aubrey's art, who would love to have one. He is a great collector, and rich. So you might send him a copy and name a price, and also deal with him for drawings by Aubrey. His name is Serge de Diaghilev, Hotel St James, Rue St Honoré, Paris.' In fact, not only was Diaghilev a great admirer of Beardsley's work, but he also went on a pilgrimage to meet Beardsley in Dieppe and published Beardsley copiously in his magazine, *The World of Art*.

Beardsley was an enormous influence on the circle around Diaghilev, especially his designers, Bakst and Benois. It was some time, however, before this influence made itself felt in works which fell directly within the Salome tradition. In 1907, the impresario Gabriel Astruc presented Richard Strauss's new opera, *Salome*, based on Wilde's play, at the Théatre du Chatelet in Paris, with Natalia Trouhanova and Aida Boni alternating in the *Dance of the Seven Veils*. It was the success of the Salome, more than any other of his presentations, that opened Astruc's eyes to the potential of Diaghilev's *Ballets Russes*, with their similar mixture of symbolism, spectacle and modernity. In the words of the dance historian, Lynn Garafola, 'More than any other enterprise Salome anticipated the arrival of the Ballets Russes'.

The following year, 1908, the Russian patron and performer Ida Rubinstein mounted a stage performance of Wilde's play, directed by Meyerhold, designed by Bakst, choreographed by Fokine, with herself as

Salome, dancing to music by Glazounov. Although the Tsarist censors attempted to ban the play, it was presented nonetheless, but as a mime drama rather than a spoken play. Discussing her influence on Bakst, the great dance critic André Levinson characterized her as 'this young woman with her disconcerting and mysterious beauty, voluptuous yet frigidly cold, with a will of iron underneath a fragile frame, and possessed of a haughty and cold intelligence'. Bakst himself characterized her as 'a fabulous being ... like a beautiful tulip, insolent and dazzling, proud of herself and shedding pride around her'. It was this 'insolent pride' which gave Rubinstein's performances their subversive strength.

Rubinstein was only 22 when she performed in her production of Salome. To get there she had first to survive incarceration in a Paris clinic, where she was placed by her brother-in-law, a doctor, when she refused to drop the project. After her release she still refused to compromise, working on her dancing with Fokine and even visiting Palestine to research her role. It was Rubinstein's *Salome* that led directly to her collaboration, again with Bakst and Fokine, in Diaghilev's *Schéhérazade*, the momentous ballet which set the seal on the success of the *Ballets Russes* in 1910. Rubinstein deeply impressed such Decadents as Robert de Montesquiou (who took her to visit the Gustave Moreau museum in 1909) and Gabriele D'Annunzio, whose *Saint Sebastian* she performed and who became her most demanding devotee. In 1912 Rubinstein finally performed her Salome in Paris, virtually naked except for great clusters of genuine jewels. Together with Nijinsky, Rubinstein was the dominating performer of late Decadence as it was transposed, by Diaghilev and herself, into early modernism. She was the breathtaking culmination of the Salome icon.

Although the Salome cult continued for many years, its most enduring legacy came through its impact on the *Ballets Russes*. *Schéhérazade* exemplified a mode of late Decadence which was compatible with the parallel breakthroughs of Matisse and Poiret. The solvents which made this possible were orientalism, eroticism and dance. The Salome motif had been isolated as a subject for specialized dance performance as early as 1895, when Loie Fuller danced three short pieces under the joint title of *Salome*. However, it was not till the time of the Strauss Salome that women dancers appropriated Salome for themselves and for modern dance.

Strauss had been inspired to write an opera of Salome after seeing Max Reinhardt's stage production of Wilde's play in a small theatre in Berlin in 1903, with Gertrude Eysoldt in the title role. In his notes for the dance Strauss explicitly invoked Gustave Moreau. It is through Strauss that Nietzsche's vision of a dancing Zarathustra encountered the literary modernity of Wilde, as Julius Korngold noted in a review of the Vienna production of Strauss's *Salome*, with Moreau's symbolist vision of Salome at the centre. Like Wilde and Rubinstein, Strauss had to fight off the censors but, unlike them, despite some setbacks, he largely succeeded in this. The opera opened in Dresden in 1905 and toured widely throughout Europe and in America. It had an enormous impact.

The American musician Maud Allan, a student of Busoni, began to dance in public to famous pieces of Romantic music in 1903, touring Germany with a programme drawn from Chopin, Schubert and Mendelssohn. The following year, she too saw Reinhardt's production of Wilde's *Salome* and began to work on a dance version, with music composed by Marcel Rémy, who she had met through Busoni. The first performance of *The Vision of Salome* took place in Vienna in December 1906, under the aegis of Gustav Mahler, then director of the Court Opera. Her Paris debut, in May the next year, was deliberately timed to coincide with the Paris production of Strauss's opera. It supplied, as it were, the eroticism and grace missing from the opera, in which the dance was performed by an opera singer rather than a specialized dancer. Later that year Maud Allan, now on her way to success, performed before Edward VII, the King of England, while he was taking the waters at Marienbad. She also appeared as a dancer in the Wagner opera at Bayreuth. Allan was a musically literate dancer, who was able to give a gloss of artistry to a performance which drew on the example of Isadora Duncan, combined with a pastiche of Arab dance. It proved to be a potent mixture.

By 1908 Maud Allan was dancing Salome all over Europe, reaching the pinnacle of her success in London. The same year Gertrude Hoffmann danced Salome in New York, after being sent to England by the theatre owner to study Maud Allan's version. Then, in November 1909, Ruth Saint Denis transposed her *Radha*, based on Indian dance, to the now fashionable Salome in a rival New York theatre. Soon America was full of aspirant Salomes. Madame Dazi, who danced Salome for the Ziegfeld Follies, even opened a Salome school. By the summer of 1908 she was sending 150 Salomes a month out into the world—or at least the world of vaudeville—each, in Elizabeth Kendall's words, 'with the same routine—an incoherent mix of gestures and undulations addressed to a papier-maché head'!

It was at this point that the 'descent' of Salome from the recondite circles of the Decadence to the vernacular world of popular culture was complete. The Salome of Moreau and Huysmans and Wilde was being mass produced. Salome allowed young American women to express a dynamic will and sexuality while remaining distant and even virginal, emerging triumphant over the world of men. Thus Salome dancing was differentiated implicitly from the raunchier success of cooch dancing, which subordinated the dancer, so to speak, to Herod's gaze.

In 1893 the Chicago World's Columbian Exposition had featured a series of ethnographic villages along the Midway, with a menagerie and the newly invented Ferris Wheel. Among these strange popular-yet-educational attractions were two from the Arab world, the 'Streets of Cairo' and an Algerian village. It was here that belly dancing, popularly known as cooch dancing, was featured for the first time in America. As the Midway's director later recalled, visitors to the Exposition 'delightedly concluded that it must be salacious and immoral. The crowds poured in. I had a goldmine.' Soon the burlesque stage was flooded with a horde of Fatimas and Little Egypts. Thus, as the Dance of the Seven Veils descended downwards into vaudeville, it was, in effect, presenting itself as the 'high-class' and cultured version of an already existing 'low-class' form of burlesque entertainment. In the end, the Salomes and the Fatimas drove each other out of business. Exotic dancers only survived in the lowest sphere of all—the bump-and-grind sex show.

The Salome epoch came to an intriguing end with three striking spectacles, all produced by Russians. In 1917 Alexandra Exter designed a production of *Salome* (played by Alice Koonen) at Tairov's Kamerny Theatre in Moscow, choreographed by Mikhail Mordkin, best known as Pavlova's partner. In 1922, Kasian Goleizovsky, also in Moscow, choreographed a modernist ballet of *Salome* to Strauss's score, with a performance by Tarnovskaya notorious for its stylized eroticism. The same year, in distant Los Angeles, Alla Nazimova, a Russian émigrée, adapted, starred in and, to all intents and purposes, directed her own film of Wilde's *Salome* with costumes by Natasha Rambova (later Valentino's partner) which were based explicitly on Beardsley's drawings. It was a strange concoction but, after censorship battles, was more or less suppressed by the studio when it was finally released in 1923. Rambova herself was not, in fact, Russian but adopted her name when she danced in the American ballet company led by Theodor Kosloff, a former Diaghilev dancer. This curious provincial version of Salome was the gallant last survivor of Russian symbolism and Beardsley-esque Decadence, somehow persisting in the Californian hinterland, long after Diaghilev himself had moved on to embrace Cocteau and cubism.

The dominant view of the Salome tradition, expressed by writers as various as Mario Praz, in his path-breaking 1933 study, *The Romantic Agony*, Bram Dijkstra in his 1986 *Idols of Perversity* and Elaine Showalter, in her feminist *Sexual Anarchy* (1990) is that it expressed male fears of women, modulating from troubled anxiety and fascinated fear of castration to rampant misogyny. This is certainly true, but it is not the whole story. In the first place, the Decadence had a subversive charge that is too often overlooked. Thomas Laqueur has shown how, in the nineteenth century, a two-sex model of humanity dominated thought about sexual difference, postulating a clear-cut, incommensurable and supposedly natural dichotomy between the sexes. For example, in Laqueur's words, 'in these new discursive wars feminists as well as antifeminists sacrificed the idea of women as inherently passionate,' assuming that men, by nature, were sexually active, women pure and passionless.

Plainly, Salome contradicted this cornerstone of nineteenth-century ideology, all the more so if she was somnambulist and hysterical in her perverse desire to kiss the lips of Jokanaan's severed head. The Decadents articulated a view of sexuality which rigorously refused any conventional ascription of sexual nature. They portrayed a world of androgyny in which desire could run, against the grain, in the wrong direction and towards the wrong object. They contested the conventional division of sexuality into active and passive. This scandalous disruption of conventional sexual stereotypes allowed modern women to identify with Salome and, along with parallel identifications with the maenad (Isadora Duncan) and the witch (Mary Wigman), to lay the foundations of modern dance, the single art form dominated by women, from Loie Fuller and Ruth Saint Denis, through Mary Wigman and Martha Grahame, up to Pina Bausch and Yvonne Rainer, and beyond.

As for men, there are two telling photographs which survive from the 1890s. The first, reproduced without background information in Richard Ellman's classic biography, is of Oscar Wilde dressed as Salome, in flowing skirt with bare stomach and jewelled brassiere, tresses running down the length of his back beneath an elaborate head dress. Wilde kneels, his beringed hands outstretched towards the severed head upon its salver. The other photograph shows Robert de Montesquiou, the original of Des Esseintes and Proust's Charlus, friend of Whistler and Mallarmé, devotee of Moreau and Beardsley. The photograph, probably taken in 1886, depicts its subject as the head of John the Baptist. Tinted blue— the colour of his favoured flower, the hydrangea—de Montesquiou's head, placed so as to appear severed, rests on a salver framed within a window and surrounded by hangings decorated with oriental motifs and, below, a Morris fabric drapery with blue honeysuckle flowers. On either side of the window there is an inscription. On the left we read, in gold lettering, 'J'Aime Le Jade Couleur Des Yeux D'Hérodiade' and, on the right, 'Et L'Amethyste Couleur Des Yeux De Jean-Baptiste'.

These two extraordinary photographs, representing two male aesthetes in their contrary identifications with Salome and Jokanaan, establish in the clearest possible way the paradoxical complexity of sexual desire, the elaborate scenography through which we recognize ourselves. In these two photographs we see that the image of Salome impinged on masculinity quite as subversively as it did on femininity. The story of Salome, as represented by writers, painters and dancers at the turn of the century, offered a variety of different positions for the identification of both sexes.

This period of intense preoccupation with the image of Salome coincided both with the foundation of psychoanalysis and the dynamic development of the women's suffrage movement. Although there were surprisingly few explicit connections between these three movements, all of them, in their own ways, undermined established ideas about differences between the sexes. In this sense, the Salome cult played a crucial part in the formation of modernity, as an emancipatory force and as a challenge to nineteenth-century assumptions about the proper roles of the sexes. Its effects are still being felt today, as, over a century later, we continue to work through these questions of sexual difference and desire.

9

BLUE

1. A PRIVATE PROGRAMME OF THE VOID

Derek Jarman's film *Blue* opened at the Camden Parkway cinema in London on 23 August 1993, and was shown the next month on Channel 4 Television, with a simultaneous broadcast of the sound-track on BBC Radio 3. A few months later Jarman was dead, from complications derived from Aids. *Blue* is an autobiographical film, which deals directly with its director's experience of Aids, his blindness, and his awareness of his approaching death. At the same time, it should be seen in parallel with his book *Chroma*, which is a meditation on colour, completed in June 1993 and published the next year. The text of *Blue* consists almost entirely of material from the book's section 'Into The Blue', plus one brief passage from the 'The Perils of Yellow' and a single new paragraph in which Blue is engaged in a death struggle with his mortal foe Yellowbelly. The film consists of the projection on screen, for its entire 75 minutes, of pure blue light, accompanied on the sound-track by the film-maker reading his text and a music score by his collaborator, Simon Turner.

Blue had been in Jarman's mind as a possible project for many years. In 1987, after the success of *Caravaggio*, which had been released the previous year, he floated the idea of making a film about Yves Klein, a painter whose work he had admired since his days as an art student at the Slade School of Art in the mid-sixties. Nothing came of this, but in

1989 he was approached by a television producer (from a 'loathsome inept youth-orientated arts program') to appear in a documentary about Klein. As he recorded in his journal, 'I agreed to co-operate only if the work explained Yves and didn't turn him into a circus—perhaps an interview followed by as many minutes or seconds of blank blue soundless TV.' Jarman hated the program, a 'travesty', when it came out, even though Simon Turner had composed the music for it. He noted that Klein's own works—such as the *Symphonie Monotone* and the *Anthropometries*,

> were for a select invited audience, who were requested to show their respect by arriving in evening dress—this the fifties, Paris, and that was what it was about, exclusivity. The photos are the evidence, the performance a secret. The enemy is the spurious egalitarianism and lack of concentration of the media. Maybe the best way would be to black out TV sets. Furious phone calls: 'I've paid my license.' Yes, but it doesn't give you the right to pry—this is a private programme of the void, if you wish to see it you'll pay the dues as well and if you fail you'll be fined.

IKB
spirit in matter

IKB refers here to International Klein Blue, the unique blue paint, a deep ultramarine, which Yves Klein himself invented, patented, and used exclusively in his series of monochrome blue works.

A week later, on 1 June, Jarman noted in his journal that 'Blueprint becomes Bliss—dedicated to St Rita of Cascia, patron of lost causes. Into the blue. Wandered through the bookshops and bought The Book of Changes to construct the script.' This entry is significant both because 'Into The Blue' eventually became the title of the section on blue in *Chroma*, which is reproduced in the film *Blue*, and also because St Rita is mentioned in a crucial passage in the text of *Blue*. St Rita was a medieval saint to whose shrine at Cascia, in a remote region of Umbria, Yves Klein's aunt and grandmother both made pilgrimages from their home in Nice, followed eventually by Yves Klein himself. He made four visits during the 1950s and left an art-work there with the prioress in return for the saint's favour. Jarman spent the next day, 2 June, planning an installation for a gallery in Glasgow—a room which 'turned in my mind from white to black, then blue, then white again', with a 'tomb/cenotaph' and other elements, which included a monochromatic painting, alluding to the Aids epidemic and to the Thatcher government's proposed anti-gay legislation (Clause 28). Thus IKB was now linked to Aids.

Next, on the Saturday 3 June, Jarman noted that 'the blue columbine', which he had planted in his garden at Prospect Cottage, Dungeness, and was now in flower, had been 'one of the herbs used against the Black Death in the 14th century'. Then, on Sunday 4 June, he 'gilded a small pocket book for Blueprint' and noted some ideas that had occurred to him while walking on the beach, which seem mainly to have pointed towards *The Garden*, the next film he was to make, rather than towards *Blue*. He did, however, wonder whether these new ideas could 'be resolved with the Tao Te Ching: great fullness seems empty?', and—surely a coincidence—quoted a passage from *The Gardener's Labyrinth* which claimed that the blue-flowering sea kale he had planted 'cureth the soreness of eyes'. Throughout this summer, Jarman was preoccupied with his gardening, the campaign against Clause 28 and the preparations for his film, *The Garden*. However, he still continued to work on *Blueprint/Bliss*, as well as thinking about the bluescreen matte background effects for *The Garden* and pasting up the script in a notebook which he then painted cobalt blue.

In 1990, when *The Garden* went into post-production, Jarman finally made some pilot reels of lab-generated blue film in the hope of raising money for *Blueprint/Bliss*. As Michael O'Pray remembers, 'He was falling over with glee in Dean Street at the thought of offering up just a blue colour field—he was always cheered up by the thought of shocking his potential backers.' Soon afterwards, however, he got enough backing to make *Edward II*, from Marlowe's play about the king's favourite, Piers Gaveston, which he jokingly said that he wanted to be 'a blue film in the porno sense'—an association of the colour blue which remains constant, along with the connections to Yves Klein, to blue sky, sea and garden flowers, and to the blues.

Jarman still persisted with the idea of *Blue*, now in a different form. When *The Garden* was finally completed and premiered at the Lumière cinema in St Martin's Lane, on Sunday 6 January 1991, the screening was accompanied by a performance piece, titled *Symphonie Monotone*, after

Yves Klein, which took place before the main film was screened. During the performance, 35mm film of a Klein blue painting, shot at the Tate Gallery, was projected on to the screen, with slides projected over it from time to time. To the left of the screen, Derek Jarman and Tilda Swinton sat behind a table and read extracts from a series of writers on the theme of blue, also stroking wine-glass tops with their fingers to make a musical sound. Beneath them, in the space between audience and stage, a group of musicians assembled by Simon Turner played his music score for about an hour. From time to time, the young boy who appeared in *The Garden* ran into the packed hall and handed out pebbles, painted blue or gold, to members of the audience. This was the first realization of Jarman's project of *Blue*, although one which was still dominated by the idea of a tribute to Yves Klein and a meditation on colour.

In 1989, Jarman had observed that 'I only go to the cinema now out of friendship or nostalgia. I cannot watch anything that is not based on its author's life. Acting, camerawork, all the paraphernalia, bring me little pleasure without the element of autobiography.' Acting, camerawork, 'all the paraphernalia', had already vanished from the project of *Blue*. However, it was not till the summer of 1991, when Derek Jarman was struck with Aids-related blindness, that the film *Blue* arrived at its final form, with the writing of a new autobiographical text, a meditation on blindness and death, which brought Klein blue together with the experience of Aids in a definitive new form. Money now came from the Arts Council of England, then from Channel 4 and BBC Radio. Brian Eno lent his studios for the sound recording and the original blue film loop was replaced by a video-generated blue field. Meanwhile, under Simon Turner's direction, the live performances continued separately— in Japan, including one at the Golden Pavilion in Kyoto, using the film loop, Turner's music and a recorded reading of Jarman's poems, and, later, in Italy, now using blue gels instead of the film loop and with a simultaneous recitation of the final film text.

2. THE MONOCHROME ADVENTURE

Yves Klein started painting blue monochrome works in 1955. He had started talking about International Klein Blue (IKB) around 1957 or early

1958 and patented the actual process of making the paint itself in 1960. In essence, IKB is a slab of ultramarine pigment suspended in a clear commercial binder, Rhodopas. The effect is to preserve the granularity of the pigment and to seal it so that a thickness of pure pigment can be hung vertically on the wall, like an upended tray. The origins of IKB, according to Klein himself, are twofold, and both significant for Jarman's re-use of this particular medium. First, the idea of monochrome came to Klein while he was playing a jazz improvisation based on the thought of Max Heindel, a Rosicrucian philosopher, or cosmogonist, who profoundly influenced Klein. Heindel, in his exposition of Rosicrucian beliefs, claimed that blue was the highest of the colours, that of spirit freed from material form. Klein believed that his IKB monochromes symbolically presented the prospect of release from materiality and entry into a world of pure spirit. In art-theoretic terms, Klein considered that art should consist simply of pure colour and that the invention of drawing and image-making, the rival tradition to that of pure colour, represented, in effect, a fall from paradise. Historically, painting had begun with pure pigment. Others, like Malevich, had shown the way back to colour, but were still bedevilled by the idea of composition. Only Klein himself, however, fully understood the true meaning and role of monochrome.

In conjunction with this mystical belief in the spiritual power of monochrome, Klein also derived his insistence on pure pigment from his intense personal experience of the materiality of paint. In 1949, aged 21, he had worked for about a year in London, in the Old Brompton Road frame-shop of Robert Savage, a friend of his father. There he experienced what he called 'the illumination of matter'. As he wrote later,

> I disliked colours ground in oil. They seemed dead to me; what pleased me above all were pure pigments, in powder, such as I saw them in the windows of retail paint-sellers. They had brightness and extraordinary, autonomous lives of their own. This was essential colour. Living tangible colourmatter. It was depressing to see such glowing powder, once mixed in a distemper, or whatever medium intended as a fixative, lose its value, tarnish, become dull. One might obtain effects of paste but after drying it wasn't the same; the effective colour magic had vanished.

Traditionally, ultramarine was the most precious of pigments, which for centuries could be obtained only from lapis lazuli quarried at a single mine in Afghanistan, shipped to Europe via Venice or Aleppo. The mine was first described in the west in 1837, by which time it was exhausted. To IKB Klein later added gold leaf, which he had worked with in the same frame-shop, when gilding frames for Savage, and then rose, to complete his colour repertoire, as a tribute to the Rose Cross. Klein's approach to colour and pigment combined many elements: an obsession with its spiritual meaning, an optical delight in its intensity and granularity, an occult interest in its symbolic interpretation, a fascination with the precious and the antique. I think that all these approaches were congenial to Jarman in one way or another. His own work is full of references to magic, alchemy and occult lore; it is also intensely sensual and, as we see from his film *Wittgenstein*, concerned with pure chromatic effect; there is an aspect which we might almost call 'precious'—for example, in the way Jarman carefully chose the opulent, encrusted colours for the covers of his notebooks and the use of gold and glass in his own paintings. (Wittgenstein, I should add, was himself the author of a book on colour, his *Notes On Colour*—in fact, his last book—written in manuscript in 1950 and 1951, immediately before his death.)

However, there were more specific reasons for Jarman's growing fascination with Klein. Jarman always had an ambivalent relationship with film and particularly, as we have seen, with television. Towards the end of his life he made it clear that he was only interested in films which were deeply personal, which were about the film-maker's own life. *Blue* is just such an autobiographical film, dealing with Aids directly as an experience lived by its maker. Blue was the colour Jarman saw when eye-drops were put in his eyes in the hope of alleviating his blindness. Paradoxically, blindness allowed Jarman to see, beyond the distraction of images, directly into the realm of colour, as Yves Klein had wished. Aids was too important to Jarman for it to be represented by images.

> It was always going to have to be the best film I had ever made. And to make matters even more complicated, there was never a situation that presented itself as the obvious scenario. I was always stuck with images. I could have made the film with actors, I suppose, but there's always the question of

whether the audience will identify with them. You'd have to get past that hurdle before you ever got close to the experience. And, at this late stage in the game, I simply wasn't prepared to short-change myself. The key to *Blue* was to do away with the images altogether, and to integrate the personal by integrating diary entries into the script.

In this emergency situation, Jarman turned to Yves Klein as Klein had turned to Saint Rita, 'saint of impossible and hopeless causes', to show the way forward, beyond images, beyond representation. There is a tendency to see monochrome, as the Soviet critic Tarabukin saw the red, blue and yellow works of Rodchenko (shown in 1921) as signalling 'the end of painting'. It would be easy to make a connection to Jarman's impending death, and, in general, to post-modern ideas about the end of history. But Klein saw monochrome as a return to a lost origin and an embarcation on a new adventure. He talked of 'infinite possibility' and his wish to overcome 'fear of the void'. 'For me a painting must create around itself, permanently, a deep, immense joy, a great illuminating, delirious, and especially immaterial happiness on the surface of the canvas.' Jarman was always opposed to facile optimism about Aids, preferring to talk about dying with Aids, rather than living with Aids, admitting the experience of physical and mental breakdown, his thoughts of suicide, his weariness with it all. At the same time, he saw *Blue* as a way of 'keeping the illness at bay', reasserting an immense joy in the face of dreadful disaster, an illumination in the face of death.

Looking back on Jarman's career, we can see how he always insisted on the present-ness of film. His exasperation with Peter Greenaway's film *The Draughtsman's Contract* was an exasperation with the painstakingly accurate representation of the past, a tradition which he saw as derived art-historically from Poussin. In *Caravaggio*, he went out of his way to set the past clearly in the present. Similarly, his *Tempest* is placed in a world which we recognize as our own, rather than in the antiquarian extravaganza of Greenaway's *Prospero's Books*. In *Jubilee*, one of the characters, Amyl, played by Jordan, observes that, 'Our school motto was *Faites vos désires réalités*; "make your desires reality". Myself I preferred the song "Don't dream it, be it". In those days desires weren't allowed to become reality. So fantasy was substituted for them—films, books, pictures, they called it art. But when your desires become reality you don't need fantasy any longer, or art.' Another character, Viv, who lives in an empty and entirely black room, announces, 'Painting's extinct, it's just a habit. I started when I was eight, copying dinosaurs from a picture book. It was prophetic.'

In 1983, soon after finishing *Jubilee*, Jarman wrote in his notebooks that

> All art is dead, especially modern art. Only when art is demoted to the ranks again, treated as nothing remarkable, will our culture start to breathe. The spurious individualism of the Renaissance, which both engendered and was born of capital, is dieing. An art which began by collaborating with the banks of the Medici ended in bankruptcy on Wall St. On the way, it destroyed the sublime anonymity of the Middle Ages and replaced it with stolen goods. Creativity in the future will be measured differently, no longer tied to commodity and worldly success.

In the face of death, 'commodity and worldly success' lose all their meaning. Speaking about *Blue*, Jarman once remarked, 'I always said I would end up painting again. And I suppose in a sense that's what I'm doing.' *Blue*, which is a rejection of the exhausted image-laden cinematic tradition, is a return to pre-modern painting in the tradition of Yves Klein's 'Monochrome Adventure'. In Klein's work, Jarman saw a way of painting which escaped the trap of the Renaissance and enabled him to return to the Middle Ages, when the Virgin's cloak was always painted in lapis lazuli, because it was the most precious of pigments, and the sky was always rendered in gold leaf. Klein had shown the way to escape (or, perhaps, aestheticize) the involvement of art with the market, when, shortly before his death in 1962, he invented a ritual procedure for the relinquishment of what he named 'zones of immaterial pictorial sensibility'. These immaterial zones could only be exchanged for gold and would magically lose their immateriality unless the receipt given to the owner by Klein was burned during the course of a ritual which concluded when Klein himself threw half the gold into a river or 'some place in nature where this gold cannot be retrieved by anyone'.

Thus, in the end, Jarman found his way back to art, through the example of Yves Klein, art in a form which stood at an opposite pole to the death of true art in the media and its interminable surplus of futile images. On New Year's Day 1974, Jarman envisaged an art-work, which he described in his journal for the day under the heading,

> *Ars Mortis* [Art of Death]. The End of Tradition. *The Disaster of War*. Bring the Goya etching from Norwood and burn it. Film and tape the event. The ashes framed between two sheets of glass and exhibited with the film. The resulting work to be exchanged for another work of art which will be similarly processed. A legally binding document to go with the work to prevent its resale unless an exchange is made and further work processed.

In the spirit of Klein's late work, which similarly involved magic and ritual, death and immateriality, Jarman was already developing an 'Ars Mortis', which would paradoxically restore life to the extinct art of painting, revive it through dematerialization and death.

3. THE TERRESTRIAL PARADISE

Recently, in the airport at São Paulo, I chanced on a twice-yearly publication called *View On Colour, The Colour Forecasting Magazine*. It was No. 7, the special issue on Monochromes. It had a cobalt-blue cover—the exact shade was Pantone number 19-3950. Inside, there were fashion photographs, mini-features on the colour of Christ, Chinese celadon ware, Pina Bausch and coloured beetles, a life-style section on monogamy, a think-piece 'on Monochromatic Merchandizing: Communicating With Colour', and, last but not least, there was also a series of introductory illustrations of work by Yves Klein, Ellsworth Kelly, Robert Ryman and Andres Serrano. Here was the nightmare, the definitive spectacularization of the monochrome canon, recycled as 'an in-depth information package on colour that will inspire the reader and help him meet the needs and demands of his customer and today's increasingly knowledgeable consumer.' For Jarman, *Blue* was a protest against what we have learned to call, after Guy Debord, 'the society of the spectacle'. As Debord himself might have put it, *Blue* was intended as 'the negation of the spectacle', a spectacle which had first surrounded and then colonized the artworld. In fact, Debord's own very first film, *Howls In Favour Of De Sade* consisted of 90 minutes of blank screen with a voice-over.

In the last few moments of another film, *The Society of the Spectacle*, Debord showed a long night sequence of American police beating up black rioters, with the added subtitle: 'However, let's consider the content of this experience in its entirety; this content is the Work which disappears .... The fact of disappearance is also quite real, it becomes attached to the work and itself disappears with it; the negative penetrates the positive of which it is the negation.' With *Blue* too the feature film disappears into the monochrome adventure, but its disappearance is in the tradition of Ficino and Blake rather than Hegel and Marx. In the text of *Blue*, Jarman puts it quite plainly—'If the doors of Perception were cleansed then everything would be seen as it is'. Jarman's project was to return the viewer to a way of seeing which was true rather than false, 'no longer tied to commodity and worldly success'. In many respects, this project seems to recapitulate that of Ruskin, who wrote that 'the whole technical power of painting depends on our recovery of what may be called the innocence of the eye; that is to say, of a sort of childish perception of these flat stains of colour, merely as such, without consciousness of what they signify—as a blind man would see them if suddenly gifted with sight.'

Ruskin too wished to affirm, as Jonathan Crary put it, 'a kind of primal opticality', his belief that vision could be freed from all the social conventions and ancillary knowledges which limited it, restored to its origin before the Fall. The idea of a return to paradise runs throughout Derek Jarman's journals. In February 1989, for instance, soon after his public announcement that he was HIV positive, he wrote down his reactions to reading a new biography of the sculptor Eric Gill, who seemed

> to have set off on that old straight track, a road pioneered by Mr and Mrs William Blake playing Adam and Eve nude in their London garden. Blake and William Morris ... all of them look backward over their shoulders—to a paradise on earth. And all of them at odds with the world around them. I feel this strongly, chose a 'novelty' medium—film—in which to search. The reels turn, every foot appropriated by commerce until I am dizzy.

Not long before Jarman had begun work on his own Paradise Garden at Prospect Cottage, which was itself a conscious version of 'Adam's wooden hut'—thus placing himself in a long tradition of revolutionary utopians and outsider artists.

In *Techniques of the Observer*, his study of the historical relationship between theories of perception and regimes of painting, Jonathan Crary cites a passage from Goethe's *Farbenlehre*, his treatise on colour: 'Let a room be made as dark as possible; let there be a circular opening in the window shutter about three inches in diameter, which may be closed or not at pleasure. The sun being suffered to shine through this on a white surface, let the spectator from some little distance fix his eyes on this bright circle thus admitted'—and, Goethe continues, the result of the experiment will be that

> the middle of the circle will appear bright, colourless, or somewhat yellow, but the border will appear red. After a time this red, increasing towards the centre, covers the whole circle, and at last the bright central point. No sooner, however, is the whole circle red than the edge begins to be blue and the blue gradually encroaches inwards on the red. When the whole is blue the edge becomes dark and colourless. The darker edge again slowly encroaches on the blue till the whole circle appears colourless ...

Today, it is easy enough to note the passage from white to black via the three optical primaries—yellow, red, blue. To Goethe, this was the discovery of a new realm of colours, the 'physiological' colours, to be seen irrespective of the external object world, colours which, in Goethe's phrase, 'belong to the eye'.

In 1843, Turner painted his extraordinary work, *Light and Colour (Goethe's Theory)—The Morning After The Deluge*, an intensely subjectivized and physiologized depiction of vision, in which great swirls of light and colour seem to spin in front of the eye. As Crary points out, Turner was living out Goethe's experiment and trying to capture the immediate physiological intensity of sight in dazzling sunlight, the 'primal opticality' of which Ruskin spoke. In this context, it is fascinating to find a passage in Derek Jarman's *Blue* in which he describes his own experience of the progression of after-images through the spectrum: 'The shattering bright light of the eye specialist's camera leaves that empty sky-blue after-image. Did I really see green the first time? The after-image dissolves in a second. As the photographs progress, colour changes to pink and the light turns to orange.' Jarman's sky-blue was the physiological vision of a man who was losing his sight, living in reverse the situation known to historians of philosophy as 'the Molyneux problem'—the question which William Molyneux asked his friend John Locke, as to whether a blind man suddenly gifted with sight could recognize objects correctly, just from looking at them, a question which assumed a clear distinction between adequate and inadequate perception and asked whether innocence could ever be adequate. Locke thought it could not.

On one level, then, Jarman's monochrome indeed derives from the *Farbenlehre* (he cites Goethe several times in *Chroma*) and it is certainly possible to see *Blue* as an evocation of pure vision—to equate Jarman's own blindness, caused by his proximity to death, with a return to the 'childish perception' purified, for Ruskin, by proximity to creation. *Blue* literally originates from an after-image—'The doctor in St Batholomew's Hospital thought he could detect lesions in my retina—the pupils dilated with belladonna—the torch shone into them with a terrible blinding light./Look left/Look down/Look up/Look right./Blue flashes in my eyes.' But this founding moment of physiological vision is immediately followed by the statement, 'I step into a blue funk', and a poetic meditation on his associations of blue with love: 'Blue Bottle Buzzing/Lazy days/The sky blue butterfly/Sways on a cornflower/Lost in the warmth/Of the blue heat haze/Singing the blues/Quiet and slowly/Blue of my heart/Blue of my dreams/Slow blue love/Of delphinium days.' Here Jarman goes far beyond Ruskin, invoking very different experiences of blue.

Jarman's blue is not purely optical. It is saturated with history and meaning. It is the blue of the crystal grotto in Riefenstahl's *The Blue Light*. It is the blue of ancient Britons daubed with woad. It is the blue of the virgin's robe in Renaissance art. It is the blue of the dark blue gendarme capes everyone liked in 1972. It is the blue of Elvis Presley's blue suede shoes and Levi jeans. It is IKB. And, at the very end of the film, it is once again the blue of delphiniums and a lover's eyes—'I place a delphinium, Blue, upon your grave.' Except for Yves Klein, its closest kin are to be found, not in the monochrome canon, but in Wittgenstein's musings on colour, Eisenstein's suggestive essay on 'Colour And Meaning', with its epigraph from Walt Whitman, 'Forms, colours, densities, odours—what is in me which corresponds with them?' or William Gass's 'philosophical inquiry', *On Being Blue*, 'written for all those who live in the country of the blue' to celebrate the productivity of language, the 'blue of the Bloomsday book', the blue of poets and philosophers, who 'shout and celebrate before the shade conceals the window: blue bloods, balls and bonnets, beards, coats, collars, chips and cheese ...' and all the other blues with which language abounds, giving up 'the blue things of this world in favour of the words which say them: blue pencils, blue noses, blue movies, laws, blue legs and stockings, the language of birds, bees and flowers as sung by longshoremen, that lead-like look the skin has when affected by cold, contusion, sickness and fear ...'

Words give new meanings to monochrome. Words bring with them the sense of difference, complexity and contingency which monochrome seems to deny. They fill the void with personal associations and public symbolism. Looking back into the nineteenth century, we can see how monochrome developed out of a long tradition of painting the sea and the sky, rather than the earth, reducing definition and line to the single trace of the horizon. This is particularly clear in Whistler's earliest *Crepuscules* and *Harmonies* and *Nocturnes* and it is reiterated a hundred years later in Brice Marden's *Grove Group*. Sea and sky are the two features in nature which present stretches of one single unvarying colour—the cloudless sky even more so than the sea, because the sea is always slightly in movement, glimmering with subtle tonal differences. Monochrome is the site of pure luminosity, uncluttered with objects, unmarked by history or humanity, deprived of complexity of meaning. His monochrome white paintings, Rauschenberg wrote to his dealer, were 'presented with the innocence of a virgin'. This search for purity, so basic to the monochrome adventure, implies a search for stasis, for the void—for pure being, the absence of difference and becoming. Monochrome white is plenitude. Monochrome black, on the other hand, is the absence of colour, its nihilation. This was the black of Ad Reinhardt's 'Ultimate Paintings', monochromes which are seen nowadays, in their renunciation of the sublime, as pointing forward to minimalism and a return to objecthood, to the idea of the painting itself as simply a blank thing in the world, representing nothing. Just 'the last painting' as Reinhardt liked to put it.

Of course, the last is never definitively the last—its meaning can never be eliminated. It mutates into the ironic trope of the last, as in the work of Sherrie Levine or Blinky Palermo or Stephen Prina's exhibition of Monochrome Paintings, a series of works spray-painted black with industrial paint in a Los Angeles auto-body shop on N. Western Avenue (known for its 'Professional Work on All Makes and Models') and exhibited as the *Stations of the Cross*, from *Christ Condemned To Death* through to *The Death Of Christ, The Deposition* and *The Entombment*. Each is identical, except that each is the exact dimensions of an original work from the monochrome canon—Malevich, Rodchenko, Strzeminski, Newman, Rauschenberg, Kelly, Klein, Manzoni, Reinhardt, Fontana, Marden, Ryman, Richter and Palermo. 1918, 1921, 1931–32, 1949, 1951, 1955, 1956, 1959, 1960–66, 1961, 1966, 1967, 1972, 1973—so many makes and models, each with its own date but each black, an arbitrary sequence drained of historical meaning, difference subordinated to a parodic representation of the death of art—Calvary, the Entombment. And on the Third Day? Derek Jarman's *Blue* seeks, in contrast, to restore monochrome to life, to history and meaning. His film is not simply pure monochrome. It is also a critique of the very idea of purity.

At the end of Jarman's film *Wittgenstein*, John Maynard Keynes talks to the philosopher as he lies on his death-bed. He tells the story of 'a young man who dreamed of reducing the world to pure logic. Because he was a very clever young man, he actually managed to do it. And when he'd finished the work, he stood back and admired it'—as a monochrome painter might have stood back to admire—'It was beautiful. A world purged of imperfection and intedeterminacy. Countless acres of gleaming ice stretching to the horizon'—the reflective luminosity of Robert Ryman's white paintings—'So the clever young man looked around the world he had created, and decided to explore it. He took one step forward and fell on his back. You see, he had forgotten about friction. The ice was smooth and level and stainless, but you couldn't walk there. So the clever young man sat down and wept bitter tears. But as he grew into a wise old man, he came to understand that roughness and ambiguity aren't imperfections. They're what makes the world turn. He wanted to run and dance. And the words and things scattered on the ground were all battered and tarnished and ambiguous, and the wise old man saw that this was the way things were'—the clutter of life rather than the purity of monochrome—'But something in him was still homesick for the ice, where everything was radiant and absolute and relentless. So now he was marooned between earth and ice at home in neither. And this was the cause of all his grief.'

'Don't think I'm afraid of dying,' Wittgenstein tells Keynes. 'It is death which gives life its meaning and shape.' *Blue* too invokes death to give meaning and shape. It tells what it feels like to die, walking slowly in old shoes, eyes stinging with belladonna, but it also holds out hope. Derek Jarman never lost faith in the future. My own most vivid memory of Derek, rather than Sloane Square or Dungeness, comes from a visit to the former Soviet Union, which we made in the fall of 1984, as part of a small delegation of film-makers—Sally Potter, Ed Bennett, Derek and myself. One day, in Azerbaijan, we went to see an extraordinary folly, a spiral tower built on the beach as a monument to his daughter, drowned in the Caspian, by a retired mason. It was like the Watts Towers, 'no longer tied to commodity and worldly success', and I believe it inspired Derek to start his own outsider garden at Prospect Cottage. On the way there we stopped for a while to visit a Zoroastrian fire temple, where the flame of the sacred fire was never extinguished. That's how I remember him best, with his Super-8 camera in his hand and the flame forever burning. His published testament, *At Your Own Risk*, ends with a paean to love:

> I am tired tonight. My eyes are out of focus, my body droops under the weight of the day, but as I leave you Queer lads let me leave you singing. I had to write of a sad time as a witness—not to cloud your smiles—please read the cares of the world that I have locked in these pages; and after, put this book aside and love. May you ... love without a care and remember we loved too. As the shadows closed in, the stars came out. I am in love.

Jarman's *Blue* was a magical act of resurrection through love, an ideal and Utopian vision in the great tradition of Marsilio Ficino and William Blake. 'Blue is the universal love in which man bathes—it is the terrestrial paradise.' As such, it reaches far beyond minimalism or colour field into the realms of poetry, symbolic discourse, and, yes, politics.

10

MAGRITTE AND THE BOWLER HAT

Visiting Brussels a few years ago, to see the centennial exhibition of Magritte, I was amused to find the city festooned with images of bowler hats, on banners, posters and placards. There were even real bowler hats in window displays. Magritte had become, so to speak, the patron saint of Brussels and the bowler hat had been chosen as his emblem. It was an apt choice. Magritte painted several dozen images of bowler hats, as well as a large sheaf of drawings and a quantity of recycled versions of the paintings as gouaches. Moreover, Magritte himself was frequently photographed, and filmed, wearing a bowler hat. It seems quite plausible to consider many of these paintings as self-portraits, as his dealer, Alexandre Iolas, did. In that sense, Magritte chose his own emblematic attribute, his own trademark headgear. He consciously became 'The Master of the Bowler Hat'. Why? And what did it mean? Most accounts stress the ordinariness of the man in the bowler hat, his unindividuated character as Everyman, his classlessness or perhaps, more precisely, his petit bourgeois character, neither cloth-capped nor top-hatted, nor even trilbied or homburged or boatered. I would like to approach the meaning of the bowler hat in a different way, stressing its rich semantic complexity rather than its banality or its blankness.

Magritte's first major work to feature a bowler hat was *The Musings of A Solitary Walker*, which dates from 1926, when the artist was in his late twenties. It is dusk. A bowler-hatted man stands with his back to the viewer, silhouetted against a cloudy greeny-blue sky, looking out across the gloomy landscape towards the horizon. To his (and our) left runs a river, the same colour and tone as the sky, with light glinting off its surface. Some distance down, there is a simple wooden bridge, just where a clear view is broken by some trees, illuminated by some hidden source of light. In the foreground, at the level where the bowler-hatted man's hands have delved into his pockets, floats the naked torso of an androgynous man, rigidly horizontal, his ribs clearly marked and his long neck leading to a shaven head. He has no hair. His eyes are closed and only the lips show any colour. He appears to be floating or levitating, with no visible means of support. His pallid form appears top-lit by some unknown source of illumination, possibly even from within, since it does not affect the ground beneath him, which remains dark. Some commentators have wondered whether this painting might not be related to Magritte's memory of the night his mother committed suicide by jumping from a bridge into the river Sambre and drowning, but he himself always denied any reference of this sort. This is the first appearance of the man in a bowler-hat, the characteristic figure, back turned, face invisible, eyes gazing into the distance.

His next appearance is in *The Meaning Of Night*, painted the following year. This time there are two figures, one facing away, the other towards us, standing with exactly the same posture, as though they were twins or doubles. Again it is dark. They are standing on a cliff, a few yards from the edge, overlooking the sea, whose white-crested waves are catching the light, like those of the river in the previous painting. Fluffy clouds litter the ground, which is illuminated from a light source, high up to the left, casting shadows diagonally to the right towards the sea. In the foreground is what I can only describe as an erotic apparition, floating at knee height above the ground, all fur and lace, feminine with a single white glove, fingers outstretched reaching towards the top of two pale silk-stockinged thighs, pulling back the fur to reveal the lace. The silhouette turned away from us, gazing away, is more or less the same as the one in the previous painting. The double, the one turned towards us, is more or less as we might have expected, almost like a fashion plate, hands in pockets, overcoat with five buttons fastened, stiff white collar, with neatly knotted dark tie. It is the face which is striking—mask-like, white with no trace of colour, completely symmetrical, a long narrow nose, eyes shut tight beneath arching eyebrows. It is the figure of a dreamer or a somnambulist. If his eyes are closed, we might presume, so are those of his double. He is not gazing out over the cliff and the waves towards the horizon. He is dreaming.

We will never see this face again. It is the only image we have. In this painting, we have been privileged to see the dreamer and the dream. In all the many that follow, we shall have to imagine the dream for ourselves. The next painting with bowler-hatted men is very different. In *The Threatened Assassin*, painted the same year, 1927, we see a murder scene. This time, it is an interior. A woman's body lies stretched out on a couch, naked, blood streaming from her mouth. A man, presumably her murderer, is standing idly, at his ease, one hand in his pocket, listening to a record being played on a phonograph with a horn. His overcoat and hat (not a bowler) are draped over a chair. In the distance, through an open frame we can see a mountainous landscape and three identical faces, witnesses, peering over a balcony into the room. In the foreground there is a similar proscenium frame opening onto the room, somehow as if it was a stage-set. Lurking, pressed up against the wall on either side are two bowler-hatted men, dressed exactly like the somnambulist, but with eyes open, looking at an angle in our direction, unable to see the murder scene. One is carrying a cudgel, the other a heavy net. It is often remarked that these two men are detectives of some kind, waiting to apprehend the killer, positioned as if they already knew he had committed the crime, although he still remains hidden from their eyes.

Also in 1927, or possibly the next year, 1928, Magritte painted *The Reckless Sleeper*, another painting with a bowler-hat, related to those I have described, but different in that the bowler-hat is depicted as an isolated object, enclosed in a bowler-hat-shaped hollow in what is generally described as a lead tablet, with an irregular curved shape of a kind Magritte often favoured. There are a number of other objects enclosed in hollows in a similar way—a bird, a lit candle, an apple and so on. The lead tablet takes up about two thirds of the picture. Above it, in the remaining third, separated by a clean horizontal line is a wooden box, rather like a coffin, marked in whorls and stripes by dark wood-graining. Inside the box, a man with a bald head is lying asleep under a blanket, his head resting on a pillow. Most viewers have assumed that the objects beneath are somehow elements of his dream or, at least, objects we might imagine as such. In fact, a bowler-hat soon reappears in an oneiric context in the 1930 painting, *The Key To Dreams*, a reprise of a 1927 painting with the same title and structure, but no hat. This time, the canvas is divided into six equal rectangular spaces, two across by three down, in which six objects are represented—an egg, labelled 'the Acacia'; a woman's high-heeled shoe, labeled 'the Moon'; a bowler hat, labelled 'the Snow'; a lit candle, labelled 'the Ceiling'; a glass, labelled 'the Storm'; and a mallet, labelled 'the Desert'.

Magritte did not paint another bowler hat for eight years—a work in which the hat is worn by a horseman, followed by one in his 'Renoir' or 'Plein Soleil' period, another horseman and then three, I think, in his 'Vache' period. All the rest, the overwhelming majority, were painted in the '50s and '60s. The foundations, however, were laid in the works I have just described, all executed between 1926 and 1930. In my view, the bowler hats in these crucial early paintings can already be interpreted within five different frames of cultural meaning. In using the phrase, 'cultural meaning', I am talking not about reference or denotation— obviously an image of a bowler hat refers to the everyday object we call a 'bowler hat', even if it is labelled, disjunctively, as 'the Snow'. Nor am I talking about 'connotation', in Roland Barthes's sense, of the way in which an image can support a rhetorical or mythological construction. I am more sympathetic to Carlo Ginsburg's controversial idea, outlined in his account of the hat worn by the Emperor Constantine in Piero Della Francesca's fresco cycle of the Legend of the True Cross, in Arezzo, that we should look for a trail of clues in the historical and social context which will enable us to establish a specific interpretation, rather than treating it as an abstract emblem. It is a happy coincidence, of course, that Ginsburg's iconographic analysis concerns a hat.

In his essay on the Arezzo cycle, Ginsburg seeks to explain the significance of the Emperor's 'white hat coming to a point on front' by relating it to the very similar hat worn by Pope John VIII Paleologus as depicted on two commemorative medals designed by Pisanello. This connection, in turn, serves as a clue which enables Ginsburg to develop a train of argument leading to an overall re-interpretation, via the hat, of the meaning of the cycle. Rather than seeking a single, precise signification for Magritte's use of the image of the bowler-hat, I want to suggest that he drew on a variety of different sources from different discourses—discourses which we could see as compressed like the rabbit fur and shellac which are the raw materials of a bowler hat, in order to make the dense amalgam which we know as felt. This amalgam carries a polyvalent cultural meaning, not so much a delimited 'signified' in Saussure's or Barthes's sense as a complex field of signification. There are five quite different discursive sources that I want to discuss, each of which, I believe, fed into Magritte's iconography of the bowler hat. These are the discourse of detective fiction, the discourse of the performing arts, the discourse of Purism, the discourse of fashion and the discourse of patriarchy. The relevance of these particular sources should come as no surprise when we consider Magritte's own valuation of 'mystery', his abiding interest in film, both as a viewer and as a performer, the importance of his family background, his origins as a modernist artist and the impact of his commercial work as an illustrator.

First, detective fiction. Magritte, it is well established, was a fan of crime mysteries. He was an avid reader of the adventures of Judex and Fantomas and viewer of Feuillade's serial film versions, the explicit source of his *The Flame Rekindled* and *The Barbarian*, alongside which he posed to be photographed wearing his bowler hat. He also treasured the Nick Carter and Nat Pinkerton stories which were neighbours of Poe, Lautréamont and Breton on his bookshelves. Magritte must have been aware that the detectives in both the Fantomas and Judex cycles wore bowler hats, as was customary for fictional detectives in general. Back in 1908, Kenneth Grahame, author of *Wind In The Willows*, described the party chasing Toad of Toad Hall after his escape from prison as led by 'shabbily dressed men in pot-hats, obvious and unmistakable plain-clothes detectives even at this distance, waving revolvers and walking-sticks'. Ernest Shepard's vivid illustration of the scene clearly shows that the 'pot-hats' were, in fact, bowlers. The bowler-hatted figures in *The Threatened Assassin* are just such a pair of plain-clothes men, armed, not with revolver and walking-stick but cudgel and net, denizens of an uncanny and mysterious realm whose unsettling and dream-like quality Magritte hoped to emulate in his own art.

In this context, it is also worth mentioning another pair of bowler-hatted Belgian detectives—Dupont and Dupond (or, in English translation, Thomson and Thompson) who first made their appearance, as yet unnamed, in Hergé's second Tintin story, *Tintin In The Congo*, published in 1930, just three years after Magritte had painted *The Murderer Threatened*. Albert Algoud, in his entertaining survey of the Dupondts career, traces the ancestry of Hergé's pair back to Jules Verne's novel of 1879, *The Tribulations of A Chinese in China*, with its twin pair of lookalike and bowler-hatted agents, Craig and Fry. He also mentions the possible influence of Laurel and Hardy, whose first films together in bowler hats were actually made in 1928, two years before Hergé launched his farcical double act, but one year after Magritte's painting. Hercule Poirot, another Belgian detective, who made *his* first appearance in 1931, is also represented in visual images as wearing a bowler hat, although I have not yet been able to find any textual warrant for this—the first book in which he appears, *The Mysterious Affair at Styles*, confirms that he was something of a dandy and indeed wore a hat, but never specifies precisely what sort of hat it was. The tradition of the detective in a bowler hat, I am glad to note, lasted right through to the 1960s, with Steed in the British television serial, *The Avengers*, a kind of latter-day *Fantomas* fully in the Feuillade tradition.

Dupond and Dupont themselves combined the discourse of the detective with that of the performing arts, specifically the knockabout comedian. Their hats are jammed down over their eyes, sat upon, knocked into the water, exchanged by accident, dissolved into glop and repeatedly subjected to ludicrous disaster. The great precursor of the comic use of the bowler hat, of course, was Charles Chaplin, who first donned his 'Tramp' or 'Little Fellow' costume in February 1914, either for *Mabel's Strange Predicament*, as Chaplin himself recalled, or for *Kid Auto Races In Venice*, which was released earlier, but probably shot later. Chaplin had often worn a bowler hat, on and off stage—there is a photograph of him sporting one in 1906, a young man appearing in *Casey's Court Circus*, a knockabout musical act, and he certainly wore one when he was featured in Fred Karno's troupe. But the 1914 costume went beyond just wearing a bowler hat as a comic accessory. It created a character. As Chaplin remarked, it was based on the formal idea of contrast—at the extremities, a hat which was too small and boots which were too large, in the middle, a tight jacket and a pair of baggy trousers, all topped off with a 'hooky malacca cane'. Chaplin is important, not so much because we can demonstrate any specific influence on Magritte, but because he dominated the iconography of the bowler-hat in general. Perhaps if there was a direct relationship, it lies with the importance of the back-view silhouette that became Magritte's favoured pose for his own bowler-hatted man, with the difference that Chaplin's silhouette was dramatically mobile whereas Magritte favoured the ponderously static.

Most important of all, Chaplin fixed the image of the bowler hat firmly in the public consciousness in a number of contradictory ways, reflecting the paradoxical character of Chaplin's own screen persona. Chaplin combined knockabout comedy with pathos and childlike innocence. He could be both cruel and sentimental. His behaviour was often futile and ludicrous, but he retained a threadbare dignity and stubborn self-confidence throughout. Chaplin's antics had both an ethical and a nihilist dimension. He appealed to intellectuals as well as to vulgarians. Magritte, like almost everybody else, was an admirer of Chaplin, as well as Laurel and Hardy, whose films he collected on Super-8 and whose bowler-hatted comedy routines he enthusiastically imitated in his own home movies. Old music hall routines like the exchange of bowler hats re-surface in Magritte's films just as they do in Beckett's *Waiting For Godot*—and at roughly the same time too. Bowler hats, umbrellas, tubas and pipes are all repeated elements in his film farces—he mimics his paintings by putting a bowler hat on a shrouded head, he puts a series of hats on a bust, he uses the shadow silhouette of a bowler hat. In one sequence, his wife Georgette (wearing a Von Stroheim-style spiky military helmet) salutes a painting of a bowler-hatted man standing with his back to us. Magritte's art is often treated as though it was always basically serious. We should not forget that it was often ludicrous and absurd, even stupidly so. As his close friend Louis Scutenaire put it, 'his genius lies in his imbecility'.

Chaplin's influence also penetrated the artistic avant-garde, particularly after the success of *The Kid*. Moreover, it was in France that the first recognition came—in Cocteau's script for the ballet *Parade*, his 'Little American Girl' did a Charlie Chaplin imitation as well as dance a ragtime, composed by Satie. But Picasso's pantomime horse took the theme further than Cocteau had intended—instead of being a thundering charger, it turned out to be a dilapidated beast that only provoked hilarity. In Cocteau's words it was a 'fantomas taxi horse mounted by Charlie Chaplin'. At Picasso's insistence the horse stayed. (A footnote: Picasso had already painted a *Still Life With Bowler Hat*, back in 1910, usually construed as a joking reference to Georges Braque, who habitually wore a bowler at that time, in its turn a homage to Cézanne, whose own tall bowler, known as a 'Kronstadt', figured in his self-portrait of 1883–85.) Then, in 1921, Louis Delluc's book *Charlot* came out, applauding Chaplin for turning the cinema into a modern art form. It was translated into English the following year and its influence spread world-wide. In 1923, Fernand Léger made his famous drawing of Charlot for Ivan Goll's *Chaplinade* and, the same year, bowler hats figured prominently in his film, *Ballet Mécanique*, as they also did in another 1923 avant-garde film, Hans Richter's *Imps Before Breakfast (Vormittagspuk)*, with its bewitched bowlers flying through the air, tormenting their would-be wearers. Soon after came two more major Léger still lives featuring bowlers and the first of his life-long series of *Three Musicians*, with the tuba player always bowler-hatted. Léger's original Chaplin is clearly puppet-like, not simply a figure for a modern *commedia dell'arte*, as in *Parade*, but rather more like Mr Punch.

The same is true of the bowler-hatted stick figures that inhabit the Lancashire mill towns painted by L. S. Lowry. Lowry too was a great music hall fan, a particular admirer of Chaplin's mentor, Fred Karno, whose troupe made him laugh 'until the tears ran down his cheeks'. His bowler-hatted figures, he agreed, were like marionettes, 'and if you pulled the strings they would cock their legs up', as Chaplin did, of course, when he skeetered round a corner. 'I look upon human beings as automatons', Lowry once observed. 'They all think they can do what they want, but they can't you know', which makes them 'funny beyond belief'. At the same time, he 'liked the working-class bowler hats, the big boots and shawls'. Lowry was a great admirer of Magritte's work, especially the bowler-hatted figures, 'because they all looked so ordinary', as John Rothenstein recalled. About his own work, he noted that 'all the people in my pictures, they are all alone, you know. They have all got their private sorrows, their own absorption. But they can't contact one another. We are all of us alone—cut off. All my people are lonely. Crowds are the most lonely thing of all.' He could almost be discussing Magritte's figures. Léger represented Chaplin with this same object-like quality, turning him into a marionette, just as Magritte's figures often remind us of tailor's dummies. In his 1953 *Golconda*, serried ranks of bowler-hatted men float in front of an urban backdrop, all staring forward. Golconda, Magritte explained, is 'a magical city'. 'The bowler, on the other hand, poses no surprises. It is a head-dress that is not original. The man with the bowler is just bourgeois man in his anonymity. And I wear it. I am not eager to singularize myself.' Wigan—working class anonymity and somnambulism. Brussels—bourgeois. The same lonely crowd, each imprisoned by self-absorption, free only in their dreams.

In his early pre-surrealist years as an artist, Magritte went successively through the influence first of purism and then of dadaism. During the purist period, he became a close colleague of a fellow painter, Victor Servranckx. Servranckx was artistic director of a wallpaper manufacturing firm in Brussels, Peeters-Lacroix, and obtained a job there for Magritte, work which supported him for a number of years. Servranckx considered himself a purist and contributed to the central journal of the movement—Corbusier and Ozenfant's *L'Esprit Nouveau*, as well as co-writing an unpublished purist manifesto with Magritte, *Pure Art, in Defence of Aesthetics*. Perhaps the primary tenet of purism was its insistence that everyday manufactured objects were the proper subject for modern art—and indeed were aesthetic objects in their own right. Léger's purist works of this period are full of such objects—keys, ball-bearings, jugs, balusters, bowler hats, bottles, pipes and so on. In this context, it is worth looking too at Le Corbusier's impact on Magritte. Not only did Corbusier programmatically wear a bowler hat, as a good purist should, but he wrote a crucial manifesto celebrating it as an aesthetic object. The point I wish to make is that Magritte's later use of the bowler hat owed a great deal to purism, as indeed did surrealism in general, although Breton's cult of the 'poetic object' may seem, at first sight, the polar opposite of Corbusier's rationalism and functionalism. The crucial point of shared reference was their interest in everyday objects, first as evolved 'types' and then as sites of magical power.

In Le Corbusier's polemical book, *The Decorative Art of Today*, a collection of essays written in response to the massive 1924 Paris Decorative Arts Exhibition, a crucial chapter was headed 'Other Icons— The Museums'. Corbusier's purpose was to attack the underlying assumptions of contemporary decorative arts museums and suggest an alternative aesthetic program that they should adopt forthwith. I quote:

> Let us imagine a true museum, one that contains everything, one that could present a complete picture after the passage of time, after the destruction by time (and how well it knows how to destroy! So well, so completely, that almost nothing remains except objects of great show, of great vanity, of great fancy, which always survive disasters, testifying to vanity's indestructible powers of survival). In order to flesh out our idea, let us put together a museum of our own day with objects of our own day; to begin:
>
> A plain jacket, a bowler hat, a well-made shoe. An electric light bulb with bayonet fixing; a radiator, a table cloth of white linen; our everyday drinking glasses, and bottles of various shapes, in which we keep our Mercurey, our Graves, or simply our ordinaire .... A number of bentwood chairs with caned seats like those invented by Thonet of Vienna

—and then on to the wash-basin, the watch, the suitcase, the filing cabinet and the illustration of a pipe.

The importance of Corbusier's manifesto, of course, in the context of Magritte's development as an artist, lies in its unremitting stress on the significance and aesthetic value of the ordinary and its distaste for show, for vanity and for fancy, all things which Magritte strongly distrusted— including surrealist fancy, like that of Delvaux. In fact, towards the end of his book, Le Corbusier goes on to discuss the surrealists' attitude to the object. He comments that 'the supremely elegant relationships of their metaphors—as they impress one who is not such a "high dreamer"—are all the time very clearly dependent on the products of straightforward conscious effort, sustained and logical, cross-checked by the necessary mathematics and geometry—the necessary exactitude for the functioning of mechanisms, etc.' Magritte, too, fiercely resisted automatism and always insisted that he worked consciously and precisely. Le Corbusier went on to conclude:

So the poets of Surrealism can only base their poetics on realism, this realism which is the magnificent fruit of the machine age and of which we are still so far from tired that they themselves hook onto it in the skein of their dreams. The product of the machine age is a realist object capable of high poetry. We approve so much of this object, we are so fond of it, we would so much like to live with it, that our desire adds to its utility the higher dignity of beauty! The realist object of utility is beautiful. Such is the final conclusion of the spirit forged in the labours of the age. So we have to reconsider what is beautiful for us, to recognize what is beautiful for us. A beauty that is made from objects whose relationships exalt us.

Magritte's conversion to surrealism did not require as great a rupture with purism as one might have imagined. He took from Purism, of course, only those elements necessary to the new vision that surrealism imparted, but among those images that crossed the divide was that of the bowler hat. From the start, the bowler was intended to be functional—it was designed at the request of an English landowner as protective headwear for his gamekeepers, made of compressed felt and fitting snugly, so that it was securely fixed on the head. (He was worried it might be dislodged during an encounter with a poacher.) As such it was a model of simple, purified design, a hemisphere resting on an annular brim shaped in a symmetrical wave pattern. At the same time, this masterpiece of functionalism was open to a multitude of metaphoric expansions of meaning. The hard, shaped, static, black object could be labeled as 'snow': soft, shapeless, mobile, white. Its very ordinariness could become mysterious. In the '50s and '60s, when Magritte painted the great majority of his bowler-hatted figures, their poetic beauty emerged from their being, as Le Corbusier put it, hooked on to the skein of their dreams—dreams which themselves involved everyday objects—the moon, the glass, the loaf of bread, and even the *Primavera* of Botticelli, which Magritte preferred as a mass-produced image on a postcard, rather than as a great painting, a unique masterpiece. He was not impressed when he saw the showy original in Florence.

From early on, through his work as a fashion illustrator, Magritte must have thought of the bowler hat as a functional and commercial object. While he never designed posters simply for bowler hats as such, he did work on advertisements for a wide range of everyday products, which are represented in a precise geometrical purist style—cigarette packs, glasses, bottles. In 1924 he had left his job at the wallpaper company and begun to work for the fashion designer, Norine, the wife of Paul-Gustave Van Hecke, an art dealer and close friend of Magritte's own friend E. L. T. Mesens. As Carine Fol has pointed out, a number of Magritte's familiar motifs are first introduced in his Norine fashion plates, such as the picture within a picture and the stage curtain framing a scene. We might add the Stockman 'form' or display dummy, often converging with Magritte's familiar *bilboquet* shape. Then, in 1926, he also began to work for the Samuels fur company. His images, at that time, became much more realistic, moving away from the last, lingering post-cubist influences— 'Around 1925, I decided only to paint objects with all their visible details because this was the only way in which my research could develop.' In the second Samuels catalogue, on which Magritte worked closely with Paul Nougé, he collaged a photographic image of himself with eyes closed, playing the somnambulistic dreamer, while, in the background, we see a model wearing a fur coat, foreshadowing *The Meaning of Night*. And in 1928 he illustrated a Norine gown for *Psyche, le miroir des belles choses*, while on the directly opposite page there is an ad for Maison Basile, Piccadilly's Hatters, featuring a bowler hat.

The confusion of dummy, *bilboquet* and human figure can also be seen in Magritte's 1926 painting, *Nocturne*, in which a man dressed in black and white, with a high collar and black tie, leans over a female figure sitting up in bed—each of them with the familiar, spherical *bilboquet* head, like a chess piece. In *The Conqueror*, also from 1926, a dummy with white shirt, stiff high collar, black tie and black jacket occupies the foreground of the painting. In the place of his head there is a simple wooden plank, protruding up from the collar. The *Denizens of the River*, painted in 1927, also features a clothed headless dummy. These amalgams of fashion plate with surrealist scene lead directly on to the very first bowler hat paintings, in which mannequin and human figure merge in the bowler-hatted man. I would like to suggest that Magritte favoured the bowler hat precisely because of its hemispherical shape, rhyming, so to speak, with that of the 'head' of the chess-piece, itself a stylized anthropomorphic form of the *bilboquet*. It is, after all, the natural hat to place snugly on a mannequin's bald head—like those in *The Face of Genius* or *An End to Contemplation*, both works from 1927, which was also the year in which groups of isolated objects first appeared in Magritte's repertoire, as in the suggestively named *One Night Museum*.

It is significant too that Magritte's parents were both employed in the garment business. His grandfather had been a tailor and his father, Léopold, was described as a commercial traveller, thought to mean that he was a garment salesman, since on Magritte's birth certificate he is described, more grandly, as a merchant tailor. On the marriage certificate, Magritte's mother, Régina, was designated a *modiste* and other sources characterize her as a milliner who specialized in hats. His father was even photographed in a shirt with a stiff, high collar and an overcoat, carrying what could be either an umbrella or a cane and wearing, of course, a bowler hat. This brings us, in turn, to the fifth form of the discourse of the bowler hat—the patriarchal. A surprising number of artists who used the bowler hat in their work themselves had fathers who wore bowler hats—not only Magritte, but also Beckett, Lowry and Hergé, for example. (Hergé's father was actually one of a pair of bowler-hatted twins.) The wearing of the bowler was passed on from father to son, and failure to comply could lead to family drama, as Samuel Beckett discovered when he returned home from Paris wearing a beret. Among Irish protestants, of course, the bowler hat had long carried a particularly strong emotional charge, as we are still reminded every year by the ritual marches of bowler-hatted Orangemen through the streets of Ulster. Beckett was also expected to undertake the definitive act of filial piety, of full incorporation into the world of the bowler hat, by going into the family business. In a way, Magritte did just that, if we can interpret his fashion illustration for Norine, Samuels and the others as entering the fashion trade. He had fulfilled his duty and earned the right to wear his bowler hat.

In Beckett's story *First Love*, the narrating monologuist recalls that 'they gave me ... a hat. Now the truth is they never gave me a hat, I have always had my own hat, the one my father gave me, and I have never had any other hat than that hat. I may add it has followed me to the grave.' In another story, *The Expelled*, the monologuist asks,

> How describe this hat? And why? When my head had attained I shall not say its definitive but its maximum dimensions, my father said to me, Come,

son, we are going to buy your hat, as though it had pre-existed from time immemorial in a pre-established place. He went straight to the hat. I personally had no say in the matter, nor had the hatter. I have often wondered if my father's purpose was not to humiliate me, if he was not jealous of me who was young and handsome, fresh at least, while he was already old and all bloated and purple.

It was a sign of premature aging, of loss of freedom. Hats for Beckett, and particularly bowler hats, are also associated with civility (straightening, adjusting, tipping, touching, albeit gingerly, doffing, removing, the flurrying of hats at funerals), with separation (grabbed, seized, snatched, fallen to the ground, trampled on, sailing through the air, flying off but not getting far because of the string), with protection (against stones, against rain, against the roof of the cab), with exchange (for the phial of calmative which will ease eventual death, for a kiss, for another hat or series of hats, tendered and taken), for study (peering into, examining, contemplating, feeling into, judging), for emptying (shaken, knocked on the crown, blown into) and finally, for display (mincingly, like a mannequin). Beckett's hats also suffer from re-functioning, practical or metaphoric—as begging bowl, as milk pail, as helmet, as chamber pot, as frisbee (shades of Oddjob!), as cathedral dome, as a second pustular skull.

Magritte's hats, in contrast, are usually just bowlers, sitting on the head or exhibited as simple objects. The only exceptions I have noticed were the 1952 *Everyday Magic*, showing a smouldering bowler hat with a baby suspended above it in the smoke, and two works from the 'Vache' period, one featuring a hat with an eye looking out on the world, the other with a protruding tap as if from a cistern. Then there is *The Patch of Night*, a bearded bowler hat from 1965, and *The Horrendous Stopper* (1966), a single bowler labelled 'For External Use Only', as though it were the stopper for a container filled with something dangerous—for a mind, perhaps, filled with dreams or subversive thoughts. (After he was crowned, Babar, the elephant king, gave his bowler hat to his chief minister, Cornelius, because Cornelius was good at thinking.) *The Horrendous Stopper* is the same Magritte work, incidentally, which the young British artist Gavin Turk, best known for his waxwork of himself as Sid Vicious, included in his slide piece on the theme of Britishness, a cascade of metaphoric

British objects—the bowler hat, even if Belgian, following logically after a cup of milky tea, Stonehenge, fish and chips, William Morris's Red House, etc., etc. Magritte, however, eschewed metaphor. He always claimed that his objects were just ordinary things, like his figures who were not 'characters' or 'individuals' but generic 'human beings'— and yet there are still many affinities between Magritte and Beckett. Primarily, I think, this is because their sense of the bowler hat as typically a patriarchal object leads both of them to associate it with the traditional—the singular, after all, is usually associated with the new, the commonplace with the old.

In his 1938 work, *The Endless Chain*, painted for Edward James, Magritte depicted three riders on a single horse, each representing, as he explained to his patron, one of three historical epochs—the first, a curly-headed rider in a short tunic, representing antiquity; the second, a gallant musketeer, 'all top-boots and plumed hat'; the third, 'our modern cavalier, with bowler hat and flowing cravate'. Here, in contrast, Magritte explicitly assigns the bowler hat to modernity, to the period since 1850 when Lock's of St James sold their very first bowler to William Coke. Yet already, even at that time, the bowler was inscribed into the register of tradition. William Coke, after all, was a landed aristocrat, the future Earl of Leicester. Gradually the bowler hat seeped down through the social order, from aristocracy to gentry, to bourgeoisie, to petit bourgeoisie, to proletarian, to underclass. In this sense, as Fred Miller Robinson argues in his pioneering book on *The Man In The Bowler Hat*, it became the universal classless hat of modern times. Yet, from another point of view, it began and remained a traditional hat, a hat which always aspired upwards, towards the world of the aristocracy, with its timeless, unchanging, fetishized values. A dyed-in-the-wool traditionalist like King Edward VII of England would expostulate with rage when he saw a bowler hat being worn in London. He considered it a country hat. In the country it began and there it certainly should remain, on the heads of the gentry and their gamekeepers. In the late nineteenth century, so the story goes, a traditionalist French lawyer would wear his bowler on the train into Paris. At the station he would hand it to a servant, who would hand him his top hat in exchange. All day, he would wear the top hat and then in the evening, at the station, the exchange would be repeated in reverse and he would return to the country in his bowler. On the side of the future, Lenin himself wore a bowler hat as he played chess with Gorky in Capri. Yet, 30 years on, the actor Maxim Straukh would wear another bowler hat as period costume when he portrayed Lenin in Stalinist films. The bowler could never quite shake off the echoes of the past and, in the end, it was fated, once again, to be seen as traditional.

George Melly tells a story of how, while Magritte was in England, painting for Edward James, Mesens tried to persuade him 'to buy a superior bowler hat from Lock's in St James's Street, but that Magritte had indignantly refused on the grounds (which the choice of objects in his work makes obvious) that he preferred a mass-produced model'. Magritte, Melly notes, was forced to shop at 'cheap gent's outfitters' from poverty, but then made a virtue of necessity by turning his 'clerk-like off-the-peg appearance' into a trademark. When Magritte became richer, in the 1950s, as a result of his increasing fame and the exertions of his dealer, he stuck with the trademark. But by now the bowler hat was no longer the anonymous headgear of Everyman. On the contrary, it stuck out. It signaled an allegiance to 'retro' traditionalism, whether for defiantly reactionary or for studiously parodic, even camp reasons. Bowler hats disappeared from the Simpson's, catalogue but clerks in the City of London still went on wearing them as Pooter's colleagues had worn them in the Grossmiths's *Diary of A Nobody*, as T. S. Eliot had worn a bowler when he worked for Lloyds Bank at 17 Cornhill, and later at Faber and Gwyer, just as MacHeath in *The Threepenny Opera* had worn a bowler to show his ambition to become a banker. British Guards officers were instructed to wear bowler hats and carry rolled umbrellas when in mufti. In the '60s, outrageous reactionaries like 'Lucky' Lucan, with his closets full of identical Savile Row suits, and Evelyn Waugh, in his loud checked tweed and Gilbert Pinfold period, both affected fetishistic bowlers. At the same time, reactionary Edwardianism was parodied by the dandified wave of 'mods'. Across the street, so to speak, the 'trad' fans of revivalist jazz musicians like Acker Bilk wore bowlers as a cult item, harking back nostalgically to the great black musicians who had clowned their way into the affection of whites by using their derby hat as a mute.

The bowler hat was now entering the period when it became an erotic fetish-wear for women—dancers and singers in Bob Fosse movies,

Madonna on the stage, Armani models on the catwalk. The key artistic reference here is to *The Unbearable Lightness of Being*, first published in 1984, but largely set in the 1960s, when Magritte's assembly-line production of bowler hat paintings was reaching its greatest intensity. It is a book which centres around two symbolic women—Tereza, the protagonist's wife, and Sabina, his mistress, standing respectively for the 'heaviness' and 'lightness' which mark the extreme poles of 'being'. Tereza returned to eke out her days in her native village. Sabina's ashes are scattered into the Pacific off the California coast. It is Sabina, of course, who wears the bowler hat, as an erotic come-on and a fetishistic prop in her sex life. Tereza is unfamiliar with bowler hats. Kundera notes, writing of her first encounter with the hat on a fraught visit to Sabine's apartment, that 'it was the kind of hat—black, hard, round—that Tereza had seen only on the screen, the kind of hat Chaplin wore'. It takes her far back over the years, back to what now seem like a golden age, those happy but distant Chaplinesque times. For Sabina, in contrast, the hat has a number of very personal meanings, which Kundera carefully expounds for us:

> First, it was a vague reminder of a forgotten grandfather, the mayor of a small Boheminan town during the nineteenth century.
>
> Second, it was a memento of her father. After the funeral her brother appropriated all their parents' property, and she, refusing out of sovereign contempt to fight for her rights, announced sarcastically that she was taking the bowler hat as her sole inheritance.
>
> Third, it was a prop for her love games with Tomas.
>
> Fourth, it was a sign of her originality, which she consciously cultivated. She could not take much with her when she emigrated, and taking this bulky, impractical thing meant giving up other, more practical ones.
>
> Fifth, now that she was abroad, the hat was a sentimental object. When she went to visit Tomas in Zurich, she took it along and had it on her head when she opened the hotel room door. But then something she had not reckoned with happened: the hat, no longer jaunty or sexy, turned into a monument to time past.

In an uncanny way, all five of these meanings also apply to Magritte—the bowler as patriarchal heirloom, the bowler as fetishized object, the bowler as witness of dandyism, the bowler as sign of eccentricity and, last but not least, the bowler as 'monument to time'. 'The bowler hat' Kundera notes, 'was a motif in the musical composition that was Sabina's life. It returned again and again, each time with a different meaning and all the meanings flowed through the bowler hat like water through a river-bed.' Each 'semantic river', Kundera explains, would give rise to a new meaning, 'though all former meanings would resonate, like an echo, like a parade of echoes, with the new ones.' It is with this metaphor in mind, that we can best understand the complex meanings which the bowler hat acquired for Magritte. The different echoes were often incongruous and, as time went by, their resonance changed. The first time Magritte's bowler-hatted man stared out over the landscape he was 'light', in Kundera's terms, mysterious and mobile. But by the time that Magritte's repetition compulsion had worked its way through year after year and image after image, he had become 'heavy', recognizable and rooted.

For Seurat, Lautrec, Cézanne or Caillebotte, the bowler hats they painted were simply part of everyday life, the leisure wear of a Sunday tripper at Asnières or the habitué of a Montmartre dance-hall. For the cubists, for Picasso and Braque, painting a bowler hat involved an element of homage. For Corbusier and Lowry and Chaplin, all born at the end of the 1880s, it had become an everyday 'type', a commonplace. For Ernst and Raderscheidt and Magritte, it could be invested with a certain mysterious melancholy. For Beckett, the Chaplinesque was re-invented, imbued with melancholy and even abject despair. For Kundera, the bowler hat had become a monument. By now it was useless rather than useful, eccentric rather than universal, fetishistic rather than poetic. Magritte entered the chain in the 1920s, but unlike his co-evals he was still stubbornly painting bowler-hatted men 40 years later, at the end of the 1960s. In the very last paintings of this lifelong series, their figures have become completely transparent. In each, only the familiar outline silhouette is left, cut into a monochrome background, with stormy sea or moonlit night or mountainous landscape inscribed luminously within. It is as if the bowler-hatted man himself has vanished clean away. He is less than a phantom now. He is an empty screen.

11

MAPPINGS:
SITUATIONISTS AND/OR CONCEPTUALISTS

When I was first asked to write about the relationship between the Situationist International and conceptual art my immediate reaction was one of considerable scepticism. I could not see at first how they had anything very much in common. To begin with, the project of the Situationist International preceded the beginnings of conceptual art by a whole decade—the founding issue of the SI journal was published in 1958, while the path-breaking 'Xeroxbook' show organized by Seth Siegelaub and Robert Wendler took place fully ten years later, in 1968. As I have argued elsewhere, conceptual art only took off as an art movement in the following year, 1969. The foundation of the SI, in contrast, coincided closely with the first Happenings in New York and the first stirrings of the Fluxus group in North America. Of course, it would be possible to argue that Fluxus, in particular, was itself a crucial predecessor of conceptual art and, indeed, that there was a definite historical overlap between them, but the situationists had a quite different kind of artistic history, one that derived principally from the post-war break-up of surrealism and the appearance of a spectrum of successor movements such as CoBrA and Lettrism, which in turn split into a competitive array of small, even minute, post-surrealist groupings.

While I can see that some of the tendencies within conceptual art might seem to have converged politically with the Situationist International —itself an explicitly Marxist group—the conceptualist movement as a whole stayed broadly within the limits of the art world, even though many artists became personally involved in the Civil Rights movement, anti-war activism and feminism, or became interested in various new currents within Marxist theory. The situationists, on the other hand, under the leadership of Guy Debord, consciously left the art world behind and mutated into a primarily political and philosophical grouping, a vanguard '*groupuscule*', whose 'artistic' contribution to the events of 1968 was restricted to painting slogans on walls. This kind of activity may have been salutary in itself—and it eventually contributed to the punk graphics of an artist such as Jamie Reid—but it was clearly not an 'art practice' of the kind that the more politicized elements within conceptual art veered towards, such as the Art & Language movement or the group gathered around *The Fox* in New York. The situationists consciously cut off all their past ties with the art world and turned instead towards ultra-left politics, calling for revolutionary mass struggle, and to developing their own political theory. The single exception to this was Guy Debord's own work as a film-maker, which was largely related to his theoretical work on the 'society of the spectacle' and its reception, and very different in its intent from, say, the structural films of Michael Snow or Hollis Frampton, which could plausibly be seen as cinematic analogues to conceptual art.

As I pondered all this, however, I was struck by one strange overlap between the interests of the situationists and those of the conceptual art movement: their fascination with maps, as a form of documentation, but also as a form of design. If I could understand this common interest in cartography, I somehow felt, I might be able to uncover a submerged shift which linked the two movements, a pointer towards subterraneously shared artistic and cultural strategies. Maps, after all, are a form of graphic art, one which is particularly complex but inevitably carries with it a certain perspective on the world around us. Maps, it has often been pointed out, convey information in visual form, just like other forms of visual art, but they do this in a particularly complex way. They always have a threefold character, involving a subject, data relevant to that subject, and a theme which orients our understanding of it. As Denis Wood has proposed in his sketch of a rhetoric of cartography, maps typically involve the use of five distinct types of semiotic code: iconic, verbal, tectonic, presentational and temporal. The 'iconic code' refers to the way the map presents a visual analogue, scaled down and projected, which matches the subject of the map and its topography. The 'verbal code' is used to label the various features of the map and sometimes to add comment or further information. The 'tectonic code' covers the various ways in which information is symbolized—different types of lines used (dotted, broken, etc.), areas of colouring or shading, the symbols used to indicate special features, such as crossed swords for ancient battlefields or clusters of slanted lines for rainstorms. The 'presentational code' covers the ways in which display and design features, not integral to the map itself, provide a meta-language to convey its import. Finally, the 'temporal code' shows how features, such as the weather or epidemics, change over time.

A map, in fact, can be viewed as a complex type of semiotic text with many possible frames of reference (political, medical, meteorological, demographic, military ...) and many different purposes. In fact, it is precisely because maps are needed for such a wide variety of purposes, covering such a wide variety of topics and uses, that they have developed such intricate and complex semiotic features. To read a map and to understand why it looks the way it does is also to understand its underlying goal. As I began to think about the specific differences between the kinds of map and mapping used by the situationists and those used by a wide range of conceptual artists, it became clear to me that these differences were directly related to their differing goals. In the case of the situationists, maps were overwhelmingly used in the context of their critique of post-war forms of city planning, predominantly rationalist and functionalist in their approach, dividing the city into functional zones and demolishing whole neighbourhoods in order to construct 'modernized' but socially and psychologically destructive new traffic systems.

In sharp contrast to the dominant planning ideology, the situationists developed three principal theoretical ideas of their own—those of the *dérive*, psycho-geography and unitary urbanism. The *dérive* referred to an experimental technique of 'transient passage through varied ambiances', a kind of chance wandering from area to area, in the hope of finding provocative interlocutors or strange and moving encounters. Psycho-geography referred to 'the study of the specific effects of the geographical environment, consciously organized or not, on the emotions and behaviour of individuals'. Unitary urbanism was the theory of the combined use of arts and techniques for the construction—or preservation—of environments in which the *dérive* and psycho-geographical experiments would prosper. In fact, all three of these concepts were actually pre-situationist in origin. Gilles Ivain's pioneer *Formulary for a New Urbanism* was actually written in 1953 (although it was first published in the SI journal fully five years later, in 1958). Guy Debord's *Introduction to a Critique of Urban Geography*, which launched the idea of 'psychogeography', first appeared in *Les Lettres Nues* in 1955 and his *Theory of the Dérive* appeared in the same journal the following year (republished in the second issue of the SI journal in 1958).

As Simon Sadler points out in his indispensable book, *The Situationist City*, these ideas first originated in reaction against city planning schemes for the modernization of Paris, which threatened the old bohemian areas on the Left Bank in which the future situationists themselves were then living—and indeed many other neighbourhoods which they frequented and to which they felt strong emotional attachments. These schemes, for example, eventually brought about the destruction of the old market area (les Halles) in order to replace it with a transportation hub and a shopping mall. For this reason, the maps used by the situationists were predominantly maps of Paris (or, in the case of the important Dutch and Danish groups, maps of Amsterdam or Copenhagen). For instance, in 1956, Debord, working with his Danish colleague Asger Jorn, produced a folding map, the *Guide Psychogéographique de Paris*, subtitled *Discours sur les Passions de l'Amour: pentes psychogéographiques de la dérive et localisation d'unités d'ambiance*, followed the next year by another jointly produced psycho-geographical map of Paris, *The Naked City*, as well as a screenprinted book, *Fin de Copenhague*, with text and imagery collaged together from magazines and newspapers acquired at a single Copenhagen news-stand. Two years later, in 1959, Debord and Jorn collaborated again, this time on *Mémoires*, a retrospectively psycho-geographical account of Paris. This book, unlike the first, contains collaged chunks from maps, as well as texts and illustrations. Both works, I should add, also have a strongly cartographic appearance due to the dribbled lines of coloured ink which link the images, as canals or river might link landmarks within a city.

The two psycho-geographical street maps of Paris produced by Debord are both collaged from two pre-existing Paris maps—the extraordinary 1956 *Plan de Paris à Vol d'Oiseau*, drawn by G. Peltier, and the 1951 Guide Taride de Paris, a conventional street atlas. The Peltier map shows the centre of Paris, with the two diagonal axes crossing at what seems to be a point very close to where the Mona Lisa hangs in the south wing of the Louvre. All the buildings, parks, bridges, stretches of river, are depicted from a point of view apparently located high over Paris to the south of the area mapped, with the perspective adjusted so that there are no distortions. Debord and Jorn cut sections out of this map, chosen on psycho-geographical grounds from the areas immediately north and south of the Seine, just to the east of the Louvre, and then pasted these together as if they were islands, joined by prominent red arrows which point directions from one zone to another across an empty space—reminding us, as Michelle Bernstein had suggested in 1954, that a *dérive* through one zone could best be continued by taking a cab to another and then starting again on another tour. 'Only taxis', Bernstein noted, 'allow a true freedom of movement. By travelling various distances in a set time, they contribute to automatic disorientation. Since taxis are interchangeable, no connection is established with the "traveller" and they can be left anywhere and taken at random. A trip with no destination, diverted arbitrarily en route, is only possible with a taxi's essentially random itinerary.' The second map, based on the Taride guide, covers the same area of Paris but is less ornate in its design.

It might be useful, at this point, to return to the five cartographic codes which I mentioned above. The iconic code is heavily marked in the *Psychogeographic Guide*, which is based on a bird's-eye view of the city, representing not only the street lay-out but also the buildings, bridges, monuments, clumps of trees and other features which are enclosed by those streets. In *The Naked City* there is a street-plan alone. The verbal code, in both maps is divided into two elements—the conventional lettering of the original map, concentrating on street names, and the lettering of the map's title, added by Debord. With the *Guide*, this characterizes the purpose of the map directly as psycho-geographical and presents it as a kind of love-letter to selected neighbourhoods within the city. With *The Naked City*, on the other hand, the title directs us back to Jules Dassin's film of the same name, a drama-documentary about detectives in New York. As Sadler points out, this could be construed as claiming a certain investigative role for the *dérive*, seen as a process of evidence gathering, as the strollers researched 'the condition of contemporary Paris', perhaps with the city planners in mind as guilty wreckers of the precious ambiances they were mapping. *The Naked City* also has a subtitle, reading *Illustration de l'Hypothèse des Plaques Tournantes de Psychogéographie*, a phrase which refers to the situationist claim that the neighbourhoods they loved were pivotal zones (*plaques tournantes*) in the sense that they linked the wanderer to neighbouring zones with which they shared an emotional affinity.

The tectonic code in these maps has two unconventional features—the stereometric perspective of the *Guide* and the red arrows which feature in both the *Guide* and *The Naked City*. The bird's-eye view, I would suggest, directs us to the idea of 'unitary urbanism', giving us a sense that, seen from above, each fraction of the city is integrated, through the red arrows, with all the others, thus creating an ideal unity which exists in contrast to the everyday fragmentation of the city, and which is based not on traffic planning schemes, but on what we might call elective affinities. The presentational code designates the *Guide*, through its status as a folding map, as a critical variant of the tourist guide, designed to be carried in a pocket while exploring the city—while, of course, substituting the image of psycho-geographer for that of typical tourist. The street atlas connotation of *The Naked City* has a similar, if less marked, effect. The durational code, I think, is particularly important as we consider these two maps. First, of course, there is the date of the maps themselves, produced at a time when Paris was beginning to undergo a process of massive change as the planners assumed control. As Sadler points out, from the early 1950s onward Paris began to undergo a process of reconstruction unprecedented since the time of Haussmann. The two situationist maps both commemorate the old Paris and issue a warning against future trends, sadly unheeded. Looked at today with hindsight, they assume an elegiac quality, probably intended even at the time of their making.

There are a few comments I would also like to make in relation to three other maps which were important to the situationists. The first of these is a map 'plotting all the trajectories effected in a year by a student inhabiting the 16th Arrondissement', first published in Chombart de Lauwe's massive *Paris et l'Agglomeration Parisienne*, vol. 1 (1952), a book which deeply influenced Debord. This shows all the routes traversed by a single student within a year, dominated by a single thick triangle with, at each apex, his domicile, the place he went for piano lessons and the School of Political Science lecture room. Debord discussed this map in his *Theory of the Dérive* (1956), pointing out how it illustrates 'the narrowness of the real Paris in which each individual lives', a narrowness to be opened up by the situationists' use of *dérive*. The second is a 1656 *Map of the Land of Feeling*, reproduced in the SI no. 3, in 1959, as an illustration accompanying an unsigned article on *Unitary Urbanism at the End of the 1950s*. Clearly, this map presents, in cartographic form, the relationship between the passions and the lived environment suggested by the whole concept of psycho-geography. Thirdly, there is the map by the Dutch situationist Constant of his massive New Babylon project, depicting the outlines of a floating aerial city superimposed above the undisturbed traditional neighbourhoods beneath, which strides on stilts, so to speak, above the very same city centre of Amsterdam illustrated in the SI journal, an area favoured by the Dutch situationists for their own *dérives*. Here the temporal code, though still referring us to the future—almost to a kind of science-fiction future—is utopian rather than elegiac, a mapping of hope rather than despair.

What emerges from a consideration of these maps is that they were presented in a double context—that of a pessimistic critique of contemporary society, combining defiance with elegy, and, at the same time, that of an optimistic utopian futurology, combining a basically Hegelian teleology with a resolutely buoyant utopianism. This strange manic-depressive timbre of situationist thinking, always passionate, but veering between highs and lows, affected situationist cartography as well. In this respect, it is very different from the cartography favoured by conceptual artists, which was much more distanced from issues such as city planning or urbanism, much less activist in its mentality, although conceptual artists sometimes also used city maps for purposes which might almost be called psycho-geographical. Let us look, for example, at the maps used by such key conceptual artists as Douglas Huebler and On Kawara, as well as a second-generation conceptualist Fiona Templeton, all of which involve the mapping of a city and the tracing of an itinerary within it. These maps, however, differ in significant respects from the situationist maps, not only because they are unconcerned with any critique of city planning, but also because the itineraries which they trace are conceived not in terms of psycho-geography, but in terms of a specifically artistic concept of 'performance'. With the exception, perhaps, of Templeton's work, the passions, in Debord's sense, are no longer at play. Instead there is a kind of scientificity, an almost clinical mind-set, based on an obsession with theoretical methodologies for documenting behaviour.

Conceptual art maps began appearing in 1968, at the very outset of the movement. 1968 saw both the launch of On Kawara's I Went series in Mexico City and Douglas Huebler's Site Sculpture Projects, such as *42° Parallel* and *Windham College Pentagon*. Kawara's work involved tracing an itinerary on a xerox taken from a city map, using a red ball-point pen. The number of maps in any one sequence depended on how many days he spent in each particular locality, until he departed and the pages were sheathed in transparent plastic and put together in a loose-leaf binder. Like other similar series produced by On Kawara, such as I Met or I Read, I Went was a form of self-documentation, which used maps because the behaviour documented traced the artist's trajectory through the city. These were not *dérives* because although some may have been random strolls, some of them were clearly not—as, for instance, the journey he made to the airport on leaving or his walk to the end of a promontory overlooking a lake with, I would suppose, a fine view. In effect, Kawara's series form part of a kind of elaborate diary or personal journal which uses the semiotic system of mapping alongside that of verbal text. The theme of these maps, rather than an experience of the city as such, is the experience of On Kawara's own life, one aspect of which involves moving around within a particular city.

Huebler's maps, in contrast, are about the nature of art itself. His Site Sculpture pieces, for instance, instantiate a particular geographical site, marked on a map, as the site of a particular sculpture. Thus his *42° Parallel Piece* is defined by him as follows: '14 locations ("A" through "N") are towns existing exactly or approximately on the 42° parallel in the United States. Locations have been marked by the exchange of certified postal receipts sent from and returned to "A"—Truro, Massachusetts." The full piece consisted of the defining statement, plus the map, with the parallel and the 14 cities marked on it, together with the postal receipts and other ancillary documents, including two city maps. Obviously, the main impact of this piece consists of Huebler's radical redefinition of the term 'sculpture' to include such constituent elements as postal receipts or maps. Another Site Sculpture project, *Windham College Pentagon*, executed the following month, consisted of removing a small quantity of dirt from five points (A, B, C, D, E), each of which was located about $1\,^1/_3$ miles from a designated central spot located on the college campus, and then setting the five collections of dirt in epoxy, each in a five-sided shape which would form a small pentagon isomorphic with the pentagon created by the sites A, B, C, D, E. The finished piece consisted of the five-sided shape, two maps locating A, B, C, D and E, as well as five Polaroid photographs of the sites. While this piece retained an element of conventional sculpture (the shapes) these were not part of the finished piece, since they were returned to the earth. Huebler did, however, consistently use maps as a site for drawing, adding a performance-related diagrammatic feature—a pentagon, for instance, an arc or three concentric squares.

At much the same time, however, Huebler executed two other projects—one of which, conceived in 1968, used a Shell road map to document a proposed round-trip drive to be made between Haverhill, Massachusetts and Rochester, Vermont, and back again, using a route marked on the map by Huebler, which might be followed either clockwise or anti-clockwise, according to personal preference. The piece would consist of the map plus 'whatever is seen when the trip is taken'. In his 1969 *Location Piece #1*, Huebler's work included an American Airlines system map showing, among other features, the route flown between New York and Los Angeles. Huebler himself took this flight and photographed out of the airplane window what he designated as 'the airspace over each of the thirteen states' which were crossed by the plane. For this piece, Huebler pointed his camera 'more or less staight out of the airplane window (with no "interesting" view intended)'. The piece thus consists of the photographs plus the map. In both of these pieces, Huebler documented an actual trip or journey, thereby moving closer to the situationist aesthetic of the *dérive*. Unlike the situationists, however, Huebler presented his journeys completely dispassionately. Far from having any psycho-geographic content, the journey is seemingly bereft of any emotional content or any interest in the landscape as an aestheticized object of the traveller's gaze. As Huebler has noted, his work 'forecloses the possibility that its subject can be regarded as just another aestheticized object of consumption'. In this respect, he went even further than the situationists in rejecting any form of visual pleasure.

In discussing his use of maps, Huebler specifically recalled the time he spent as a non-commissioned intelligence officer on Peleliu Island in the South Pacific during the Second World War, attached to Marine Air Group II. There he

> wrote the group's diary, which was a daily account of the details and results of our ongoing bombing strikes against the islands of Koror and Babelthaup .... On a number of occasions I accompanied pilots on observation flights in order to determine if targeted anti-aircraft gun positions had been either destroyed, or moved, as was often the situation. Whatever new information we brought back was displayed on our large map with coloured push pins, and that information played an important role in the intelligence briefings delivered before each strike.

Huebler notes that the verbal briefing combined with 'the several kinds of visual imagery provided by the map' to convey 'a mental picture' to the mind of each pilot, 'so that he would know what he would expect to see' during his mission. Searching, many years later, for 'alternative methodologies' that he could use in his art work, Huebler 'began to sense the significance of the map as a most essential kind of conceptual model'.

Maps, Huebler noted, 'include both "aspects of time" and culturally developed "propositions in language"'. Put another way, he was interested not only in the iconic code but also in the verbal and temporal codes involved in making and understanding maps. The tectonic code was also relevant through the choice, say, of magic marker to show the round trip route on the map prepared for *Rochester Trip* (compare the red arrows on Debord's map). The presentational code was one which directed the viewer to look at the map in the context of art, rather than military strategy (an approach sometimes favoured by Debord, who was an avid reader of Clausewitz) or a critique of urbanism. Maps, together with verbal language, could be used to convey the conceptual elements of his project as an artist—actions performed in a specific location for a specific period of time. Maps were thus a necessary element both for planning many of Huebler's pieces and for documenting them. From an ensemble of verbal, photographic and cartographic data, the 'viewer' could then conceptually reconstruct the actual performance—which involved a programmatic journey in the real world 'outside of my studio', as Huebler insisted, rather than a traditional studio-bound way of making art. Maps thus created a new frame of reference for art, whose possibilities were subsequently explored by artists such as Long and Fulton, renowned for their programmatically mapped walks and journeys ...

Templeton's work, *YOU—The City*, was a piece produced in New York City in 1988 and repeated in various other cities. She describes it as a 'play', albeit of an experimental kind, but it would normally be regarded as a kind of interactive performance piece. The audience at any one performance consists of one person (the 'client') who checks in at a starting location and is then directed from one interlocutor or companion to another, who form a kind of human chain passing the audience from one interaction to another. These interactions also structure a physical journey that lasts until the client reaches the final destination, and the play ends. As in Huebler's *Rochester Trip*, a map is included in the published play text but the route it traces is structured not by an arbitrary protocol, but by a series of human encounters, as with a situationist *dérive*. In fact, it could be argued that Templeton's piece is located conceptually somewhere between Debord and Huebler—as with Huebler, the itinerary is predetermined but, as with Debord, it consists of a series of chance meetings with 'clients' who arrived, one by one, as audience but ended up turning into performers as they were manipulated by actors who already knew the script—chance meetings, that is, to the 'client', while in reality each encounter had been carefully planned and scripted by Templeton. For the artist, the point was to create a situation in which an 'intended' structure (the script) encountered an 'unintendable', or unpredictable one (the client's response).

The map, like the script, is clearly programmatic, like Huebler's maps, but it only determines one dimension of the play. Templeton's map falls within the tradition of the map made in conjunction with an artist's 'happening' or 'event'. Thus, nearly 30 years before, Wolf Vostell, who obviously loved the look of maps, had used a loosely painted map of Cologne to advertise his 1961 *Cityrama* event, and a Paris bus map for his

Petite Ceinture happening in July 1962, a bus trip which he turned into an art event by suggesting that the participants 'keep a look out for the acoustic and at the same time optical impressions' available on their trip, paying particular attention to the sight of *décollages trouvés*, 'walls with placards torn or hanging down', thus foregrounding within the cityscape a form of chance visual composition (or decomposition) which he himself consciously favoured and practiced as an artist.

Later, Nam Jun Paik drew a map of *Fluxus Island in Décollage OCEAN*, which is in the tradition of the maps for *Treasure Island* or *The Lord of the Rings*, but showing the location of such odd and fantastic features as the site where 'The jewel box of wife of Syngman RHEE is buried here and lost', 'the ministerium for developing the electronic television', 'the cinemathek of all the censored parts in the 20th century' and 'the pyramid, higher than Egyptian pyramid, made of AUTOMOBILE WRECKS (10,000)', and other such wonders. Perhaps the two most interesting map pieces within the world of happenings, *décollage* and fluxus, however, were Yoko Ono's 1962 *Map Piece*, to which I shall return, and Chieko Shomi's two *Spatial Poems* of 1965 and 1966. Yoko Ono's piece took the form of a verbal instruction, reading as follows:

> Draw an imaginary map. Put a goal mark on the map where you want to go. Go walking on an actual street according to your map. If there is no street where it should be according to the map, make one by putting the obstacles aside. When you reach the goal, ask the name of the city and give flowers to the first person you meet. The map must be followed exactly, or the event has to be dropped altogether. Ask your friends to write maps. Give your friends maps.

Both of Shomi's poems included maps, one of them (No. 2) designated as 'folding'. The first poem runs as follows: 'Write a word (or words) on the enclosed card and place it somewhere. Let me know your word and place so that I can make a distribution chart of them on a world map, which will be sent to every participant.' In the same vein, Alighiero Boetti's 1968 *City of Turin*, a photocopied city map with the residences of the city's artists (at least those known to the cartographer) marked with a line and their names written in crayon. This map, like Chieko Shomi's, is also a form of 'distribution chart', which charts the whereabouts of the artists themselves rather than of their works. Such maps are quite conventional in cartographic terms, but they originate as an art project and their underlying theme—mapping a sector of the art world—is an unconventional one.

Finally, I want to comment on three further artists' uses of maps, all of which confront issues of cartography itself, rather than using maps as a form of documentation. The first is an Art & Language map, created in 1967 and labelled 'Map to not indicate Canada, North Dakota, Straits of Florida, etc.', showing only the floating outlines of Iowa and Kentucky. Its effect comes from the idea of cartography as representing a form of non-representation and subtraction rather than of comprehensive representation and addition, as new regions or features are discovered, surveyed and included. In general terms, the Art & Language map falls within the category of what Peter Gould and Rodney White have called 'mental maps'—such as those representing 'The New Yorker's Idea of the United States of America', which shows Manhattan as larger than California, or 'How Londoners see the North', which shows a gigantic London and a road system that ends before you reach Scotland, shown as located in dog sled country north of the Arctic Circle. In the art world its distant predecessor was the surrealist map of the world, which omitted the United States completely and included instead a vast Papua. Unlike this map, however, Art & Language's radical subtraction drew our attention to the process of map-making rather than the content. In contrast, Agnes Denes's uncanny maps of the world are mathematically distorted to represent it as it would be if it were shaped as a cube, a doughnut or a pyramid, rather than a spheroid, forcing us to focus on the technique of map-making and the way in which it can alter our mental image of the world, subverting the power of the mathematical grid, forcing us to re-evaluate our whole sense of reality.

In contrast to these maps, which ask us to re-examine the assumptions which determine our mental representations of the world, the maps used by Newton and Helen Mayer Harrison are functional, goal-directed and set in a context that makes no distinction between work in art and work in ecology—the map is both an aesthetic object and a tool for developing land use policy. Thus their 1985 *Lagoon Cycle* uses huge panels as a means to display a series of maps which, along with other materials, including a poetic and dialogic text, serve as visual aids designed to provoke a train of thought which starts from the problems surrounding the development of a viable aquaculture for crab farming in Sri Lanka. The Harrisons' aim, it seems, is to provoke thought about the shifting relationship between man and nature, seeking to find a constructive way forward in the idea of participating in a dialogue with nature, rather than addressing it with a unilateral anthropocentric monologue. The function of maps within this dialogic work is to focus our attention on specific locations that provide examples of failed policies towards the natural environment, and to propose an alternative set of constructive uses for the future—a future which we might characterize, with sympathy, as unashamedly 'utopian'.

It is the political dimension of this work, of course, which brings us back to the situationists. For the Harrisons, however, it was the balance between human needs and the rural environment, rather than the equally precarious relationship between human needs and the urban environment, which concerned Debord and his comrades. As with the situationists, the Harrisons used maps for a purpose, one which erased the line between art and politics in an unprecedented way. In an essay published in the catalogue for *The Lagoon Cycle*, Michel de Certeau wrote of mapmaking as a way of envisaging a possible future, casting cartographic temporality in the mode of future possibility—utopian, perhaps, but not counter-intuitive like Denes's maps. De Certeau reminds us that early Renaissance maps combined the realistic with the fabulous, and encourages us to consider how cartographers and artists alike have repeatedly ventured into what we might call fantastic mapping, citing as an example artists' maps of imaginary countries (such as Norman Daly's 1972 map of Llhuros). Maps can serve both as political tools and as stimulants for the imagination—linked together they can delineate a utopian form of vision shared by situationists and conceptualists alike, one which offers us new ways of thinking about the world in which we live and, as a result, new ways of thinking about changing it. In their book *Mapping: Ways of Representing the World*, David Dorling and David Fairbairn note how 'resistance mapping' can change our conception of the world, citing Doug Aberley's contention that, as maps have increasingly become instruments of power, non-specialists must begin to create their own resistant counter-maps. Despite all their differences, both situationists and conceptual artists can be seen as pioneers of resistance mapping, challenging the orthodoxies of power through an alternative cartography.

12

ART AND FASHION: FRIENDS OR ENEMIES?

In his book on Mariano Fortuny, Guillermo de Osma argues that Fortuny's Delphos dresses, first designed in 1909, were practical realizations of a style of costume which had been promoted by painters some decades before. In fact, the painters de Osma names were members of a now discredited English school of art—Albert Moore, Frederick Leighton, Lawrence Alma-Tadema. These artists draped their models in an approximation of classical Greek or Roman dress, which they considered both more healthy and more beautiful than any other style. Behind their Hellenism in matters of fashion lay the Aesthetic movement and the Rational Dress movement, both of which sought to reject contemporary fashions—the crinoline, the corset, etc.— as constricting, irrational and ugly. As Walter Crane observed, '[If we regard] dress as a department of design, [then] as with design, we may consciously bring to bear upon it the results of artistic experience and knowledge of form.' In fact, Crane, and others like him, believed that dress designers should be artists. Satin 'toga' dresses 'à la Tadema' were made and sold by Liberty, the pioneer in promoting modern dress. It was not until after the turn of the century, however, that fashion as a whole moved away from Victorian body sculpture to promote the free development of the female form. The impetus, I believe, came in four related fields—from literature (Mardrus's translation of *The Arabian Nights*), from dance (Isadora Duncan and her cult of the Greek body, together with the Russian Ballet and the flamboyant orientalism of *Schéhérezade*), from painting (the paganism and orientalism of Matisse) and finally, of course, from fashion (Fortuny and, above all, Paul Poiret).

Poiret was more important than Fortuny because he was the head of a leading Paris fashion house and, therefore, in a position to exert a much wider influence than the eccentric Venetian who drifted towards theatre (where he invented the cyclorama). If we look back at the history of art in the twentieth century, we quickly discover that there was always a relationship of sorts between the two worlds of art and fashion. It began, as we have seen, with the rise of aestheticism towards the end of the nineteenth century. Aesthetic dandyism clearly played an important part in creating the culture which made possible the beginnings of both modern art and modern fashion. From Whistler's circle came E. W. Godwin, better known today as an architect, who was put in charge of the new fashion department at Liberty in Regent Street. The success of Liberty led in turn to the extension of the Wiener Werkstatte, which now set up its own fashion department, under Eduard Wimmer-Wisgrill. Klimt, the most successful Secession painter, was closely associated with the Wiener Werkstatte through his wife Emilie Floge, who was herself an outstanding dress designer in the aesthetic mode. Klimt both designed clothes himself for his models, as Whistler had done, and painted his society sitters wearing extravagant Wiener Werkstatte dresses. In turn, the Wiener Werkstatte inspired the great French couturier, Paul Poiret, after his visit to Vienna in 1910, into creating his own Martine workshop as an adjunct to his fashion house, a workshop school from which the free-style art-work created spontaneously by the pupils was used as the basis for fabric designs.

A crucial dimension of early modernism involved the development of a highly saturated palette and, aligned with this new sense of colour, a parallel re-figuration of the human body, especially the female body, in the name of emancipation and a new approach to sexuality. The turn towards orientalism which preoccupied Poiret, Matisse and Bakst (in the context of the *Ballets Russes*) should be seen as part of a general trend which involved fashion, art and performance. There were also many direct connections between these worlds—Poiret designed an orientalist gown specifically for his wife to wear at the opening of *Schéhérezade* in Paris, and

Matisse himself designed for the *Ballets Russes*. Poiret consciously cultivated his close relations with the art world. He both painted and collected paintings. He was particularly close to Dufy, Van Dongen, De La Fresnaye, Derain and, later, Picabia and Man Ray. He held art exhibitions —Picasso's *Demoiselles d'Avignon* was first exhibited in public at Poiret's gallery, before it was purchased by another Paris couturier, Jacques Doucet, on the advice of André Breton—and he also employed Man Ray as a photographer in the 1920s. In fact, Man Ray's very first *photogrammes* were made for and acquired by Poiret. This intersection of the art world with the fashion world was typical of early modernism—not only can we see the same pattern in Vienna, but also in London, where Bloomsbury artists, such as Vanessa Bell, produced both paintings and fashion, through their own Omega Workshop (itself modelled on Poiret's Martine workshop).

The next generation of artists in Paris continued on the same track— the most prominent examples would be Picabia and both Robert and Sonia Delaunay—bringing together the worlds of performance, couture and painting. Sonia Delaunay began as an artist but ended as a professional couturier, bringing a strong cubist influence to a fashion sense originally derived from Poiret and artists' balls such as the *Bal Bullier*. The same trend can be seen among the Italian futurists and, in the 1920s, the Russian avant-garde became involved in both fabric and clothes design. Simultaneously, artists began to design costumes for dance performances. Diaghilev, in particular, employed cubist painters as costume designers—Picasso, Braque and many others. Picasso regarded his work for *Parade* as central to his career as an artist, unashamed to follow in the footsteps of Bakst, Larionov and Goncharova, who herself went on, like Delaunay, to become a professional fashion designer. In Germany, Schlemmer designed his *Triadic Ballet*. Paintings by Delaunay and Léger (who wrote about fashion) follow the same trend—as the orientalist body metamorphoses into the sporting and mechanical body— a movement paralleled by the priority now given to sportswear by the world of couture (and by Chanel's costumes for the *Ballets Russes*).

The end of the 1914–18 war, however, led to a turn against pre-war colourism and ornamentalism, both in art and fashion. The preconditions for this drastic U-turn can be seen already before the war. In a sense, they represent the result of a split between the aesthetic and rationalist wings of the old Dress Reform movement. The first triumphed before the war, the second after. In 1898 the great Viennese architect, Adolf Loos, had written two extraordinary articles on this subject for the *Neue Freie Press*, part of a series which he contributed on the state of the arts and crafts in Austria, provoked by the Vienna Jubilee Exhibition of 1898. The two most telling were on the subject of 'Men's Fashion' and 'Ladies' Fashion'. Both of them were essentially part of an ongoing polemic carried out by Loos against the decorative aestheticism of his contemporaries in the Secession movement and its offspring, the Wiener Werkstatte, including, of course, its fashion department.

On the subject of men's suits, Loos made three main points. First, he attacked the idea that men's fashion should be judged on criteria of 'beauty'. On the contrary, he claimed, 'It means to be dressed correctly.' He condemns the aesthetic movement for its cult of beauty expressed 'in the form of velvet collars, aesthetic trouser fabric, and secessionist neckties'. Second, he praised English Savile Row fashion as the model of its kind. In true Brummell style, Loos argued that the Englishman dressed 'in such a way that one stands out the least'. Thus he turned Brummell's example back against the devotees of false, aesthetic dandyism, for whom 'a dandy is a man whose clothing serves only to distinguish himself from his environment'. Thirdly, Loos stressed that the tailors of London— he mentions Poole specifically—excel in cut and understanding of cloth. It is because of their technical expertise that they lead their world, just like English plumbers or shoemakers. Loos tried explicitly to separate aestheticism from male clothing, and praise instead its rational and functional characteristics, contrasted with the frivolity, as he saw it, of women's fashion. Thus he opened the way for a partisan divide to develop between women's fashion and high modernism in the arts.

'Ladies' fashion! You disgraceful chapter in the history of civilization!' Thus Loos began the second article. He goes on to note that

> the clothing of the woman is distinguished externally from that of the man by the preference for ornamental and colourful effects and by the long skirt that covers the legs completely. These two factors demonstrate to us that the woman has fallen behind sharply in her development in recent centuries.

> No period of culture has known as great difference as our own between the clothing of the free man and that of the free woman. In earlier eras, men also wore clothing that was colourful and richly adorned and whose hem reached to the floor. Happily, the great development in which our culture has taken part in this century has overcome ornament …. The march of civilization systematically liberates object after object from ornamentation.

Loos went on to note that 'only in the last fifty years have women acquired the right to develop themselves physically. It is an analogous process: as to the rider of the thirteenth century, the concession will be made to the twentieth-century female bicyclist to wear trousers and clothing that leave her feet free. And with this, the first step is taken toward the social sanctioning of women's work.' Loos concluded with a passage of burning optimism.

> We are approaching a new and greater time. No longer by an appeal to sensuality, but rather by economic independence earned through work will the woman bring about her equal status with the man. The woman's value or lack of value will no longer fall or rise according to the fluctuation of sensuality. Then velvet and silk, flowers and ribbons, feathers and paints will fail to have their effect. They will disappear.

Loos believed that modernity would bring an end to the reign of sensuality, which he associated, like ornament, with barbarism. He saw eroticism primarily in terms of seductiveness, through 'surface magic implying hidden pleasures', as Anne Hollander later characterized it. This kind of seductive and artificial eroticism would give way to a rational and pragmatic functionalism. Sexual desire would then return to a more natural and healthy mode. Hollander has described the history of fashion in a very similar way to Loos, but, unlike him, has always insisted on the eroticism of a rationalized modernity, more powerful precisely because it is more natural and more attuned to the active body. Loos, of course, was succeeded by Le Corbusier, the leading post-war prophet of modernity. 'If the Greeks triumphed over the barbarians, if Europe, inheritor of Greek thought, dominates the world, it is because the savages liked loud colors and the noisy sound of tambourines which engage only the senses, while the Greeks loved intellectual beauty which hides beneath sensory beauty.' Le Corbusier's staggering pronouncement, yoking classicism to racism and imperialism, was made in 1918, at the end of the war, in the Purist manifesto, *Après le cubisme*. With his partner, Amédée Ozenfant, here he staked out the ground for their campaign in favour of a radical neo-classical modernism. For Ozenfant and Jeanneret (as Le Corbusier still called himself) the war ('The Great Test', 'The Great Competition') had given France, the 'inheritor of Greek thought'—and Europe—a new sense of purpose, organization and rigor. Cubism itself, they maintained, had 'remained, no matter whatever anyone says of it, a decorative, ornamental and Romantic art'. It must be further purified and classicized, freed of its residue of the bizarre and the 'original'.

The same line of argument had already been directed against Paul Poiret, who had been accused of 'German' taste, as early as 1915: 'After the war, M. Poiret will have to seek pardon from Frenchwomen; he will most certainly need it.' Poiret sued the journal which had attacked him, *La Renaissance*, which, in turn, welcomed the law-suit as an opportunity to return to the fray and explain what they meant by 'German influence on the decorative arts and fashion'. The burden of the aesthetic charge against Poiret was that his art was decadent, strident, discordant, theatrical, exotic (i.e. un-French) and based on fantasy. In particular, orientalism came under specific attack because of the German–Turkish alliance. Poiret was not to be forgiven for his decadent One Thousand And Second Night Ball, during which, as sultan of fashion, he released his wife, Denise, from a gilded cage in which she was imprisoned, a symbol of the corset and the crinoline that he had banished in favour of loose pantaloons and kimonos *à la Japonaise*. One journalist warned Marianne, the symbolic Frenchwoman, against unheard-of dresses, odalisque's trousers and sultan's turbans, direct references to Poiret's fashions. Eventually Poiret's case was settled out of court, nearly two years later, but his career never recovered. Thus France had its revenge on a rebel spirit, condemning of course in the name of reason and nation. Others, like Cocteau and his friend Picasso, repented and called for 'a new order', willing and able to navigate the new currents, painfully stung by the attacks launched against *Parade*, the war-time ballet they devised for Diaghilev, with its extraordinary late cubist costumes by Picasso.

Poiret's eclipse during and after the war evidently left a vacuum from which 'Coco' Chanel was one of the main beneficiaries. Poiret himself denounced what he saw as her 'misérabilisme de luxe', her cunning combination of luxury and poverty. Herself closely attached to the ancien régime, to the society of dukes and, indeed, grand-dukes, she nonetheless was able to capture an image of modernity and even democracy, to set a look appropriate for working women, while, at the same time, welcomed by the traditional clients of haute couture. She made use of her Anglophilia as well, through her concern with tailoring, in a way that inevitably reminds us of Loos. The aristocracy, at this critical juncture in history, when thrones toppled and revolution threatened, was happy to wear clothes which, on the face of it, were simple and far from extravagant, but whose luxury of cut and fabric would still be noticed by the discerning eye. Hence the success of the little black dress and the real jewels worn, as recommended by Chanel, to look as if they were junk. At the same time, there was a genuine recognition that the twentieth century was indeed becoming the American century and that Henry Ford was its emblematic figure. The holders of wealth and power in Europe ignored this at their peril. An orderly modernization was not only necessary, but desirable. Here, too, the modernization of fashion had its symbolic role to play: the little black dress as 'A Ford signed "Chanel"'.

In parenthesis, it is worth mentioning that the return of masculine black and white associated with Chanel, the flight from the rich palette of Poiret, Bakst and Matisse, was made possible by the effect of the First World War on traditional patterns of mourning. Up to that time, fashion journals and designers continued to include mourning clothes in their collections, designs and prescriptions, although by the year 1916 *Modes Illustrés* was already noting that 'never has the code of mourning been less strictly applied, than in these days of anguish. Women are unable to interrupt their daily occupations in order to observe the absolute seclusion that used to be the custom, whilst in deepest mourning.' Not without irony, Marcel Proust, always an alert observer of fashion, noted in *A La Recherche du Temps Perdu* that even when young women did observe mourning—'the fact and propriety of which there is no need to remind Frenchwomen'—they now wore satin or chiffon rather than the heavier, duller and more traditional cashmere.

It was because they never stopped thinking of the dear boys, so they said, that when one of their own kin fell they scarcely wore mourning for him, on the pretext that 'their grief mingled with pride' had permitted them to wear a bonnet of white English crêpe (a bonnet with the most charming effect 'authorising every hope' and 'inspired by an invincible assurance of final victory').

In December 1919, Coco Chanel's English and aristocratic lover and patron, 'Boy' Capel, having survived the war, died in an automobile accident. Three months later, Chanel moved ino the new house she had bought at Garches, in Normandy. Still in mourning for 'Boy', she had her bedroom decorated completely in black: the walls, the floor, the ceiling and even the bed-sheets. But, according to the story recounted by her biographer, Edmonde Charles-Roux, the first night she spent in the room, Chanel summoned her butler shortly after retiring and ordered a bed made up for her elsewhere in the house. In the morning, the black hangings were removed and the order was given to decorate the room in pink. There is a way in which this symbolic gesture made possible the little black dress she was to design a few years later. The rejection of black as a mourning color was the necessary precondition for its adoption for everyday life.

The recuperation of white, though itself a mourning color, was less problematic than black. It signified youth, sunshine and purity—health, agility and fitness. Moreover, the association with summer sports had already been established in the nineteenth century, not only with tennis, but also with athletics, where it had classical associations. The revival of the Olympic games in 1896 preceded the hellenic tunics of Raymond and Isadora Duncan and carried the same symbolic resonances. In 1909, the five-times Wimbledon lawn tennis champion, Mrs Sterry, observed that 'to my mind nothing looks smarter or more in keeping with the game than a nice clinging white skirt (about two inches off the ground), white blouse, white band, and a pale colored silk tie and white collar'. In 1919, the first year she won Wimbledon, Suzanne Lenglen appeared in a calf-length, one-piece sleeveless white dress. In 1921 she returned in a knee-length white silk pleated skirt with a white sleeveless cardigan, designed by Jean Patou. The next year, Lenglen noted that 'if you wish to look neat in court, never wear a colored skirt, always a white one ... I will briefly detail what I consider the ideal dress: a simple piqué dress, or one of drill or white linen, made in the old Grecian style and fastened at the waist with a ribbon or leather belt. The sleeves should be short.' Patou, whose partner and brother-in-law, Raymond Barbas, played tennis for France, went on to dress both Lenglen and her successor, Helen Wills, off the court as well as on. In 1929 Joan Lycett appeared stockingless, and in 1933 Alice Marble introduced shorts at Wimbledon. Tennis fashions were crucial, not only because of the publicity surrounding the stars, but also because they combined 'life-style modernism', 'Grecian' neo-classicism and Edwardian formality: the all-white Wimbledon dress code survives to this day.

In 1924, at Cocteau's insistence, Chanel had been asked by Diaghilev to design the costumes for *Le Train Bleu*, the definitive celebration of 'life-style modernism', the Riviera, sun, beach, and body. For Nijinska, who danced the role of 'The Tennis Player', she produced a costume all white from head to toe, modelled on the Patou clothes worn on court by the great French tennis champion, Suzanne Lenglen. Nijinska studied newsreels of Lenglen as source material for her choreography. Lenglen, Chanel—this pairing signified the overthrow of the orientalist aesthetic which had established Diaghilev's pre-war fame with *Schéhérazade*, a riot of extravagance and tumultuous colour. The days of Bakst and Poiret, the designer of the harem skirt and the 'Minaret' look, the champion of rich, bright colour in fabrics, were now gone. The cult of sports, fitness and efficiency took off even in Russia, after the Revolution. The designs of Stepanova and Rodchenko evolved, like the painting, away from futurism towards constructivism. The futurist clothes designed by Balla in Italy and the simultaneist gowns of Sonia Delaunay were phased out—Balla stopped designing, Delaunay moved from Bohemia into the fashion world proper, designing for the couturier Jacques Heim. Through the twenties, black and white continued to gain ground, until by 1927, *Vogue* could write that 'the smartest clothes for spring and summer are all white or all black'. Then, with the Great Crash and the Depression, the modern movement of the 1920s went into a general crisis in the 1930s.

Both left and right abandoned modernism, either for a renewed realism and academicism or, in the case of surrealism, for a return to fantasy and dream, now construed as subversive rather than escapist, topically Freudian rather than nostalgically ancien régime. Strict modernism mutated into streamlined *moderne*, just as Fordist minimalism and productivism gave way to the consumer-oriented stylization pioneered by Harvey Earl for Alfred Sloan at General Motors: tail-fins and streamlining. In interior design, streamlined *moderne* still kept faith with black and white, which signified fashionable modernity in the ocean-liner, night-club and luxury-apartment sets of Paramount romantic comedies and RKO musicals. Jean Harlow, Martin Battersby notes, seemed made of equal parts of 'snow, marble and marshmallow'. 'White on white' (Malevich already forgotten) mutated out of high modernism to provide a 'modern' note in the nostalgic academicism of designers such as Oliver Messel or Syrie Maugham. Indeed, this current survived right up to Cecil Beaton's celebrated black and white designs for the Ascot scene of *My Fair Lady*, his homage to the black and white Ascot of 1911, held while 'society' was still in mourning for Edward VII, who had died the previous year. In the 1963 film Beaton took the stylization of court mourning right through *moderne* up to the very verge of op art.

The break from twenties modernism was already signalled in Patou's winter 1929 collection, contemporary with the Great Crash, when he lengthened hem lines, switched to chiffon and tulle and replaced black with 'Dark Dahlia', a deep copper red. As he sardonically put it, he had been inspired by Chanel to take this new direction. In 1930, Patou announced: 'I shall fight with all my my influence to banish the much too simple little black frock from the ranks of the fashionable.' Yet Patou was more of a 'stream-liner' than an anti-modernist. His alternative was a white, satin slip, cut in biased triangular pieces. The flowing, curving look was based on a new attention to fabric and cut, made possible by the innovations of Vionnet. Looking back, we can see that, in a sense, Patou was only preparing the way for the much more theatrical Schiaparelli, who brought back lurid color, extravagant embroidery, fantastic accessories—in her own words, 'an absolute freedom of expression, and a daredevil approach with no fear'. Where Poiret had drawn on orientalism and the Ballets Russes, Schiaparelli drew on surrealism. Breton replaced Diaghilev and Dalí supplanted Matisse. Like Chanel, Schiaparelli had the knack of pleasing the rich and powerful while appearing contemporary—and even subversive. Cocteau, still keeping himself at the centre of things, worked closely with Schiaparelli, as did Salvador Dalí, eager to help introduce an element of delirium and fantasy into fashion after the minimalist rigours of Chanel and the neo-classicism of Mme. Grès. Like Poiret, whom she cited as her inspiration, Schiaparelli liked to surround herself with artists and found, as a result, that the fantasy world of fashion could exploit affinities with the world of surrealism. Thus once again the pendulum swung, bringing art and fashion together again, in joint reaction against a period of rationalism and neo-classicism, with its associated vision of the body.

Man Ray, in particular, personally bridged the gap between Poiret and Schiaparelli. He worked in the early 1920s as a house photographer for Poiret, having been introduced by Picabia, whose wife, Gabrielle, was a Poiret client. For Poiret, whose fashion house was already in decline, he made his famous fashion photograph of a model—Poiret's wife, Denise—posed with a Brancusi sculpture of a stylized bird, part of Poiret's collection. He first invented his 'Rayographs' when he made a mistake while developing fashion prints for Poiret, who was naturally the first patron to purchase one. Later, Man Ray made his extraordinary print, *Fashions For Radio*, as a project for *Harper's Bazaar*, a photographic impression of new fashion appearing as if transmitted by short-wave radio. For a succession of springs, he was given exclusive coverage of Paris openings. As well as Man Ray and Dalí, another crucial figure with fashion connections was Meret Oppenheim, clearly the most fashion-oriented of the major surrealists, followed by Léonor Fini. Oppenheim made a whole series of drawings of weirdly inventive fantasy garments and accessories—her most celebrated work, the fur tea-cup and saucer, is best seen as a direct spin-off from her preoccupation with fashion. Man Ray had helped her with her project of selling costume jewellery to fashion houses, as Fini was already doing, and managed to persuade Schiaparelli to buy Oppenheim's idea of 'winter jewellery', a band of fur glued on to a simple brass bracelet. According to Man Ray's biographer, Neil Baldwin,

> a frivolous discussion at the Café Flore with Pablo Picasso and Dora Maar, who admired the bracelet and thought it quite original, led to some free-associating about what else could be covered with fur. 'This teacup and saucer I'm drinking from right now, for instance?' Oppenheim thought. She

strode off to Monoprix department store and bought a cup, saucer and spoon, which she then decorated with Chinese gazelle fur.

Schiaparelli always used accessories as the primary sites of fantasy—hats, shoes, jewellery, even buttons. Once again the body was reconfigured under the influence of surrealism, this time as the site of fantasy, realized through decorative excess, the body which could be envisaged as a chest of drawers, as Dalí envisaged it for Schiaparelli. Typically, Dalí's fantasy of shoe-as-hat shows up both in his painting and in Schiaparelli's couture. Even after the decline of surrealism, hats and shoes have remained the maximum zones for the expression of untrammelled fantasy in fashion. But after the Second World War, when New York began to replace Paris as art capital, the connection between art and fashion began to waver—although Léger's contribution to the surrealist film, *Dreams That Money Can Buy*, and the launch of Pollock as art-star in the pages of *Harpers* and *Vogue* did something to continue the traditional link. Just as Poiret had been ousted by Chanel, so Schiaparelli, in her turn, was targeted and overthrown by Dior, this time after the Second World War, when Schiaparelli returned from exile in America and tried to re-establish herself. 'Hideous styles and monstrous hats': these were the words with which Dior summarily dismissed her. 'Remember the years before the war. Remember the extravagance of those surrealist trimmings with which Mme Schiaparelli loved to decorate her clothes ... to push the frontiers of elegance until it bordered on the bizarre.' Dior's rhetoric is uncannily similar to the attacks which wounded Poiret 30 years before. Dior too described himself as initiating, along with Balenciaga, 'the return to a more classical style'. 'In 1947, it was time for fashion to forsake adventure and make a temporary return to base.' Once again, it was time for a recall to order. Now, however, Dior appealed not to the purist order of modernity, but to the timeless order of 'fashion'. Once more, there was a swing of the pendulum, forcing art and fashion apart.

'Strict is a thing of the past', *Vogue* had announced in January 1930. It took nearly two decades and a war before strictness returned with Dior and the New Look. Dior, in his memoirs, constantly stresses, not what he dubbed the 'absolute freedom' and 'daredevil approach' favored by Schiaparelli, but careful thought and planning.

I have to resist many insidious temptations: sometimes it is the color which attracts me, sometimes the texture of the material. Of the two, the latter is the more likely to captivate me because I never choose a material solely because of its exquisite shade of color but more often because its texture seems exactly adapted to the effect I want to achieve .... What examinations, what tests it has to pass before it is deemed worthy of being chosen!

Dior describes at great length the process of selection, the stretching, weighing, stroking, rubbing, holding to the light, draping, judging, discarding, reverting, re-draping, re-examining, before a material is cut for use. 'Most of the time this ritual, which would baffle an outsider, consists of choosing, from thirty black wools, all of excellent quality, the sole one which is in fact suitable.' His distrust of colour gives his clothes an austere look, despite their invocation of a nostalgic 'femininity'. His preference was for black wool, black crêpe, black velvet, black and white tweed, white chiffon with black silk. In 1952, he explicitly rejected what he called 'fashion fripperies' and announced that 'the new essential of fashion is that it should be discreet'. Dior's neo-classicism pushed him towards clarity of outline and shape, emphasized by black, and carrying echoes of an ordered, formal world, where discretion rather than spontaneity was stressed.

As fate would have it, of course, it was precisely the austerity, severity and melancholy of Dior which was challenged after his death, at the onset of the 1960s. Paris fashion by then had settled into a conventional eclecticism, dominated still by Balenciaga and Chanel, who returned to couture in 1954 after an absence of 15 years. Chanel's achievement was signalled most strikingly with her designs for *Last Year in Marienbad* (1961), a masterpiece of formal black and white, over-exposed by Resnais at the central traumatic moment, in order to blind the viewer. *Marienbad*, like *The Blue Train* near the beginning of her career, gave Chanel the opportunity once again to combine fashion with avant-garde spectacle, an opportunity which showed her work in a completely new light. The crucial moment of change, however—the decisive break with Dior, came with Courrèges's 'space age' show of 1964. Courrèges dropped black and formality. Once again, white was used against black to clear the way for colour. Meanwhile, of course, the centre of the art world had moved from Paris to New York. Relations between the two worlds became more distant, until globalization re-aligned them.

Courrèges had left Balenciaga in 1961 to open his own house and pioneered clothes in angular, geometrical shapes and stark, glaring white: very short trapeze-shaped skirts, pants suits, mid-calf boots and huge goggles. For the 'space-age' look, which Courrèges saw as embodying 'fun and laughter', models leaped and frugged in weird, exaggerated costumes of shiny white PVC, full of startling helmets and rocket imagery. In 1965, however, Courrèges stopped exhibiting and fashion was soon submerged in yet another explosion of bright and gorgeous colours, this time emanating not from Paris couture, but from London boutique designers and hippie street culture, a new wave of exoticism which fed back into the mannerist work of designers like Yves Saint-Laurent and Zandra Rhodes. Throughout this period Saint-Laurent, who had inherited Dior's mantle, oscillated desperately between different versions of exoticism and a re-appropriation for women of male formal clothes, the tuxedo and the 'smoking'. In the 1960s, high modernism entered into crisis. Pop art challenged the boundaries between high and low art, introducing the techniques and images of mass reproduction into the gallery and museum. The same crisis struck the world of fashion, which became more and more commercialized and industrialized, a trend pursued most assiduously by Pierre Cardin, the master of the brand-name. After decades of flirting with modernity, fashion was finally 'modernized'. The immediate result was a breakdown of the orthodox tradition of style and elegance, which had survived the vicissitudes of war, depression and reconstruction, held together by the implicit norms of aristocratic taste, however spiced these might be by exotic extravaganzas or 'life-style modernism'. In the '70s and '80s, the 'zazous' Christian Dior had despised finally cavorted on to the catwalk, in every variety of fancy dress, ransacking history and ethnography for novelty and surprise.

The contemporaneous revolution in New York took place, emblematically, in the summmer of 1965. Andy Warhol had just returned from Paris, where he had enjoyed a big success with his flower paintings and with his current super-star, Edie Sedgwick. He immediately set about shooting two new films, devised by Ronald Tavel and, of course, starring Sedgwick—*Kitchen* and *Beauty #2*. *Kitchen* was Tavel's second film for

Warhol, following their first collaboration, on *Vinyl*. In *Kitchen*, all the characters have the same name. 'I was trying to get rid of character', Tavel later explained. Warhol had already instructed him, it seems, to 'get rid of plot!' and it just seemed logical to get rid of character as well. Warhol had given Tavel another important instruction too. He had said, 'I want it simple and plastic and white.' That same summer, as well as making *Kitchen*, Warhol also hosted the opening party for the fashion boutique, *Paraphernalia*, launched by the designer Betsey Johnson. It was photographed by Nat Finkelstein and was an invite-only event complete with a guest list and a runway show. The next year there was another party in the boutique. Warhol's films were projected on the wall and spotlights illuminated the models, who could be seen through the plate-glass store front by the mob of spectators who gathered outside. Warhol was thrilled when the police showed up. The Velvet Underground were there as well—the newly formed rock group which provided the performance core of Warhol's *Exploding Plastic Inevitable*. (It may be worth noting that Betsey Johnson later dressed the Velvets and married one of the group, John Cale.)

Betsey Johnson had met Warhol through his then principal acolyte, Gerard Malanga, co-star of *Vinyl* with Edie Sedgwick. He had suggested inviting Johnson to the Factory to dress Warhol's entourage for a group photograph. There she encountered Sedgwick, who later became her fitting model and a walking advertisement for her clothes. Later, Betsey Johnson dressed Edie Sedgwick for her starring role in the archetypal '60s trash scene film, *Ciao Manhattan*. Apparently, Malanga and Warhol were first attracted to Johnson by her aluminum foil tank-dresses, which matched the silver foil wall-covering with which Billy Name had swathed the entire Factory. However, the affinity between Johnson and the Warhol world proved to be surprisingly deep-rooted. Warhol, of course, had begun his own career as a fashion illustrator and remained fascinated by fashion throughout his career. Johnson and *Paraphernalia* combined his interest in the quintessential '60s look with his interest in both reflective surfaces and plastics. *Paraphernalia* brought together four extraordinary women designers—Betsey Johnson, Deanna Littell, Elisa Stone and Diana Dew. All four worked with unusual materials—plastics, paper and metals—and Littell and Dew even experimented with electric light-up clothes. Elisa Stone specialized in paper dresses—they were made from paper with, in Joel Lobenthal's words, 'a porous but firm weave with a pebbly texture resembling the surface of a paper towel', secured at the back with velcro. Stone became interested in paper as a material because of her fascination with paper dolls, which were also a childhood obsession of Warhol's, perhaps even the source of his own orientation towards fashion. In 1967 Stone made a dress out of translucent theatre lighting gel, which was featured on the cover of *Harper's Bazaar*. Displayed on hangers in the *Paraphernalia* shop they resembled 'transparent candy', in Stone's own words. Stone was also interested in paper because of its obsolescence, another Warholian characteristic—'I loved the idea that my clothes were not going to last.'

Deana Littell, like Johnson, worked with plastics. 'Someone brought me a plastic, like a leather-ette, that was coated with a glow-in-the-dark film. It was used for policemen's night raincoats. They had started manufacturing it in day-glo purples and greens.' Littell used the material to make a glowing incandescent coat, an early example of the late '60s light-show aesthetic which shaped the *Exploding Plastic Inevitable*. Littell, inspired by Jasper Johns, also devised an American flag shirt, with white collar and cuffs, which was never marketed for fear of law-suits from the Daughters of the American Revolution. As Lobenthal notes, *Paraphernalia* 'resembled an art gallery more than a conventional retail space'. Its architect, Ulrich Franzen, imagined it as 'a continuous Happening', with models frugging on stages under theatrical lighting instead of conventional window display, of the kind Johns, Rauschenberg and, of course, Warhol had earlier designed for Gene Moore at Bonwit Teller. *Paraphernalia* realized a vision of the fashion world, both in design and merchandizing (Warhol's own sector) that was in synch with the Factory and his art production. It brought to New York the excitement which Warhol had earlier felt emanating from London via such friends and exemplars as Nicky Haslam, David Bailey, Jane Ormsby Gore, Jean Shrimpton and Twiggy. In a way, the London 'youthquake', along with London Pop Art, can be seen as prefiguring the Manhattan scene we associate with Warhol. The '60s was also, after all, the decade when long-haul passenger air travel became increasingly viable for the general public, the first pre-condition for the global economy and culture that was soon to follow. Not only was the fashion world dispersed, but also the art world, while, at the same time, much closer connections became possible between different cultural centres—Paris, New York, London, Milan, Tokyo.

The '60s was also the decade when the art world began to transmute. The influence of Happenings, Fluxus and conceptual art dethroned painting and sculpture from their traditional place and introduced a new landscape of mixed-media and mixed-genre work, incorporating photography, performance, sound, light and installation. Collage expanded into assemblage, and assemblage into environments which merged with the post-Duchampian strand within conceptualism to produce installation art. In this context, fashion could re-encounter fine art on much more favourable ground, as another medium to be scavenged from (or colonized, depending on your point of view) or, conversely, as a new means for fashion to re-configure itself and develop an innovative new aesthetic. This time, the dominant fashion aesthetic ('60s design energized by street style) was challenged in ways more radical than it had been at any time since Poiret, as the pendulum swung once again, carrying fashion with it. The key designers now were the Japanese trio, Rei Kawakubo (working through her Comme Des Garçons line), Issey Miyake and Yohji Yamamoto. Kawakubo, drawing on Japanese culture and clothing as well as street fashion, produced garments with concepts and shapes that were completely unfamiliar. Her first shows were seen as mysterious, even aggressively strange in their strategy. A pattern-cutter describes being asked to produce a coat 'that would have the qualities of a pillow-case that was being pulled inside-out'. Clothes are wrapped rather than tailored or draped, and take on a pseudomorphic life of their own, as though co-habiting with their wearer, rather than trying to serve or flatter. Like other designers with a strong sense of shape, Kawakubo worked a great deal in black, the crucial element in a new minimalist aesthetic.

Kawakubo viewed her clothes almost as installation pieces in her meticulously designed stores. The first number of her magazine *Six*, published in 1988, contained articles on Cocteau (the single great constant of twentieth-century fashion, evoking in turn Poiret, Diaghilev, surrealism and Schiaparelli) and also the unsung architect and designer Eileen Gray. Eileen Gray died at the age of 98 in 1976, the year in which

Rei Kawakubo opened her first store in Tokyo. In 1906 Gray had begun her career as a designer by learning the craft of lacquer from Sugawara, a Japanese artist who had come to Paris for the 1900 Universal Exhibition. In the 1920s, under the influence of De Stijl and Le Corbusier, she gave up work in lacquer and became a much purer modernist, always insisting, however, on the need to temper reason, order and utility with emotion, the personal touch and imaginative wit. Gray absorbed the formulas of purism and modernism, but saw them as transitional, as means, rather than ends. 'No, on the contrary, I want to develop those formulas and push them to the point where they re-establish contact with life; I want to enrich them, to make some reality penetrate their abstraction.'

Miyake, like Kawakubo, actively sought out connections with the art world. He was interested early on, for example, by Christo's project of wrapping, first people, then objects. He could make the connection with Japanese culture through the concept of 'wrapping' (rather than the Western mode of tailoring and fitting) and pursue his project of bringing together East and West by making contact with Christo as a European artist. From East Asia, but active in America and Mexico, Isamu Noguchi played a similar role as model for Miyake, representing a complex pattern of connections between West and East. It was Miyake who was featured on the cover of a 'Special Issue' of *ArtForum* in February 1982, with a photograph, taken by Eiichiro Sakata, of a Western model wearing a Miyake design, featuring a ribbed rattan bodice with a full-length and pleated nylon polyester skirt. The rattan was split (to make the intervals between the ribs), coloured (black and a dull red) and polished to give a reflective sheen. It had been formed 'to follow the line of the body' from broad shoulders to narrow waist, with bamboo 'woven in to hold the curve in place and prevent the rattan from separating'. It was a typical combination, for Miyake, of attention to materials and their texture; form, in relation to the body; and craft skill, in relation both to the work with the rattan and the pleating of the polyester. The design was one of a series which made up Miyake's *Bodyworks* show which traveled to Paris, London and San Francisco, where it was exhibited in the Art Museum.

The editorial for the 1982 'Bodyworks' issue of *ArtForum* was written by Ingrid Sischy and Germano Celant (who were also the two organizers, it's worth noting, of the recent Art and Fashion extravaganza, *Il Tempo e la Moda*, which formed the centrepiece of the newly launched Florence Biennale in 2000). In what now seems virtually like a manifesto, they wrote as follows:

> In the specialized realm of art a distinction was always made: art that is autonomous and for the indoctrinated [*sic*!] was opposed to art that is applied and for the masses. A reciprocal hierarchical order was established based on this opposition between serious and frivolous, high and low, pure and impure. These distinctions were determined by a dialectic between aesthetic and utilitarian values, between the unique and the multiple, between the useless and useful, between elite and vulgar. More than any other ism, Pop broke down the antagonisms and the illusions of such distinctions (which were the products of the marketplace as much as of ideology) …. The offspring of this relationship between the avant-garde and mass culture is an artistic pantheism affecting all aspects of the merchandizing of culture and the culturalizing of merchandise. Art becomes capable of appearing anywhere, not necessarily where one expects it, and of crossing over and occupying spaces in all systems.

I have quoted from this editorial at some length both because it marks a crucial turning point in the relationship between art and fashion, but also because it spells out an agenda for the incorporation of both art and fashion as allied sectors of 'the society of the spectacle'. In another way, it heralds the appearance of what is now called 'clothes art', the use of garments in installation pieces, either as designed or as found objects. At the same time, it encourages fashion designers to see themselves as potentially artists, moving across the frontiers into another area, more prestigious in cultural terms, less industrialized in institutional terms. Miyake was cast as standard-bearer for this new aesthetic/commercial age of crossover. In fact, from an artistic point of view, Clothes Art has developed by leaps and bounds since 1992. Retrospectively, perhaps, we can see Clothes Art beginning even earlier, in the 1950s or 1960s, with work like Tanaka Atsuko's extraordinary *Electric Dress* from 1956 or Nakanishi Natsukuyli's *Clothespins Assert Churning Action* from 1963, works for which performance functioned as an interface between art and clothes design. Performance played a similar role in Brazil, during the '60s, with

Helio Oiticica's capes or *'Parangolé'* and Lygia Clark's *Clothing–Body–Clothing* pieces. Perhaps Joseph Beuys's 1970 *Felt Suit* might fall into the same category, if you look at it as a performance element rather than a multiple for sale.

More recently, the falling-away of performance as an interface has led to the use of clothes in static, quasi-sculptural art-works such as Jana Sterbak's elision of the skin in pieces which fuse clothing with meat, or Gotscho's bodiless tableaux in which only the phantom forms of clothes remain. Rosemaries Trockel uses misconstructed knitwear; Beverly Semmes designs clothes with metaphoric meanings (as frozen waterfalls, as soft columns); Aganetha Dyck has used bees to create wax gowns, shoes and coats for her installation, *Extended Wedding Party*. From the other side, fashion designers have begun to move into the arena of Clothes Art. The first, I think, was Lun*nah Menoh, a Japanese couturier trained in New York, collected in the V&A as a designer (a garment covered with words) and then moving over into the art world, while retaining the exhibition format of runway shows, with a video as the permanent record and individual garments as art-objects. More recently Martin Margiela worked with a microbiologist to create a show in Rotterdam, based on the accumulation of mould on a succession of fashion garments, and Helen Storey, a designer in London, collaborated with her sister, a scientist, to design an extraordinary 'fashion collection chronicling human embryonic development', exhibited at the Institute of Contemporary Arts—a project uncannily reminiscent of Kiki Smith's *Endocrinology*, also produced the same year.

So which is it to be? Friend or enemy? I'll be brief. The answer, surely, is that the current convergence of experimental fashion with Clothes Art, the current swing of the pendulum, has created the exciting possibility of the demarcation of a new hybrid area of art/fashion, as the threads between art and fashion design tighten again, along the lines *ArtForum* had envisaged. On the other hand, the assimilation of art and fashion together into the global society of the spectacle can only cause alarm, as art-forms begin to lose not simply their formal autonomy but also their long-established distance from commercial imperatives, blended now into an ongoing, overwhelming and undifferentiated media extravaganza, driven by sponsorship, publicity and marketing. We are far away from the

Wiener Werkstatte, Martine or Omega today. From the first contacts between Klimt and Floge, between Poiret, Bakst and Matisse, we have finally arrived at a junction-point which offers us, perhaps, modest possibilities but massive perils. The possibilities are artistic, in the realm of the aesthetic, but the perils, there is no doubt, are institutional and ethical. As always, we are left, in the end, with an all-too-familiar political dilemma: how to take advantage of a new opportunity, without being simultaneously overwhelmed by it—how to question and criticize a cultural–commercial system which threatens to engulf us.

13

THE MYTH OF THE WEST

I want to begin, unexpectedly perhaps, with Mabel Dodge. Up until 1912, Mabel Dodge had been living with her wealthy husband in Florence, Italy, but that year she returned home to New York, partly because her son was now old enough to enter prep school, partly because she was finding Florence 'aesthetically and emotionally bankrupt'. In his book, *New York 1913*, Martin Green has described in detail the artistic and political salon which Mabel Dodge masterminded after her return, a salon whose habitués played crucial roles not only in the Armory Show but also in the Paterson Strike Pageant, a demonstration of support for the mill-workers of Paterson, under the leadership of the IWW (Industrial Workers of the World)—better known as the Wobblies. The Wobblies had originated out West, where they had organized, as best they could, a largely nomadic workforce of sailors, harvesters, loggers and miners that drifted from job to job and from town to town, a kind of hobo proletariat, who self-consciously lived the 'myth of the West', although they are largely absent, of course, from its mediated representation in literature, cinema and art.

Ralph Chaplin, the composer of *Solidarity Forever*, bard of the IWW, used to recall the stories his father told him as a boy—tales of wild horses, Indian raids and the frontier characters of Kansas. The world of the Wobblies was fundamentally a male world—more precisely, a young man's world—a world in which thousands of young men had travelled out West and thrown themselves there into living the political ideals of

Marx and Paine, into reading Jack London's *Iron Heel* but also Frederick Jackson Turner's histories of the West and the frontier—in Martin Green's words 'a love of the West was as dominant a passion in the IWW as a hatred of capitalism'. Turner's ideas about the frontier were important to the Wobblies for a number of reasons. First and foremost, as Green notes, 'they were empowered by the myth of moving west whenever city life became oppressive, of starting again in the infinite spaces where a man had to deal with nature, not with society'. In other words, nature was socialist rather than capitalist in its essence.

In actual fact, 'for every factory hand who had turned farmer between 1860 and 1890, there were twenty farmers who had gone into the factory'. (Renshaw, *The Wobblies*, 1967.) The Wobblies, however, were mostly itinerants, attracted by a vision of freedom—freedom to move on, to look for a new opportunity, however transient it might turn out to be. They saw themselves, in the words of Fred Thompson, editor of the Wobbly newspaper, as fundamentally footloose: 'I think they shunned stereotype in all things. Their frontier was a psychological fact—a rather deliberate avoidance of certain conventions, a break with the bondage of the past. Yet ... individuality and solidarity or sense of community flourished here together, and with a radical social philosophy.' Big Bill Haywood, the Wobbly leader, was unusual in being born in the West, in Salt Lake City. He wore a Stetson and spoke with a Western drawl and loved cowboy stories. In his autobiography Haywood told the tale of a faro table in Tuscalora, with eight men and one woman, each of whom had killed at least one man. He himself was a quick hand with a gun. As Green notes, 'Haywood's west was the site of mining, not ranching, but he tried his hand at being both a cowboy and a homesteader.' Haywood even organized a 'Bronco Busters and Range Riders' union, although apparently it didn't last very long.

Bill Haywood's father was a Pony Express rider, his mother an immigrant from South Africa. After their marriage broke up, he went with his mother to Ophir, Utah, a mining camp where the mines produced copper, gold, lead and zinc. He took his first job at the age of nine, going down the mine in Ophir. By that time the mines were more or less worked out—2,500 workings had shrunk down to 150. In one of the two or three streets remaining in Ophir, Haywood saw the shootout in which Slippery Dick killed Marny Mills and walked away. Soon afterwards, he went down to Nevada and took a job in the mines there. Haywood, however, was not a typical miner. His stepfather had introduced him to Voltaire and Byron, Burns and Milton. He played chess and, like Doc Holliday in *My Darling Clementine*, he liked to recite Shakespeare. He took the Indians' side, remarking that the massacre of Indians 'began when the earliest settlers stole Manhattan Island [right here]. It continued across the continent. The ruling class with glass beads, bad whisky, Bibles and rifles continued the massacre from Astor Place to Astoria.'

By 1913 Haywood was in New York himself, where he met the journalist Hutchins Hapgood, who brought him to Mabel Dodge's salon. Martin Green describes the scene at 23 Fifth Avenue in vivid terms:

> Her bedroom was draped in white Chinese silk and embroidered Chinese shawls, bought from smugglers on the beach at Biarritz during her second honeymoon. In the front room there was a bearskin rug in front of a white marble fireplace; there was old gray French furniture and chaises longues, old coloured glass, and a Venetian chandelier in pastel shades. When at midnight food was served, that too seems to have been often white or pastel: turkey, ham, white Gorgonzola, with hundreds of cigarettes and bottles of kümmel in the shape of Russian bears.

In Carl Van Vechten's novel, *Peter Whiffle*, there is a description of Bill Haywood's effect on Mrs Dodge's salon—Edith Dale's in the fiction— 'The tremendous presence of the one-eyed giant filled the room .... Debutantes knelt on the floor beside him.' To be taken with a pinch of salt, perhaps, but indicative of the power that radiated from the miner, gambler and Wobbly leader, who had seen the inside of at least three jails, surrounded now by artists and intellectuals. There, in Mabel Dodge's salon, they talked about both revolution and art.

As well as Big Bill Haywood, her guests included many artists: Andrew Dasburg, Marsden Hartley, Max Weber. An old friend of Gertrude Stein, Mabel Dodge was committed to modernism (Stein had even written a portrait of her—*Mabel Dodge at the Villa Curonia*). It was from the circles of Stein and Dodge that the impetus behind the Armory Show first came, though the task of organization fell to the Association of American Painters and Sculptors, who then named Mabel Dodge as one of the show's two Vice-Presidents and as writer of an introductory essay to the catalogue. However, not long after the conclusion of the show—and the conclusion of the pageant produced by the IWW in support of the Paterson strike—Mabel Dodge decided to leave New York. In 1916, she moved out of her Fifth Avenue house and re-located to the Hudson Valley—to Croton on Hudson, where she had found a temporary home for the Isadora Duncan dance company. Among her many house-guests was the painter Maurice Sterne, who had been one of the Steins' circle in Paris and whom, despite the failure of her two previous marriages and her Freud-based theories of feminism, she decided to marry in August 1917.

Immediately after the marriage, in a typical gesture, Mabel Dodge sent her new husband off to Wyoming to paint the landscape. A few weeks later, he left Wyoming and moved down to Taos in New Mexico, where he was finally joined by Mabel Dodge. Artists were already painting in Taos—in fact, it had been 'discovered' for painters, as Green points out, as long ago as 1898, by Bert Phillips and Ernest Blumenschein, although, as Green also notes, 'they were traditionalists in art. It was Mabel Dodge who brought the modernists there.' Soon, Mabel Dodge and Maurice Sterne were joined by other protégés—Andrew Dasburg and Robert Edmond Jones, who became famous as a successful stage designer. Later came John Marin, Stuart Davis (whose stay didn't last very long), Georgia O'Keefe and Paul Strand, as well as writers such as D. H. Lawrence and Robinson Jeffers. For Mabel Dodge, Taos was essentially an 'Indian place'—as Martin Green notes, 'its connections with Kit Carson, for instance, were of no interest to her'. For Mabel Dodge, the relevant myth was that of the Indian and a primeval American culture, a native and non-Cartesian culture, based on community and a reverence for nature and the earth. John Sloan summed this up when he wrote that the paintings of American Indians were 'evidently inspired by a consciousness of life, plus a thing we have not got—a great tradition'.

This tradition was essentially a landscape tradition, as interpreted by the Taos group of painters. As John Marin put it, 'the artist must from time to time renew his acquaintance with the elemental big forms which "have everything": sky, sea, mountain, plain'. Essentially, this group of modernists continued the landscape tradition which had long inspired Western painters, transposing ideas of the sublime into a more abstract or even, as in the work of O'Keefe, erotic register. Later, when Max Ernst arrived as a refugee from the Second World War and moved to Arizona, to Sedona, he brought a surrealist vision with him—the surrealists had long been interested in Native American culture, as demonstrated by André Breton's collection of Native American masks or Wolfgang Paalen's expedition to the totem poles of the Skeena valley. In fact, native American art was to re-surface as a key influence in the 1940s—on the Gallery Neuf group, on 'Indian Space Painters' such as Steve Wheeler or Peter Busa, but also, I might add, on Busa's friend, Jackson Pollock.

Western art had always been landscape oriented. Its roots were in early nineteenth-century paintings of Indian life—George Catlin's portraits and his quasi-ethnographic scenes of village life, as well as paintings of buffalo hunting, bronco riding or throwing the lasso—soon to be followed by paintings of human figures set in a vast landscape—Native Americans or perhaps trappers, riding on horseback or in canoes, set in scenes of natural beauty, with luxuriant forests or craggy mountains. In time, the human figures were left out and artists like Albert Bierstedt or James Madison Alden painted pure landscapes, often scenes of great grandeur—mountains viewed across a glistening lake or the giant waterfalls of Yosemite. Then, towards the end of the century, energetic foreground action within the landscape began to return, as in William Ranney's *Hunting Wild Horses* (with a lariat) of 1846, Alfred Jacob Miller's *Buffalo Hunt* of around 1850 or James Walker's painting of *Vaqueros at the Roundup*. The buffalo hunt painting became almost a genre in its own right, although it was not until the end of the century, in Charles Russell's paintings, that the Indian War Party became a subject and we see buffalo being shot rather than speared. Finally, in Frederic Remington's work we see Native Americans attacking a wagon train or scenes of urban slaughter, as in *The Misdeal, Barroom Scene*, with its dead and dying sprawled across the floor, amidst toppled chairs, dislodged hats and fallen guns.

By that time, of course, the Wild West show had already established an image of the West as the site of danger, brutality and vigorous action. As Paul Reddin has noted, the roots of the Wild West show can be traced back to George Catlin's exhibitions of his paintings in 1836—for which, of course, he charged entrance fees—as well as his lectures, for which he used the paintings as illustrative material. It was not long before he brought live Indians along with him, in ethnographic displays, playing their musical instruments and performing dances for the audience. Soon afterwards he assembled an entire troupe of Ojibway dancers, soon to be replaced by an Iowa troupe who erected wigwams, demonstrated the game of lacrosse and performed scalp dances, complete with tomahawks and 'real and genuine scalps'. On tour in England, Catlin eventually introduced horses and feats of horsemanship into his show—the first of these outdoor performances took place in 1844 at Lord's Cricket Ground, then as now the headquarters of England's national sport.

Just two years later Catlin ended his career as a showman and returned to his painting, after six of the Iowa contracted smallpox and died in Brussels, a city to which Catlin had been invited by the King of Belgium, following his success with the King of France. Catlin was shattered by the deaths and, to his credit, made every effort to protect Indians from any further danger, campaigning against the prospect of sending any future shows to Europe. Nonetheless, Catlin had set in motion a process that was by now unstoppable. As it happened, Buffalo Bill Cody was born near Leclair, Iowa, in February 1846. It was Cody who would develop Catlin's concept of the Wild West show, but featuring the Indians as the enemy rather than the stars of the show. As Reddin put it, 'For Catlin, Native Americans became heroic and the Westward expansion of the United States was "a headlong stampedo of half-crazy adventurers". For his part Cody would identify closely with frontiersmen who fought against Indians and cleared the way for settlement.' Catlin exploited his Indian employees, but did so somehow out of a wish to educate the world about Native American culture. Cody simply exploited them and despised them.

The scalping in Cody's Wild West show was carried out by Cody himself, dressed up in vaquero costume while killing and scalping Yellow Hand, a *coup de théatre* based on Cody's actual scalping of an Indian soon after General Custer's defeat at the Little Big Horn. Encountering a group of Cheyenne, Cody shot their leader and then, according to his own account, stabbed him to the heart, jerked his war-bonnet off and scalped him, all within five seconds. He then brandished the scalp in the air, shouting 'The first scalp for Custer!' Cody began his career exhibiting the scalp. Then he moved on to theatrical performance, re-enacting the event in a play he had written himself, *The Red Right Hand*, finally using the re-enactment to launch his first Wild West show, which opened at the fairgrounds in Omaha on 17 May 1883. After exhibitions of riding, shooting and roping came the re-enactment of a 'Startling and Soul-Stirring Attack upon the Deadwood Mail Coach'. Cody's formula mingled spectacle with melodrama, combined to provide the public with a patriotic and triumphant celebration of America's violent westward expansion. As Reddin put it, 'the show wrote frontier history in blood'. Cody presented his public with an amalgam of horsemanship, marksmanship, animal exhibitions, variety acts and acts that depicted the one-sided conflict between frontiersmen and Plains Indians—encounters from which the white frontiersmen, of course, always emerged victorious. Eventually the Wild West show faded away, to be replaced by the rodeo, a development of one aspect of the show—feats of horsemanship, with titles like 'Bucking Bronco', 'Bucking Steer', 'Steer Riding' and 'A Bucking Mustang'—as rodeo developed into a competitive sporting contest rather than a dramatized demonstration. The real impact of the Wild West Show, however, was to be found in its effect on the new art of cinema, with its continuing celebration of westward expansion. Buffalo Bill's last show took place in 1913, after the aging Cody had been bamboozled into signing his property rights away. After the intervention of law enforcement officers, Cody was forced to appear in a rival circus until it collapsed, whereupon all its effects were auctioned off to the Miller Brothers' 101 Ranch Wild West show. Cody worked for the 101 Ranch show for less than a year, finally dying at his daughter's home in Denver, in January 1917.

    By then the baton had already been passed to the film industry. The key figure was Tom Mix, born in Driftwood, Pennsylvania in 1880. As a youngster he was carried away by the Wild West Show, inspired by Buffalo Bill to practise bareback riding on the horses his father used to haul logs to the family saw-mills. Eventually, after a spell in the military, he left home to seek his fortune in the Wild West. Settled in Oklahoma, he hung out at the 101 ranch, swaggering and spinning yarns, eventually finding work in the Miller Brothers' show as the rustler who is dragged to his death behind a galloping horse. Mix was proud of what he did, asserting that 'these ranch shows are just as important as cleaning up a band of rustlers. The old ways are going fast. We've got to keep on showing people what they were.' He appointed himself keeper of the memory of the old West's heroic past, finally quitting the 101 Ranch to start a show of his own, with all the standard features of the genre—a battle with Indians, an attack on a stagecoach, bulldogging, jousting—until his big break came and the Selig Film Company hired him as stock handler for a film they were shooting, *Ranch Life in the Great Southwest*. Mix wheedled his way into performing for them as a bronco-buster and soon became a regular, moving on to Hollywood in 1911.

Mix was able to exploit his Wild West skills in the new world of movies—marksmanship, athleticism, being dragged by a horse with his foot caught in the stirrup. He soon overtook such stars as Bronco Billy Anderson, who had got an early start in Porter's *The Great Train Robbery*. In 1917 Mix joined the Fox studio and began his spectacular rise to fame. In the 1920s, when post-war disenchantment coincided with the shock of the 'jazz age', Mix saw the appeal that the Western might have as a vehicle for reassurance and nostalgia. Moreover, he was 'a wonderfully malleable man', as Reddin phrases it, equipped with a stock of tall tales and a crew of press agents. He refashioned his life story, acquiring a new birthplace (El Paso, Texas, instead of Driftwood, Pensylvania), a father who served in the US cavalry and, of course, Cherokee blood. He claimed that his childhood was spent growing up with cowboys, that he had attended military academy, fought in a series of wars—Mexico, the Philippines, China, South Africa— and served as a Rough Rider in Cuba with Teddy Roosevelt. He said he had been a Texas Ranger, a cowboy, a deputy US marshal and a fearless sheriff who arrested 113 ne'er-do-wells in one fell swoop.

Mix's movies followed a simple formula—'I ride into a place owning my horse, saddle and bridle. It isn't my quarrel, but I get into trouble doing the right thing for somebody else. When it's all ironed out, I never get any money reward. I may be made foreman of the ranch and I get the girl, but there is never a fervid love scene.' Or as his new Hollywood wife put it, somewhat sardonically—'[His films] consisted of plenty of action, a simple plot, a very white hero, an impossibly incorrigible villain, a number of dangerous schemes to be foiled, and a helpless heroine to be rescued at the last moment.' While these two versions are not exactly the same, they fit within the same general scheme, one in which Mix righted wrongs single-handed, yet never got any financial reward, becoming involved simply because of his innate sense of justice. He did the right thing because, after all, he knew it was the right thing to do. He also had a winning manner, a sense of humour and a glamorous repertoire of cowboy skills. Indians were still seen as savages, but they were not central to Mix's view of the West. After a century of harassment and genocide, the relatively few Indians who remained were no longer considered threatening and were replaced as villains by local bullies, corrupt bosses and blood-sucking creditors.

Another type of Western film, however, was soon to appear, one that eventually replaced the old Tom Mix formula. The new epoch began with a trilogy of films that showed much greater ambition—James Cruze's *Covered Wagon* (1923), John Ford's *The Iron Horse* (1924) and Raoul Walsh's *The Big Trail* (1930). *The Big Trail* was John Wayne's first major film, but his career as a whole was dominated by work for John Ford, in a sequence of films that began with Ford's classic *Stagecoach*, released in 1939. Ford had been in the industry since before the First World War, starting out as an extra and a stuntman in films made by his brother Frank, mostly Westerns. It was not until 1917 that he got director credit. In the 1920s he made a series of formula Westerns as his brother had done, including Tom Mix vehicles, but none of these films were considered seriously. His reputation before *Stagecoach* depended on the dramatic films he made during the 1930s, films like *The Informer* and *The Plough and the Stars*. As Garry Wills points out, the reputation of *Stagecoach* as a seminal Western was constructed retrospectively in the light of Ford's subsequent post-war career as a specialist in Westerns. Stagecoach then became seen as the first true Ford Western, the first to feature not only John Wayne, but also the sweeping landscape of Monument Valley, in Northwest Arizona.

When Ford first approached him to play the Ringo Kid in *Stagecoach*, Wayne saw it as a minor role. The leads were the talkative characters in the stagecoach, not the Kid, who was a stock Western character with little dialogue. Ford, however, had much higher ambitions—basically he wanted to remake Maupassant's *Boule de Suif* as a Western, bringing together the workaday genre in which he began his career with the respected drama that had crowned it, mixing Hollywood saddle tramps with seasoned character actors. Wayne, it goes without saying, was a saddle tramp. Wills compares the film to *The Lady Vanishes* or *Grand Hotel* or *Rules of the Game*, films whose characters are isolated as passengers in a train or guests in a hotel or country house. It is a film about class and how the wealthiest member of the group—the banker—is arrested and comes out worst, while Wayne as the Kid, a wronged man bent on revenge, comes out best and then leaves with the other outcast, the saddle-tramp with the prostitute. Thus the social scale within the Western is turned upside down. Elitism is trashed, egalitarianism is rewarded.

The Western setting—the landscape of Monument Valley which subsequently became the signature landscape of a John Ford Western—functions both as a stupendous backdrop to the foreground action, as in so many nineteenth-century paintings, but also as a zone of danger, a device for isolating the characters in the stagecoach and then submitting them to a series of tests, both moral and physical. The Western becomes the site of allegory—an allegory which reveals the discrepancy between the social and the ethical hierarchy, ethics perceived in terms of depth of character rather than the observation of a conventional code. In this context the Ringo Kid, like the Indians, is almost a part of the landscape, as well as acting within it. He belongs in the landscape rather than in the town—in fact, the town of Lordsburg to which the coach is travelling is a threat to the Kid, rather than a refuge, a haven of civilization. The landscape, of course, stands for 'nature' rather than 'culture', for values which are somehow innate rather than acquired, for a deeply felt sense of the right course of action, which is dependent on an inner light, a natural gift, rather than on a superficial, surface respect for the law as a social artefact. The little microcosm in the stagecoach is saved not by its law-abiding members, but by its outcasts.

A few words more about Monument Valley (talkativeness, of course, is not a Western virtue, as I am all too well aware). Ed Buscombe, in his essay 'Inventing Monument Valley: Nineteenth-Century Landscape Photography and the Western Film', notes that the first film to feature the landscape of the West was Selig's *Western Justice*, made in Colorado in 1907 and advertised in the press as set 'in the wildest and most beautiful scenery of the Western country'. He goes on to point out that genuine Western scenery rapidly became a *sine qua non* of the Western and was a principal factor in preventing other countries from making Westerns, until the belated appearance of the Italian Western, shot on location in the south of Spain. Buscombe also notes that Albert Bierstadt, perhaps the most successful of nineteenth-century Western landscape painters, actually regarded the mountainous scenes in which he specialized as similar to the Swiss Alps, and therefore suitable for a style of painting derived from German romanticism. Bierstadt also painted Yosemite, which was declared a preserve by President Lincoln as early as 1864. Shortly after this the photographers arrived and, following them, of course, came the film-makers.

Yet, as Buscombe points out, 'today when we think of the West and Westerns, it's not mountains, trees and lakes that first come to mind, but more often the deserts and canyon lands of Arizona and Utah. Since the 1860s the centre of gravity of the Western landscape has moved to the Southwest'—although, as Buscombe also points out, the director Anthony Mann went against the trend, saying, 'I have never understood why people make almost all Westerns in desert country. John Ford, for examples, adores Monument Valley, but Monument Valley, which I know well, is not the whole of the west. In fact, the desert represents only a part of the American west.' In a French study, *Géographies du Western*, a detailed map shows how the vast majority of Westerns are set in the Southwest (principally Texas, Arizona and New Mexico) although most of them were actually shot in just three states—Utah, Arizona and California—even when they represented Montana, Wyoming or Kentucky. Buscombe argues that a principal reason for this preference was the pre-eminence given to the Grand Canyon as a symbolic site. By 1899 Baedeker's guide to the United States included a map and instructions on how to get to the canyon by stagecoach. A few years later, the Santa Fe railroad built a spur to provide access by train.

Ed Buscombe also wonders whether the stories of Zane Grey, by far the most successful Western author in the first part of the century, were not instrumental in privileging landscapes of mesas and desert above those of mountains and forests. (Zane Grey's first best-seller was actually *The Heritage of the Desert*, written after a trip to Arizona and the Grand Canyon.) In 1913 Zane Grey visited Monument Valley and then wrote about it in *Tales of Lonely Trails*. As Buscombe points out, these stories, set in the desert, privilege stoicism in the face of the wilderness over the comfort and 'softness' of civilization, a preference clearly shared by Ford's *Stagecoach*. The appeal of the Southwest was based not simply on a preference for nature over culture, but also, more specifically, for the distance it provided from urban life and even from the farm community—it was attractive precisely because of its inhumanity, which automatically conferred a heroic quality on those who ventured into it and survived. The desert is also, as Michael Budd has noted, a zone of extreme contrast between light and shadow. Garry Wills notes that in *Stagecoach*, 'shadows and sources of light [actually] reconfigure human relationships'.

In his classic study of the Western film, *The Six-Gun Mystique*, John Cawelti stresses the role played by geography in the Western. Primarily, of course, he considers the role played conceptually by the frontier, traditionally the geographical meeting point of civilization with savagery and lawlessness. Most Westerns, however, seem to be set in the latter part of the nineteenth century, at a time when the battle over the doomed Indians had been more or less won and the United States had completed its triumphant and murderous march to the Pacific (and indeed beyond). Lawlessness was already in decline—the Indian as nomad was vanishing, the forces of social order had gained the upper hand. It is precisely for this reason, Cawelti suggests, that the landscape itself became such a central feature of the genre, a landscape whose principal characteristics are 'those of its openness, its aridity and general inhospitability to human life, its great extremes of light and climate, and, paradoxically, its grandeur and beauty'. These visual images of landscape, he explains, themselves exemplify the grand thematic conflict between civilization and savagery and its final resolution. The Western—as in *Stagecoach*—presents a world in which an isolated town, ranch or fort is surrounded by prairie or desert, linked to the rest of the civilized world only by train, stagecoach or a simple trail. While we can see the town as the advance-guard of an oncoming civilization, we also sense that it could be swept back into the desert. Yet, while the desert is inhospitable, its expanse and grandeur suggest that it is not simply the site of lawlessness but also a source of natural power, the 'sublime'.

The people in this landscape, Cawelti proposes, can be divided into three categories: the townspeople, who are static and defensive in their settlement; the outlaws or Indians, who are mobile and potentially aggressive, and the hero—a sheriff, perhaps, in the town; a cavalry officer, perhaps, in the desert; a hero as mobile as the outlaws, with much the same skills, yet differentiated from them by his moral character. The landscape, in its grandeur, helps us to characterize him as an epic hero. Monument Valley, for instance, embodies its own complex mixture of epic grandeur and savage hostility, which serve as metaphors for the encounter between the values of hero and outlaw. Yet in *Stagecoach*, paradoxically, it is the heroism of the two outcasts, an outlaw and a prostitute, which is contrasted with the shameful conduct of respectable townsfolk, over-eager to reach safety in the next town.

Artists, of course, have often identified with the figure of the outcast who is redeemed as a hero, in the face of rejection by respectable people. In this context, with the myth of the West in mind, it is worth making a detour in order to look at the life of Jackson Pollock, whose family moved to California when he was a teenager. Pollock was born in Cody, Wyoming in 1912, in the Big Horn Basin. In the centre of town stood the Irma Hotel, an impressive sandstone structure erected by Buffalo Bill Cody himself. The carved cherrywood bar, it seems, had been sent by Queen Victoria as a gift to her favourite cowboy. The year Pollock was born, *The Great Train Robbery* played in the local moviehouse, as Steven Naifeh and Gregory White Smith reveal in their exhaustive biography of Pollock. Pollock's father soon became a sheep ranch foreman, working up in the Big Horn mountains. This was where Pollock's elder brothers heard Rattlesnake Pete tell his stories of life on the range, stories Pollock himself would later echo as he span his own tales of the West, put on his Western boots and painted Western scenes with covered wagons and cowboys too. Not long afterwards, the Pollock family left the ranch and set off for Arizona, where they stayed five years, farming. Next, in 1917, came Chico, California—a gold rush town—followed by Janesville in the foothills of the Sierra Nevada, where the teenage Jackson hung out at the Diamond Mountain Inn, built in 1872 as a stage-coach stop on the road between Susanville and Reno. There Pollock followed the Wadatkut Indians out to their burial grounds and listened to their chants. After a series of other moves and more time spent in Phoenix, Jackson ended up living on the Carr Ranch in the south-east of Arizona, on the slopes of

Aztec Peak where his mother ran the kitchen in the big boarding house, where the fiddlers played for the cowboys on Saturday nights, and the young Apache girls from the reservation waited on tables.

It was in 1926, some time after the family had moved to Riverside, Los Angeles, that Pollock set out with Sande, his brother, and their friend, Roy Cooter, on a return trip back to Arizona, where they chanced upon a 'cowboy-turned-roadworker' called 'Red', who took them mustang-hunting. Naifeh and Smith describe the sequence of events as follows:

> With 'Red' as guide, the boys drove back across the plateau, out of the forest and into the hot sagebrush flats around Fredonia. Around noon, at Cain Springs, they turned off the road and headed west across the dry, rough ground ... By sundown they found a suitable campsite at a watering hole, where they built a fire and slept round it on the ground .... At first light, before the horses arrived, [they moved] to the narrow draw that served as a gateway to the watering hole. From there, Red figured, the shooting would be best. Before they could reach their positions, however, they heard the rustle of horses' hooves echoing from deep within the canyon. 'We were just a little late getting there', Cooter recalled, 'so Red says to get down and be real quiet or the horses might see us and get scared away.' On their knees, they crawled the final few feet into position as the tight knot of horses appeared in the draw and moved nervously toward the watering hole, just a few dozen yards away. 'They had long manes hanging way down', Cooter remembered, 'and tails that hit the ground. They were beautiful animals and they shook their long manes'. Then the shooting began. At the first thunderlike volley, the herd exploded. A few horses fell almost immediately, the rest were in full gallop within seconds, stampeding through the draw .... They could hear the rumble of hooves for a long time after the last horse disappeared, leaving a thick haze of dust and three or four dark shapes on the canyon floor .... 'They were beautiful horses', Cooter recalled, 'and I can't believe we could just shoot them and walk off. But we did. And I'm ashamed of it to this day.

Seventeen years later, in 1943, Pollock was in New York where his patron, Peggy Guggenheim, commissioned him to paint a mural on canvas. Pollock was unsure how to approach the project, and the day before the final deadline he had hardly even begun work on it. Then, Pollock told a friend, 'I had a vision. It was a stampede.' In fact, he was back there in the canyon in Arizona. 'Cows and horses and antelopes and buffalo. Everything is charging across that goddam surface ... every animal in the American West.' Fifteen hours later, at nine the next morning, the mural was finished, the black outlines filled in with white and then splattered over with colours, and Pollock was on his way to becoming America's most famous painter. Pollock, I might add, had already painted works that were influenced by his viewing of Navajo sand paintings, Tlingit and Tsimshian paintings on hide and Haida totem poles. The slaughter of the mustangs must surely have recalled to him the slaughter of the Indians, so central to the history of the West.

Pollock was well aware of the celebration of Native American art and culture in the work of the Mexican muralists—Siqueiros especially. In fact, like Siqueiros, Pollock too, we might say, tried to combine the gun-slinging cowboy and the noble Indian in his own self-image as an artist. On the one hand, his biography contains no less than eighteen entries under *Cowboy, image of.* On the other hand, Pollock was one of a group of American artists of his generation influenced by Native Americans, both for political and artistic reasons, impressed by the analogies that were made between northwest coast art and certain aspects of cubism, as well as the surrealists' fascination with Native American art. In 1946, Howard Daum celebrated the work of Steve Wheeler, Robert Barrell and Pollock's old friend, Peter Busa, under the name of the 'Indian Space' movement, and organized an exhibition in New York titled *8 and a Totem Pole.* Barrell actually carved a totem pole for the exhibition, entitled *Bird Feeding Young.* The whole group were influenced by the collection of Native American Art on display in the Museum of Natural History, and Barrell was an enthusiastic student of work illustrated in the *Annual Reports* of the Bureau of American Ethnology (copies of which Pollock also owned and treasured, keeping them under his bed). Pollock's friend Peter Busa had studied Boas's book, *Primitive Art,* and many of the Indian Space painters used the flowing black line, typical of northwest coast art, to integrate paintings otherwise influenced by the flat space of cubism.

As for cowboys in art, we can find them in the work of Manny Farber, an artist best known as a film critic—one who was especially fond of

Westerns, maybe because he was born in Douglas, Arizona, a township he evoked in his 1947 work, *Birthplace*, a painting dominated by railroad tracks and a broken line of eight cowboys and a mule. Later Farber celebrated, in paintings, the Westerns of Anthony Mann, Budd Boetticher, Sam Peckinpah and, indirectly, Howard Hawks—in *A Dandy's Gesture*. Ronald Kitaj has paid a moving tribute to John Ford, in a painting which shows the great director on his deathbed, saluted by an obstreperous but humble character from his Westerns, Sergeant Quincannon of the US Cavalry. Nonetheless, it is Pollock who comes to mind when I think of the myth of the west in the context of painting. In 1949 Pollock even told the architect Tony Smith that collectors out West would better appreciate the scale of the murals he wanted to paint.

Whitney Darrow has recalled taking a trip out across the deserts of Arizona and New Mexico with Jackson Pollock, back in 1932, through landscapes in which, as Darrow put it, 'you could tell Jackson was in his element'. After a night spent sleeping out in the desert, he would lean back in the car, his cowboy boots up on the dashboard, and play his mouth-harp 'until the coyotes complained'. (Pollock had begun to play the mouth-harp at the Benton's musicales back in New York, which featured a medley of hillbilly ballads and country blues.) Back in 1910, John Lomax had published his collection of *Cowboy Songs*, writing in the introduction that 'They loved roaming; they loved freedom; they were pioneers by instinct; an impulse set their faces from the east, put a tang for roaming in their veins and sent them ever westward.' By the 1920s singing cowboys were performing on stage and radio. In the 1930s Tex Ritter and John White, the 'Lonesome Cowboy', became national stars singing cowboy numbers on radio. Soon cowboys (or pseudo-cowboys) were singing on screen. One of the first was none other than John Wayne, who made a series of eight films for Monogram's Lone Star Productions, in which he played the cowboy part of 'Singin' Sandy', singing as many as four songs per picture.

Wayne, however, was unhappy in the role of singer, and in 1935 he confronted the head of the studio (Monogram had now merged with Republic) and told him he was refusing to sing any more, explaining, supposedly, 'I've had it. I'm a goddamned action star, you son-of-a-bitch. I'm not a singer. Get yourself another cowboy singer.' That is just what

Republic did. After a lengthy search, they chose Gene Autry, the one candidate who could both sing and ride. Autry was brought up in West Texas and began singing to while away the lonely hours while he was a railroad telegrapher, as in Porter's film. 'Discovered' by Will Rogers he quickly became a radio star and a successful recording artist. When he replaced Wayne, Autry was cast in *Old Santa Fe* and *Tumbling Tumbleweeds*, films aimed at the juvenile market, which nonetheless launched his career and made him a film star too. Soon he was selling Gene Autry song-books by the million and marketing Gene Autry Round-Up guitars through the Sears Roebuck mail catalogue. In 1938, however, he finally asked the studio for too much money and was replaced by Roy Rogers. Nonetheless, that didn't stop him from selling no less than two million Gene Autry cap pistols in 1939.

The success of Western singers on film led to an attempt by other musicians to get on the Western bandwagon. Hillbilly singers started to put on cowboy boots and Stetson hats. It turned out that it was Western 'style' and imagery that was popular with the public, rather than Western music as such. This trend, apparently, was accelerated after 1928 when Harry Stone took over the task of auditioning and booking artists. Richard Pearson, in his book, *Creating Country Music, Fabricating Authenticity*, describes how Stone 'was more concerned with producing a popular show than with adhering to tradition' and, in practice, that meant hiring bands, many of whom were dressed in 'the newly fashionable western outfits', whatever their actual origins. The main contribution of the singing cowboy was not so much the music but, in Bill Malone's words, 'the fabric of usable symbols which surrounded him'. That is to say, as Pearson has explained, 'the ten-gallon hat, the silver-studded leather wear, the distinctive cut and decoration of clothes and boots, the six-shooter, the horse with western saddle, the impassive look, and the imperious, legs-spread wide stance'. The West had become a style commodity.

Perhaps this might be true of the art world too, just a bit! Back in 1976, for instance, the Fort Worth Art Museum in Texas mounted a show called 'The Great American Rodeo'. Most of the artists involved travelled to Fort Worth the previous year to attend the Fort Worth Fat Stock Show and Rodeo. Among the works they produced were Robert Rauschenberg's *Rodeo Palace* and Red Grooms' *Ruckus Rodeo*, strongly contrasting pieces, with the Rauschenberg rustic and enigmatic, the Grooms exuberant in its coverage of a range of rodeo spectacle, including clowns concealed in barrels and a cowboy carried off on a stretcher. While Rauschenberg, a native Texan, preferred understatement, Grooms, the outsider, clearly favoured overstatement. Taken together, their works appear as allegories of cowboy as working man and cowboy as showman. The most interesting installation, however, was made by George Green, and described as 'a combined memorial to the cowboy and shrine to the commercialization that has developed around the cowboy myth'. First, the myth of the West was a spur to America's imperial expansion, then it became a dramatization of the conflicts that ensued; finally it was transmuted into a repertory of styles and images.

Pollock, at least, had a claim to authenticity. His brothers remembered questioning their father about the letters 'IWW' which they had seen scrawled on walls, and being given a sympathetic account of the Wobblies and their struggles against exploitation. The Wobblies were a key part of his Western inheritance, actors in a drama of the West, who played their mythic role alongside the cowboys and the Indians. In his memoir, *The Living Spirit of the Wobblies*, Len De Caux describes a movement of 'footloose rebels', hobos who rode the rails in boxcars, migrant labourers looking for work in the mines, in the lumber camps, in the farms at harvest time, an itinerant way of life that came to an end with the combine harvester. In the 1930s, long before Kerouac, Pollock hitch-hiked from East to West coast and back. In a letter to his brothers, he wrote that: 'My trip was a peach. I got a number of kicks in the butt and put in jail twice with days of hunger—but what a worthwhile experience .... The country began getting interesting in Kansas—the wheat was just beginning to turn and the farmers were making preparation for harvest.'

At the same time, Indians too were important to Pollock, because of his fascination with the West, his childhood, because of his Jungian therapy—hence paintings like *The Moon Woman Cuts the Circle* or *Totem Lesson*. This was the side of Pollock that was close to Mabel Dodge—the Mabel Dodge who married a Pueblo Indian, Tony Luhan, but also fought politically for Indian rights, in New Mexico and beyond. Luhan, coincidentally, had actually performed in a Wild West show, even appearing at Coney Island. He also worked closely with the Indian rights activist John Collier, accompanying him to every *pueblo* in New Mexico to translate Collier's explanations of the Bursum bill of 1922 and the effect it would have if it became law, making it possible to deprive the Pueblo of 60,000 acres of land, much of it irrigated and cultivated. Mabel Dodge herself worked hard to build a coalition of Indian rights supporters, opposing the Bursum bill and calling for 'recognition of Indian civil rights, conservation of their lands through co-operative enterprise, preservation of their communal societies, and agricultural and industrial assistance programs sponsored by the federal government'. So the spirit of her Fifth Avenue salon survived to the end, bringing together, in spirit, both the Wobblies and the Indians—as Jackson Pollock did too, in his own confused way. One day, perhaps, the art world might build upon their example—on the tradition of Mabel Dodge and the 'Indian Space' Jackson Pollock and—I should add—the example of Jimmie Durham, an American Indian Movement veteran, and Al Clah, whose film *xyz* was the centrepiece of the Navajo film-making project.

As Garry Wills has pointed out, this series of films followed the same eight-point structure: (1) *Social diversity* of the pioneers: a spectrum of ethnic stereotypes suggesting a whole people on the move; (2) *Temporal extension*: expansion through time, symbolized by changing seasons, the sequence of life from birth to death, shifts in personal relationships. As Wills puts it, 'The message is: "Life goes on, even in these trials."'; (3) *Physical Obstacle Course*: storms, river crossings, feats of endurance; (4) *External opponents*: Indian attacks, of course, although in Walsh's film the attack is prevented rather than fought off—John Wayne's first major role, as a peaceful trapper who has learnt everything he knows from the Indians and serves as an intermediary; (5) *Internal opponents*: saboteurs who want take control of the wagon train for their own selfish reasons, thereby threatening the community as a whole; (6) *Separation of the hero from the train*: threats draw the hero away from the train, damaging community morale and spoiling his romance with the heroine; (7) *The Crisis*: morale disintegrates and members of the community begin to leave the wagon train—perhaps to seek their fortune in a gold-rush rather than persevere to the still-distant farmland that had been their original goal; (8) *The Higher Goal*: to get through to the end there has to be a deep sense of purpose. In *The Covered Wagon* it is the Mormon promise of a heavenly community. In *The Iron Horse* it is a vision of national unity, bonding East and West together, as Lincoln had bonded North and South. In *The Big Trail* it is manifest destiny, as John Wayne's character cries out in a snowstorm:

> We're blazing a trail that started in England. Not even the storms of the sea could turn back those first settlers. And they carried on further. They blazed it on through the wilderness of Kentucky. Famine, hunger, not even massacres could stop them! And now we've picked up the trail again. And nothing can stop us—not even the snows of winter, not the peaks of the highest mountain. We're building a nation!

(Walsh, it is said, made up his own script as he went along, with a writer at hand to help.)

14

THE SITUATIONISTS AND ARCHITECTURE

This is not a conventional scholarly essay. Instead I am going to write about a number of topics addressed by the situationists, making in the end a kind of collage of commentaries on what seem to me key elements of their thought in relation to architecture and the city, which were, indeed, centrally important topics for them. These elements are going to be as follows: 1. The Minaret; 2. The Gypsy Camp; 3. *Dérive*; 4. Mad King Ludwig; 5. The Postman Cheval; 6. The *Merzbau*; 7. Le Corbusier; 8. Paris; 9. Psycho-Geography; 10. Love on the Left Bank; 11. White Bicycles; 12. New Babylon; 13. The Cavern of Anti-Matter; 14. Watts; 15. The Architecture of Despair; 16. *Détournement*; 17. Vienna's Place; and finally, 18. Albisola.

I begin with the minaret. In 1948 Asger Jorn wrote an article titled 'What Is An Ornament?', which was published in an obscure Danish journal. That same year he had spent time in Djerba, Tunisia, which I believe is the same place that Paul Klee visited and which had such an influence on his calligraphic style of drawing. Among the illustrations to Jorn's essay was one juxtaposing a 'horsetail' and a minaret. The horsetail is a kind of plant, whose structure is very similar to that of the minaret depicted next to it—a kind of telescopic series of towers, each with a narrower diameter than the last, piled on top of each other, finally ending with a tiny little turret at the topmost point. The picture of the horsetail used looks as if it was one of Blossfeld's famous series of photographs of plants, but I have not been able to check this. The point Jorn wishes to make is summed up in his caption: 'Horsetail and Minaret. They resemble each other, not because the minaret is a copy of a plant but because this is the natural mode of form in matter.' Underneath, there is a similar juxtaposition of a totem pole and a chestnut branch, also lookalikes. Jorn observes that 'the nature of art is not to imitate the external forms of nature (naturalism) but to create natural art. Natural sculpture which is true to its material will be identical to nature's forms without seeking to imitate.' Architecture and sculpture, I might note, here seem to be treated as if they were more or less the same thing.

Asger Jorn had gone to Djerba in order to confirm the theories put forward by the Swedish architectural theorist Erik Lundberg. According to Jorn, writing in the late 1940s, 'Erik Lundberg seems to be the first in the civilized world, America included, who has been able to give a definition of the opposition between the classical-European and the oriental attitudes to art which is correct, true to reality, and which offers a perspective for explaining works of art and their nature.' For Jorn, the pairing of European vs Oriental, ran together with other pairings, such as Classical vs Spontaneous, Idealist vs Materialist, Apollonian vs Dionysiac, and so on, with Jorn supporting the second term throughout—oriental, spontaneous, materialist, Dionysiac, and so on. Obviously these pairings are very broad-brush in their scope, but they gave Jorn a framework for developing his ideas about art and architecture, ideas which had a big effect on situationist thought, as we shall see.

Next, the Gypsy Camp. Another early member of the situationist group, back in its Imaginist Bauhaus days, was Giuseppe Pinot Gallizio, an Italian artist. Pinot Gallizio had played an important role in his home town in northern Italy in defending the rights of gypsies to set up campsites. This defence of nomadism became an important element in situationist thought. The Belgian artist, Constant, another early situationist, designed a gypsy camp as an architectural project, creating a maquette, an architectural complex which could be taken apart, transported and re-assembled. After the Situationist International had been dissolved, Debord's partner, Alice Becker-Ho, wrote a fascinating little book on the Romany language. There is an obvious sense in which this abiding interest in nomads and gypsies could also be related to Jorn's support for the spontaneous and the Dionysiac over the classical and the Apollonian. To be fixed, to be static, is to refuse spontaneous activity, to remain, in a sense, imprisoned in a single, confining location. In fact, Constant, as we shall see, designed his city project, New Babylon, to be inhabited only by transients, rather than having a settled population. In a way, it was rather like a single, city-scale mega-hotel complex.

Now, *Dérive*. Guy Debord wrote the classic text on the 'Theory of the Dérive', usually translated 'Drift' or 'Drifting', in December 1958, in the second number of *Internationale Situationniste*. He defines it as 'a technique of transient passage through varied ambiances'. Note, again, the taste for transience and spontaneity. Debord's basic idea is that this project of wandering through the city should be determined not by any pre-conceived plan, but by the attractions or discouraging counter-attractions of the city itself. It requires a 'letting-go' of 'the usual motives for movement and action'—we might almost say, a letting-go of everyday identity. Debord seems to have been inspired in part by Chombart de Lauwe's study of *Paris and the Parisian Agglomeration*, published in 1952—particularly by its maps, which are frequently used as illustrations in the situationist journal and in Debord's own art-works. He was struck particularly by a map detailing all the movements, made over a year, by a student living in the 16th Arrondissement—'her itinerary delineates a small triangle, with no deviations, the three apexes of which are the School of Political Science, her residence and that of her piano teacher.'

Shocked by this rigid repetition of a fixed pattern of mobility, Debord conceived dérive as a way of creating completely new, unpredictable itineraries, dependent on chance and the spontaneous subjective impulses and reactions of the wanderer. The recourse to chance reminds us, unavoidably, of André Breton's doctrine of 'objective chance' and especially of his great book, *Nadja*, which traces a series of just such aimless journeys through Paris, punctuated by a pattern of attraction and repulsion to certain buildings or kinds of buildings rather than others. Debord notes that this technique of *dérive* is, in a way, only necessary because his larger project of 'psycho-geography' has not yet been sufficiently far developed. Psycho-geography would make possible the creation of maps in which particular locations or regions had already been designated as favouring the arousal of one kind of affective or aesthetic response, so that a certain amount of pre-planning could then take place. Meanwhile, chance was the best method. This text, interestingly enough, was written just as John Cage was conducting his seminars on chance procedures in New York at the School for Social Research. Probably a coincidence.

A *dérive* could take place over a few minutes or even a few days. Duration didn't matter. Taxis could be used for rapid transport outside one's usual environment. (One situationist demand was for the abolition of private cars and their replacement by fleets of low-cost taxis.) As in Breton's book, the *dérive* also implied the possibility of chance encounters, meetings with strangers. Debord even suggests that the subject of a *dérive* might be invited to visit a particular place at a particular time, with the expectation of meeting an unknown person, thus being forced to introduce himself to random passers-by in an effort to identify if they were the person he or she was looking for. This was called the technique of the 'possible rendezvous'. He also reveals a taste for wandering in uncanny locations—'slipping by night into houses due for demolition ... wandering in subterranean catacombs forbidden to the public, etc.'. Here we see the *dérive* both as a kind of dream journey, even an invitation to break tabus—or perhaps simply to enjoy what we might think of, in the architectural register, as the Gothick picturesque.

Fourth, 'Mad King Ludwig'. King Ludwig of Bavaria built the palaces at Neueschwanstein, Herenchiemsee and Linderhof, strange follies perched high in the mountains, with an architectural repertory ranging from fairy-tale turrets to the Wagnerian grotto. The Mad King's follies appealed to the situationists presumably because they defied the protocols of instrumental reason. The king built exactly what he desired, in the way he wanted it, rather as if he was engaged in a kind of constructional *dérive*. The idea of the folly seems crucial to situationist thinking on architecture, just as it was to the surrealists. In a way, though, 'folly' is slightly too weak a word, conjuring up as it does Stowe or Stourhead, monuments of the eighteenth-century picturesque. Probably a better term would be 'outsider architecture'. On the other hand, a builder like Gaudí was a professional architect, despite the idiosyncracy of his work; Niki de Saint-Phalle, who has built a series of strange houses in France and Italy, is a professional artist. Perhaps the main point is that all these buildings seem to meld sculpture with architecture and to be works of the untrammelled imagination rather than controlling reason. In the pre-situationist journal, *Potlatch*, Ludwig was invoked alongside Claude Lorrain, Piranesi and the Postman Cheval as a pioneer of psycho-geography.

Perhaps the building most mentioned was the *Palais Idéal* of the Postman Cheval, another surrealist favourite, which is to be found in a small village near Lyon. A photograph of Debord at the *Palais Idéal* can be found at the museum at Silkeborg in Denmark. Instigated by a dream, based perhaps on memories of a mock Asian palace seen at a Grand Exhibition in Paris, the *Palais Idéal* falls into the category of highly ornamented buildings approved by Jorn, with a quasi-organic feel to them, as if they had grown out of the rock rather than been carefully planned and constructed by their obsessive, artisanal creator. Moreover, there are abundant references to North African architecture—to an Arabian Mosque, an Arabian House and construction in the Egyptian style, according to Cheval himself. It is important, too, that Cheval, like Constant or Pinot Gallizio—or, indeed, Ludwig of Bavaria—was not a trained architect working to a commission, but a visionary willing to devote his life to realizing his dream. Although we might think of him as a compulsive obsessive, from another vantage point he could be described as an entirely free man, whose life outside his work as a postman was devoted to his great, imaginative project. In fact, even his hours as a postman were devoted, partially, to the task. He kept a look-out for useful chunks of rock, the soft limestone of the region, as he cycled down the country lanes with his mail-bag, stopping to place them at the side of the road to be collected later in his cart for use in the building.

Kurt Schwitters's *Merzbau* in Hannover, which I revisited a month or so ago, is, so to speak, the practising artist's version of outsider art, a single room densely packed with the signs and symbols of an intensely private imaginative world. On the other hand, it also appears orderly and sophisticated, with a clear sense of geometrical design and carefully contrived focal points for the eye. For the artists who made up the bulk of the situationist group, particularly in its early years, Schwitters was a more appropriate role model than either the crazy, authoritarian king, with his apparently unlimited resources, or the strange, unsophisticated postman, with his single compulsive life's project. Schwitters was well aware of what he was doing and why, even as he was prepared to use elements of chance or to follow a sudden impulse. The scale of his work, too, was much less grandiose, almost domestic. It's not that the situationists didn't have a megalomaniac side—it is more that their truly grand public visions, of constructing whole, new revolutionary cities, were much more ambitious than those even of outsider artists, while their private projects (films, installations, models) were actually quite feasible.

The counterpart of the situationists' praise for Schwitters can be found in their hatred of Le Corbusier and modern, rationalist architecture in general. In some sense, too, Corbusier could be seen as a rival, with his own megalomaniac city plans, devised, however, on a very different intellectual basis. The dislike for Le Corbusier can be found very early in Jorn's writings. Jorn had studied painting, as a young man, with Fernand Léger, and had actually worked, at that time, on a painting-decoration project under Le Corbusier's direction. In the words of the most acute commentator on Jorn's thinking, Graham Birtwhistle, 'These experiments made a deep impression on him, stimulating both an antipathy to the kind of theory and practice he had encountered in Paris and a lasting respect for Léger and Le Corbusier whom Jorn apparently went on to regard as the most noble of foes.' Jorn's polemic against Corbusier was mainly directed at his functionalism, his reductive vision of architecture as a means to an end, rather than an end in itself. It was precisely because he was searching for a way of mounting a critique of Corbusier, so it seems, that Jorn turned to Erik Lundquist with such interest and enthusiasm. Essentially he set himself the task, never completed, of constructing a counter-theory to that of Corbusier.

One of Debord's main arguments against capitalism was contained in his film, *Critique of Separation*, released in 1961, with its call for an attack on the totality of society, because only a total revolution could overthrow the separation of subject and object capitalism entailed. Jorn, somewhat earlier, had developed his own critique of separation, but in a different context, the critique of Corbusier:

> The logical functionalists saw a value in the division of architectural elements into supporting, isolating and enclosing elements, just as they attempted to divide the towns into districts for families with children,

districts for the elderly, for students, artists, etc. It is even claimed that it is natural, as if the functions of life allow themselves to be split off from one another. Is it for example the human skeleton which supports the muscular system? Or do the muscles support the skeleton? Is it the stalk or is it the sap which is the supporting principle in a tulip? Can a skeleton stand without muscles; can muscles hold a skeleton up without blood? Can a tulip stand up without help from its sap?

As Birtwistle observes, 'Jorn's polemical point is clear: modern design needs to learn anew the lesson of organic unity from natural, material life'. Jorn himself summed it up as follows, in another paper: 'The functionalists have defined urbanism as the creation of our framework for living. If this good idea is to be developed further we must substitute for a rationalist framework an artistic way of working, in which all branches of art co-operate in an organic "art of unity".' This, of course, was what Schwitters attempted in uniting painting, sculpture and architecture in the *Merzbau*. Looked at another way, Jorn's underlying claim was that 'the framework for living' was not one that could be imposed from outside, externally, by city planners and architects. It had to be built in co-operation with the inhabitants of the city themselves, whose free input was needed, just as the skeleton needed the muscles and the stalk the sap. In this way, a critique of Corbusier developed into a theory of 'unitary urbanism', which developed into a critique of the totality of capitalist society, which in turn led to the political doctrines of councilist democracy and workers' control which characterized the uprising of May 1968.

The focus of situationist thought, of course, was Paris. Paris was the city in which they lived, aspects of which they both loved and hated, and Paris was the city where the barricades went up in May. The situationists paradoxically combined a revolutionary concern, even a utopian concern, to create an entirely new Paris of the future, with a strong conservationist streak, endlessly condemning the destruction of old streets and protesting the bureaucratic 'modernization' of the city. For instance, the destruction of the Rue Sauvage in the 13th Arrondissement was specifically mourned in *Potlatch*. Later, the destruction of the old market area around *Les Halles*, to create a shopping centre and an art museum, was fiercely attacked by Debord. When I co-organized the situationist exhibition at the Beaubourg, Debord indicated that he would not be able to attend because he had sworn never to set foot in the building. First, it bore the hated name of Pompidou, the accursed foe of 1968, and second, it was the poisoned fruit of the destruction of the previous huddle of street and café life beloved by Debord and his comrades.

A number of areas of Paris, on the other hand, were singled out for positive attention. The 7th Arrondissement was favourably invoked—the district around and behind *Les Invalides*. The Square des Missions Etrangères, near the junction of Rue de Babylone and Boulevard Raspail, was specifically recommended; 36 Rue des Morillons was praised. This could be the abbatoir, according to my map. I have always meant to tour these, and other, situationist locations but, sadly, I have never yet done so. In fact it would be easy to carry out a situationist tour of Paris, because Debord's two folding maps of the city specifically pick out the areas worth wandering in and indicate with bright red arrows possible directions for taxi journeys between them. Areas of the city suggested for special attention and research were the Butte-aux-Cailles, near the Place d'Italie; the 'Continent of Contrescarpe', presumably the area round the Place Contrescarpe; the Morgue, Aubervilliers, just outside the city limits to the north; and the Désert de Retz. In this sense, we can see that the apparent call made by the situationists for 'total' revolution needs to be somewhat nuanced. While social relations should be totally transformed, the best of the past should be honoured and preserved. In fact, in many of Debord's texts, there is a strongly elegiac note and an intense involvement with the past—not only its struggles and failed revolutions, but also its literature and its monuments.

A brief word on psycho-geography, the field of research which guided the situationists in their appraisal of the city and its architecture. It is first introduced into situationist discourse, by Guy Debord, in the following way:

> The word *psychogeography*, suggested by an illiterate Kabyle as a general term for the phenomena a few of us were investigating around the summer of 1953, is not too inappropriate ... *Psychogeography* could set for itself the study of the precise laws and specific effects of the geographical environment, consciously organized or not, on the emotions and behaviour of individuals. The adjective *Psychogeographical*, retaining a rather pleasing vagueness, can

thus be applied to the findings arrived at by this type of investigation, to their influence on human feelings, and even more generally to any situation or conduct that seems to reflect the same spirit of discovery.

Then follows an example in the form of a question: 'It has long been said that the desert is monotheistic. Is it illogical or devoid of interest to observe that the district in Paris between Place de la Contrescarpe and Rue de l'Arbalète [the Continent, again?!] conduces rather to atheism, to oblivion and to the disorientation of habitual reflexes?'

At this early stage of situationist thought, the principal idea was simply to make delirious proposals with as much seductive power as possible, with the long-term aim of transforming 'the whole of life into an exciting game'—the play principle before the work principle—*homo ludens*, in Huizinga's words—before man as thinker or worker. Chirico's arcades could be models for a new city architecture: Claude Lorrain's paintings of harbours at dusk have a strange beauty—not 'a plastic beauty—the new beauty can only be a beauty of situation—but simply the particularly moving presentation, in both cases, of a *sum of possibilities*'. Thus, from the start, psycho-geography was bound up with the creation of situations, and the concept of situations was expanded, in time, to cover not just the city, but the whole of society—the totality of possibilities open in an unalienated community. Debord goes on to broach some further practical projects. For instance, all the equestrian statues in Paris could be taken down and re-assembled somewhere in the midst of the Sahara, arranged as if for 'an artificial cavalry charge'. Not just all the statues in Paris, in fact, but all the statues 'in all the cities of the world'! The new ensemble should be 'dedicated to the memory of the greatest massacres of history, from Tamburlaine to General Ridgway. Here', Debord concludes, 'we see reappear one of the main demands of our generation: educational value.' In the city itself, a new awareness of the emotional, atmospheric effect of streets would make it possible to create exciting new varieties of emotional experience, by creating urban décors in a way 'analogous to the blending of pure chemicals in an infinite number of mixtures'.

Ed Van Der Elsken's book of photographs, *Love On The Left Bank*, gives us a fascinating insight into the life actually lived in Paris by the future situationists, then still rebel Lettrists or Imaginists. The central character, a Mexican—whose point of view the photographer seems to take—has arrived in Paris as a hitch-hiker, sleeping out on a bench. Soon he makes some new friends and wanders from café to café with an Australian girl, in search of the scene. The book consists mainly of photographs taken in Left Bank cafés, portraits of their denizens, napping, embracing, drinking, putting money in the juke-box, playing chess, whispering, selling hashish, reading psychology textbooks, acting as nightclub guides for tourists, begging, playing the guitar, handing out publicity leaflets in the street, painting, grinning, eating cheese sandwiches, sleeping in a news cinema or the metro, arguing, singing, smoking hashish, flirting, getting drunk, picking a fight, dancing, making up, listening to music, just waiting, being sent to jail, dreaming, falling in love. Finally he returns to Mexico. In fact, it is a very confined life, limited by lack of money and, I suppose, lack of focus, if that's the word. It seems to be dark all the time. Who knows what happens in the daylight?

It is the same world—or at least overlapping—as the one Debord celebrated in his film, *On the Passage of A Few People Through A Brief Enough Period of Time*, made in 1959, also a kind of documentary—an avant-garde documentary—made two or three years after Van Elsken's book. Already a lot has changed. Debord begins by invoking the architecture of the quarter, Saint-Germain-des-Prés, on the Left Bank. In tall buildings live the ordinary, nondescript people, the petit bourgeois—buildings designed to shelter them from the street-life below. The people down below, the young people we saw in Van Der Elsken's book, are members of a kind of provisional micro-society. They are on the margins of the economy. They are consumers rather than producers—above all, they are consuming their own time, their own *free* time. Life doesn't change very much. They go back to the same places over and over again. No one wants to go to sleep. They are looking for a way out. They are lost in a kind of labyrinth. They have no sense of the future. They will never again be so free. Everything seems impermanent, including relationships. Their freedom is really only a dream. Their sense of play is inherently unstable. Any moment, everyday life can reclaim its rights. The game they play has strict spatial limits imposed upon it.

Outside their little area, there is a whole city in which you would never meet anyone you know. Sometimes the police come and take people away, perhaps to an institution, perhaps to return them to their detested families. At least these people, the subjects of the film, are aware of the inadequacy of the area in which they live. They (now Debord switches to 'we') want to find another way of using the urban landscape, they want to find new passions. The atmosphere of the places they frequent makes them feel the potential power of an architecture which has still to be created, its power to provide a basis and a framework for less pointless games. The present urban environment simply proclaims, with violence, the requirements and the tastes of the dominant society. Everything has to be changed. Here the screen goes blank.

What is interesting about Debord's film is the way in which the call for revolution follows directly from a critique of spatiality and architecture. It is as if architecture is the point where the hidden power of the dominant society imposes itself most directly, and yet in a way which is unnoticed. It is at this point that we can begin to see how the critique of city architecture, the project of a unitary urbanism, could have been transformed into a call for social revolution. He begins with a marginal micro-society, outside the world of work, scraping by, street-selling, stealing, and then goes on to analyse the way in which, although they all dream of leaving, going back to Mexico (so to speak) they are really trapped in their little area. The only way out is in the police van. They are trapped, not simply because of their own lack of vision, although this is part of the story, but also because of the spatial fragmentation of society, its segregation into different micro-societies which never really meet. Hence the project of unitary urbanism, which itself is then seen to imply social revolution. Society as a whole, totalized society, has to be transformed before particular micro-societies can change themselves.

When the revolution came and the micro-society broke out of its limits, in May 1968, when re-totalization seemed to be on the agenda, it nonetheless failed. Perhaps the only practical project which remained was the White Bicycles project in Amsterdam, organized by the Provos, for whom Constant was an important source of ideas. White bicycles could be ridden by anyone, left in the street when the journey was over and then picked up by someone else to use for another journey, and so on. Free, spontaneous transport anywhere in the city. It resembles the idea of the *dérive*, rather than that of unitary urbanism, but for a short while, as long as there was goodwill, it seemed to work. Perhaps it was the nearest the situationists came to changing the urban environment. The main activity of May 1968, however, was the promotion of occupations and, most celebrated of all, the painting of graffiti. Occupations changed the relations of power, temporarily, but didn't change the architecture. Graffiti entered the popular memory, but in the end they were scrubbed off.

The situationists' wilder projects for *détournement* never took off. In *Potlatch*, there had been any number of visionary proposals—the Metro should be running all night, special aerial runways should be constructed to facilitate journeys across the rooftops, churches should be turned into children's playgrounds (or Chambers of Horror), railway stations should be left exactly as they are—except that all timetables and travel information should be removed from them. Graveyards should be abolished. Prisons should be opened. Street-names should be changed. All museums should be closed and the art-works distributed to be hung in bars and Arab cafés. *Détournement* had already been outlined as a strategy in *Les Lèvres Nues* (Bare Lips), back in May 1956, in an article on its methods co-written by Guy Debord and Gil Wolman. Essentially the idea was something like Bertolt Brecht's concept of re-functioning. (In fact, Brecht is cited positively in the article, on the subject of making changes to the classics, so perhaps there was a direct connection.) The two basic ideas underlying *détournement* were those of re-contextualization and active plagiarism—ideas found subsequently in the writings of Kathy Acker, who had certainly read Debord and the situationists.

The article is mainly about literary re-functioning—inserting passages from one text into another in order to change their meaning and effect, creating new, unexpected meanings by juxtaposing well known passages in a surprising way, changing the sense of existing texts by making a series of word changes, and so on. But there are also sections on film (the power of montage) and architecture:

> To the extent that new architecture must apparently begin with an experimental baroque stage, the *architectural complex*—which we conceive as the construction of a dynamic environment related to styles of behaviour—will probably re-function existing architectural forms, and in any case will make plastic and emotional use of all sorts of re-functioned objects:

calculatedly arranged cranes or metal scaffolding replacing a defunct sculptural tradition. This is shocking only to the most fanatical admirers of classic French gardens.

On the scale of the city, Debord and Wolman outlined an ambitious plan for transferring whole neighbourhoods from one city and inserting them, exactly as they were, into another. 'Life can never be too disorienting: refunctioning on this level would really make it beautiful.'

Some time later, Pinot Gallizio developed a plan for 'Industrial Painting', in effect a re-functioning both of painting and the assembly line by yoking both together. He devised a kind of Heath Robinson machine which, using industrial paints, could cover rolls of canvas fed through it with arbitrary spatters of paint. In some ways, of course, it was intended as a conceptual re-functioning of Jackson Pollock, inserting his style of painting into an absurd industrial context. Pinot Gallizio then developed the idea by suggesting that immense roles of industrial painting could be used as road surfaces on the autostrada, until Italy's motorways were all paved with abstract expressionism. More modestly, Pinot Gallizio actually constructed a 'Cavern of Anti-Matter' out of his industrial paintings, which formed the walls and the ceilings, creating a cavern or grotto which was entirely man-made—or, rather, machine-made—an entire painterly environment. I found it a strange experience standing there, when it was re-constructed in the Beaubourg, after Gallizio's son found the original rolls stored away in a cellar. I felt there had been a re-functioning of painting, not simply as architecture, but even as nature, as the cavern walls sagged and seemed to be covered with some strange deposit, about to crumble or drip.

Constant's *New Babylon* project, on the other hand—the most ambitious attempt to envisage the possible implications of Unitary Urbanism—seemed completely futuristic and even rationalist, if I dare use the term. The title, *New Babylon*, was taken from Kozintsev and Trauberg's post-revolutionary film, made in Russia, about the Paris Commune. Thus Constant's name for his utopian city invoked two revolutions—one in Petersburg, the other in Paris. Constant's visionary city was essentially linear, and seemed to be designed primarily for a nomadic population. Helicopters and aircraft of the future could arrive at landing pads and travellers could stay as long as they liked, before proceeding on what, I suppose, was a kind of futuristic, inter-urban, aerial *dérive*. While in New Babylon, however, they could democratically decide how to allocate the structure's space, since all the walls were movable at the touch of a switch. Similarly, the internal climate was completely controlled—anything could be ordered up from sauna to snowstorm. New Babylon in fact combined features of council communism or workers' control (only with travellers rather than workers, since everything was automated) with a commitment to transience and a confident vision of the power of technology. In fact, Constant's project seems much more plausible now, as we read about intelligent heating systems and so on, than it did back at the time when it was first conceived, 40 or so years ago.

Of all the futurist cities devised at that period—and there were a great many—I still find Constant's the most fascinating. Aware, of course, of the critique of architecture made by his colleagues, he took care to build the inhabitants into his project as democratic controllers of its practical form, changing it day by day to suit their needs or, I suppose, in psychogeographical terms, their desire to experience new emotional states. He even allowed for the programming of coloured light and perfumes. At the same time, following Pinot Gallizio's lead, he envisaged a society of gypsies, nomads who moved, whenever and wherever their fancy took them, travelling, I presume for free, as if futuristic aircraft were like the white bicycles Constant later promoted. The plastic models were also designed to be both architectural and sculptural, to work as aesthetic objects in their own right, as well as intimations of future constructions.

Constant, however, seems to have abandoned altogether the wish to retain the already existing cities we have today, or even elements of them. He worked with a *tabula rasa*. Perhaps he imagined that the cities we live in now had all been destroyed in some kind of catastrophe—or perhaps they had been burned to the ground in a mass uprising, a kind of global Watts riots. The situationists, of course, welcomed the Watts riots when they occurred, in mid-sixties Los Angeles. They were evoked again recently by two expelled ex-situationists, T. J. Clark and Donald Nicholson Smith, as a welcome revolutionary model. There seems a difference, however, between destroying your environment and transforming it, however great the pressure under which you act. There is something eerie about the absence of the past in *New Babylon*, a sense somehow that the concept of the new has been taken too far as polar opposite of the old, a long way further than Debord was willing to take it. Debord identified himself with Lacenaire, the assassin in Marcel Carné's great film, *Les Enfants du Paradis* (*Children of the Gods*). Leaving aside Debord's identification with a figure which Mary Joyce has described as that of the 'dandy/outlaw', I was struck once again by the nostalgia for a vanished Paris, one in which an unalienated crowd thronged the streets and enjoyed a spectacle which spoke both from and to their condition.

Recently, thinking about what kind of architecture the situationists might be interested in today, I found myself faced with a problem. Hadn't architecture definitively become part of the spectacle, at least in its most recognized forms? Spectacular office blocks in London or Kuala Lumpur, spectacular museums in Los Angeles or Bilbao, spectacular new airports in Tokyo or Hong Kong. Perhaps it should all be razed to the ground? Only the classics should be preserved. On the other hand, there were new types of architecture which had emerged elsewhere in the same society. I thought of Margaret Morton's project, *The Architecture of Despair*, sections of which have been published in Diana Balmori and Margaret Morton's book, *Transitory Gardens, Uprooted Lives*, published by Yale University Press in 1993. This is a book about the gardens created and nurtured by homeless people on the desolate ground where they have built their makeshift huts. Or there is another, similar project, Anthony Hernandez's *Landscapes of Despair*, published by the Sprengel Museum in Hannover in 1995, another photographic study of the abject and transitory dwellings of the homeless, this time in Los Angeles, mainly in the wilderness running alongside the freeways. These are the outsider architects of today.

As for Debord's own attitude, I was struck how in his last film, he quotes from Nicholas Ray's movie, *Johnny Guitar*, specifically the scene where the outlaw figure—a travelling musician, a nomad, Johnny Guitar himself, played by Sterling Haydon—shows up unexpectedly at Vienna's place, a saloon and gambling house in the middle of nowhere, owned and run by a former lover, Vienna, played by Joan Crawford. It is as if the nomad has to stop wandering in the end, to try and come home at last, however alien it may seem. Of course, it is a doomed hope. Vienna's place is burned to the ground by an angry lynch-mob. There's no option—the nomadic life is the only one there is. Perhaps in the end Debord's view of architecture was a tragic view, that there was no grand solution, that you were fated to play the role of the wandering outlaw, but that this was, after all, the most honourable role there was. Vienna's place was the dreamed-of home but, in the end, it had to go up in flames, just as the May Events had to end in failure. Still, there was little to regret and much, in elegiac mood, to be proud of.

I want to end, however, on a more optimistic note. In 1973 a book was published in Turin on Asger Jorn's garden at Albisola. Basically, Jorn, before his death, had transposed a group of vernacular buildings overlooking the sea by turning them into a kind of ceramic garden, with painted sculptures, mosaic tiles, murals of found materials and so on—together, of course, with beds and pots of flowers. Guy Debord wrote an essay for the book, titled *On Wild Architecture*. He began by reminding us that the situationists had called for the construction of new types of city, environments favourable to the expression of countless new passions. Naturally, he continues, this wasn't easy to achieve and, as a result, the situationists felt compelled to try and achieve another goal, one even harder to carry through. As a result, all their projects had to be abandoned and their great capacities were wasted, as happens to many hundreds of millions of others.

Debord then turns to consider Jorn's Outsider Garden. He reminisces about Jorn and about the importance of his role in the history of the Situationist International. He recollects how Jorn, as is often forgotten, was one of the very first to develop 'a modern critique of the most recent forms of repressive architecture'. In Albisola, he continues, Jorn showed that, whatever our failures on the grand scale, each of us can appropriate our own space, make the world in a small way what we desire it to be. Out of what might seem at first to be a chaos of debris and odds and ends, Jorn had succeeded in making a complex and unified work. For those who remember the passionate conflict there had been between situationists and architecture, Debord suggests, Albisola can be seen as a kind of inverse Pompeii: the outlines of a city which has not yet been born. It had been a collaborative work, which provided at least an insight into the forms of 'collective play' which could alone put an end to the separation between culture and everyday life, typical of our society. Debord went on to invoke, once again after so many years, the example of the Postman Cheval, who built a monumental architecture entirely on his own, and the king of Bavaria who had done the same with much greater means. Jorn had shown what could be done with 'just a little time, a little luck, enough good health, enough money, some thought, and also, some good humour'.

The situationists, he notes, had badly needed reserves of good humour, given the scandal they created. To those who ask pointlessly whether it wouldn't have been better for everyone if the situationists had never existed, he suggests another kind of question: Wouldn't it have been better to give them two or three towns to reconstruct, instead of frustrating them to the point where they tried to overthrow society? But then others might explain that the result would have been just the same. Trying to buy them off would simply have whetted their insatiable appetite for change. That's it. My *dérive* from minaret to outsider garden has finally come to its end.

15

BARTHES, HITCHCOCK, BURGIN

In 1967 Victor Burgin returned to England after spending two years in America at Yale University's School of Art and Architecture. Soon after he arrived back, he discovered Roland Barthes's extraordinary little book *Elements of Semiology*, newly translated into English by Annette Lavers. I remember this book very well, although I seem to have mislaid my own well-thumbed copy. It had a pale blue cover and it was much smaller than the average paperback—genuinely pocket-size, in fact. Barthes's book had originally been published in 1964 by the French journal, *Communications*, a gathering point for young French scholars embarked on what Louis Jean Calvet has called 'the semiological adventure'. Barthes had been introduced to semiology in 1949 in the Egyptian city of Alexandria. I am sure Victor Burgin would appreciate this topographic twist to his pre-history as an artist, given his own fascination with the strange interactions that resonate between text and place. Alexandria reminded Barthes of Marseilles, a city which, many years later, came to fascinate Burgin, becoming central to much of his recent artwork.

It was Algirdas Greimas who first brought semiology to Barthes's attention. Lithuanian by birth, Greimas had studied in France at the University of Grenoble, where he specialized in lexicography and wrote a dissertation on the vocabulary of fashion, a topic which Barthes himself would later explore in depth. Grenoble, as chance dictates, is also a city to which Burgin was later invited, by the local Museum of Painting and

Sculpture, to create an art-work that could establish a link between the contemporary city and its collection of seventeenth-century art—between, as Burgin envisaged it, the utopian landscapes of Claude Lorrain and the utopian architecture of Grenoble's new satellite township, Villeneuve. Establishing unexpected links has been crucial to Burgin's career—links between people and places, books and images, cities and stories. The link with Greimas led Barthes to read Saussure, Hjelmslev and Jakobson, theorists of language whose work became central to his future projects, and thus to Burgin's own fascination with theories of signs and images. 'Who's Saussure?', Barthes had asked his friend. 'He's essential reading', Greimas replied. For Burgin, it was Barthes who now became essential reading.

If we look at Burgin's early work, what do we find? First, there was a love–hate relationship with conceptualism, the logical sequel to the minimalism that he had encountered at Yale, where Donald Judd, Robert Morris and Ad Reinhardt were among his teachers. Burgin was sceptical about minimalism, and had further reservations about reducing art to purely conceptual terms. He felt that a complete break with modernism was needed, with a way of thinking he associated with the critical writings of Clement Greenberg, which saw each new generation of artists as facing 'a problem which was then solved by the following generation, but in solving it they raised another problem', thus creating an endlessly recurring process of problem-solving in which each solution simply led to the next problem, and so on, ad infinitum. He could learn from conceptualism, but he also wanted images and a sense of place. Burgin's first works after his return from Yale included *Photo Path*, a piece in which a series of photographs of the floor were laid down across the same portion of the floor of which they were photographs, and an exhibition at the Camden Arts Centre in which he placed sheets of paper on the walls, each with a typed sentence drawing attention to an aspect of the otherwise completely empty room.

Soon, however, he came to a more radical conclusion. What was needed now was a true paradigm shift that would change the whole terms of the debate, breaking out completely from the mind-set imposed by Greenberg's modernism and its legatees. Among these he included the new wave of conceptual artists, such as the Art & Language group, whose program responded to minimalism by reducing art even further, viewing themselves as artists who tested the boundaries of art by using a philosophical meta-language which was exclusively verbal rather than visual. Burgin's own conclusion was rather different, as he subsequently explained in a conversation with John Roberts published by *Camerawork*: 'My own feeling was that, just as my art should be in direct engagement with the forms of imagery found in the outside world (hence my turn to advertising imagery and to the rhetoric of text–image relations) art theory should engage with bodies of theory being developed in allied areas. This led me to semiotics.' In other words, he wanted to break out of the narrow confines of the art world, in terms of theory as well as of imagery.

For Burgin, writing in 1972, it was Roland Barthes who showed the way forward, rather than philosophers and logicians such as Wittgenstein or Husserl or Carnap or Russell or Ryle. He argued that no art activity can be understood as an object in itself, somehow existing 'apart from the codes and practices of the society which contains it' and appealed to semiology, as the only way forward if the 'already over-historized, ingrowing, and mystificatory discourse of the art community' was to avoid 'total fossilization'. Art should be seen as both a social practice and a semiological practice, whose signs, codes and meanings could not be segregated from those of other, dominant forms of imagery, including advertizing and the media. As a socially and aesthetically critical activity, art required a theoretical understanding of the codes which governed popular imagery, in order to challenge or subvert them. In 1973, due to a chance encounter in a Charlotte Street restaurant (in London's Fitzrovia district), Burgin was invited to teach photography at the Central London Polytechnic where, the next year, he delivered a lecture on 'Photographic Practice and Art Theory', subsequently published in *Studio International*.

In this crucial essay Burgin cited Saussure, Hjelmslev, Jakobson and Barthes, as we might expect, along with a number of other linguists and semiologists. The citations from Barthes came, of course, from *The Elements of Semiology*, as well as from his earlier book, *Mythologies*, but there was a special emphasis on a crucial later essay, 'Rhetoric of the Image', as well as some references to Barthes's book on the discourse of fashion, *Système de la Mode*. 'Rhetoric of the Image' is one of Barthes's typically dense, yet illuminating essays, in which he analyses the rhetorical strategy of a single advertising image. The photographed image shows a carefully arranged display, a kind of still life (and thus an 'aesthetic signified' in its own right), featuring a string shopping bag filled to overflowing with packets of Panzani pasta, a sachet of parmesan cheese, a tin of pasta sauce and various assorted vegetables. Barthes's principal concern, however, was with the image's rhetorical and coded connotations of 'Italian-ness', freshness and what we might call 'whole meal-ness'. These connotations provided a coded superstructure which added an implicit rhetorical meaning to the purely denotative photographic image.

Burgin followed Barthes in arguing that it is precisely through connotation that an ideological message is communicated. At this point in his career, he had begun looking for ways of giving his photography a political relevance, not simply by exploiting the rhetoric of the image in a propagandistic fashion, but by contrasting verbal text with rhetorical imagery, in order to provoke questions rather than encourage automatic assent. In 'Rhetoric of the Image', Barthes had suggested that 'the common domain of the signifieds of connotation is that of "ideology"' and that the photographic image 'naturalizes' the ideological message which it is made to carry. The problem which faced Burgin, therefore, was how to find a way of creating images which would compel us to question this apparently natural collusion between photography and ideology. Burgin's work throughout the 1970s was based upon his search for strategies which might undermine or deconstruct the rhetoric and mythologies of conventional public imagery, thus conducting a kind of artistic guerrilla war from within the art world, which he saw as irretrievably marginal in comparison to the massive power wielded by the media spectacle.

During this period, Burgin began to produce photographs that alluded to advertizing through their combination of text with image, but which used text to question or undercut the image rather than to support it. In March 1976 he published a further article in *Studio International*, citing 'Rhetoric of the Image' once again, but now preceded by a double page spread showing an image of a sculpture in the pose of Rodin's thinker, brow furrowed, chin on hand, while opposite it, to the right, there is a photograph of an equally thoughtful young man. The text begins, 'It's worth thinking about ...' and ends 'Class consciousness think about it.' In between there are six paragraphs of small print which question the idea of 'classlessness' and explain how middle-class standards of living are actually supported by structures of debt which further enrich the wealthy. Later that year he exhibited his most notorious work, *Possession*, 500 copies of which were posted in the busy city centre of Newcastle, as if they were conventional commercial advertisements. They showed the image of a young couple embracing, with the text: 'What does possession mean to you? 7% of our population owns 84% of our wealth.'

The following year, 1977, in *Newcastle Writings*, Burgin published another new theoretical text, 'Modernism in the *work* of art', in which he reiterated his critique of Clement Greenberg, discussed the 'factography' espoused by many left-wing photographers of the 1920s and 1930s, and then returned once again to Barthes, this time to discuss his essay 'Diderot, Brecht, Eisenstein', published in France in 1973 and translated shortly afterwards in the theory-oriented film magazine *Screen* which, like Burgin, was preoccupied with the politics of the image. Barthes's article began by discussing Diderot's concept of the theatrical *tableau*, a visual picture contained within a scenographic rectangle, into which has been compressed an image designed to totalize the entire content of a narrative—'a pure cut-out segment with clearly defined edges' whose central meaning could be understood at a single glance, as if it were a 'hieroglyph', visual, yet also textual. This kind of 'tableau' was characterized by Barthes as a 'fetish-object' and the lesson Burgin drew from the essay was that 'dominant attitudes to photography valorise the fetish', thus introducing psychoanalytic terminology into his verbal armoury.

Burgin made the link between Diderot and photography through Henri Cartier-Bresson's celebrated concept of the 'decisive moment', which he saw as recycling Lessing's concept of the 'pregnant moment', itself derived from Diderot's original idea of the 'tableau'. Both commercial and 'art' photography now came under attack—'the "glossy" effect of the former having its fetishistic counterpart in the "quality print" of the latter'. Then, in 1984, Burgin published a critical essay of his own, 'Diderot, Barthes, Hieroglyph', a clear allusion to Barthes's 'Diderot, Brecht, Eisenstein'. He also cited another of Barthes's essays, in which the concept of the *punctum* was introduced—the apparently insignificant detail in a photograph that nonetheless strikes some strange unintended chord in the viewer, as opposed to the *studium*, which carries the photograph's obvious and intended meaning. Burgin went on to distinguish between Diderot's 'tableau', aligned with *studium*, the conscious reading, and his 'hieroglyph', aligned with *punctum*, the unconscious cue. Freud was beginning to replace Barthes, psychoanalysis was beginning to replace semiology, as Burgin sought out viable new antidotes to the power of the *studium*.

These alternatives would appeal not to the conscious and rational judgment of the viewers, but to their unconscious and unacknowledged memories and desires. Burgin became increasingly absorbed not only by Freud, but also by the new psychoanalytic thinking of Jacques Lacan. Barthes, it might be worth mentioning, had become interested in Lacan at the end of the 1960s, after Lacan's *Ecrits* was published. Barthes's own student, Julia Kristeva, had encouraged him to think seriously about Lacanian psychoanalysis, and Barthes had actually gone to Lacan for psychoanalysis, in the mid-seventies, although Lacan had turned him down. Nonetheless, the impact of Lacan, along with Kristeva and Derrida, can be seen in Barthes's switch from an interest in semiology to one in textuality, beginning in 1970 with S/Z, the product of a two-year seminar. By 1975, Burgin too was citing Freud and Lacan and, by the decade's end, Freud had clearly become a dominant influence on Burgin's work as an artist. In making *Zoo 78*, a photo-text series set in Berlin, Burgin was thinking not only about the great semiologist Victor Shklovsky, whose book *Zoo, or Letters Not about Love* inspired the work, but also about Freud's theory of scopophilia and the drive to mastery which links voyeurism with sadism, gaze with power.

In Lyon, a photo-text work made in 1980, carries his interest in Freud much further, openly invoking Freud's theories of paranoia, voyeurism/scopophilia and the primal scene. The narrative text which accompanies the image is derived directly from Freud's *A Case of Paranoia Running Counter to the Psychoanalytic Theory of the Disease*. Burgin describes the work as a 'condensation' (Freudian term) of a complex of images 'centred around the imbrication of the psychic and the social, of sexuality and politics'. These artworks are presented much as if they were dreams, to be interpreted as if by analysis, using psychoanalytic techniques. In *Gradiva* and in *Olympia*, both made in 1982, Burgin's debt to Freud is even more explicit. The first draws directly from a novel, *Gradiva*, which Freud himself wrote about, although Burgin's reading of the text differs significantly from Freud's, focusing more on fetishism and scopophilia. *Olympia* is drawn both from Hoffman's well-known tale of the automated doll and from Freud's analysis of the case of Anna O. Again the work appeals to a 'dream-logic', open to interpretation.

In the course of his essay on *Olympia*, Burgin describes how, in Hoffman's original story,

> the young student who falls in love with Olympia rents a room overlooking hers and spies on her through a telescope. This reminds me of *Rear Window*, where a photographer spies on the apartment opposite him with the aid of a telephoto lens; so let James Stewart now play the part of this student, aiming his lens (through the 'window' of the frame) across the triptych towards Manet's model.

Olympia: Hoffman, Manet, Freud, Hitchcock, Burgin. From now on Hitchcock becomes an increasingly important source for Burgin, as the master who ties the knot that binds together photography, scopophilia, fetishism, dream and psychoanalysis. The path first traced by Roland Barthes, especially in his post-Kristeva works, now became an essential element of Victor Burgin's own artistic journey, as Alfred Hitchcock now joined with Sigmund Freud as his point of departure.

In 1983, Burgin completed *Hôtel Latone*, one of his most complex and curious works. Shot in Malmö, Sweden, a city Burgin had visited some years earlier, although purportedly in New York, it tells the story of a couple watching TV in a hotel, intertwined with the tale of Phaedra, who builds the 'Temple of Peeping Aphrodite' in Troezen so that she can look down on Hippolytus as he exercises in the gymnasium. As well as a voyeur, she is also, of course, a photographer. Subsequently, now in Paris, she reminds an admirer of a voyeuristic passage in the writings of the Marquis de Sade. The work ends with a citation on 'The Obsessional and His Desire', before returning to the TV set in the hotel room, which now shows a scene of childbirth, in close-up. Then, in 1984, Hitchcock returns once more, this time in relation to what I can only describe as a photographic tableau, *The Bridge*, which is based both upon the drowning episode in *Vertigo*, an attempted suicide set under the Golden Gate Bridge in San Francisco, and Millais's celebrated Pre-Raphaelite painting of Ophelia drowned in her madness, her body floating in water strewn with flowers. Once again, voyeurism is invoked, this time in relation to 'the obsessional man, the one who is driven to investigate the enigma of the woman, who is often represented by the figure of the detective'. Thus the detective investigator merges with the obsessive voyeur, Scottie, played once again by James Stewart.

The text that accompanies *The Bridge* actually cites Freud's 'A Special Type of Choice of Object made by Men', a study of men who fall in love with a woman of bad reputation in order to 'rescue' her, a woman already attached to another man. Freud also notes that this type of man tends to seek out a specific type of woman, one who resembles a previous object of desire. As Burgin notes, all these criteria are met by Scottie in *Vertigo*. Besides the Freudian implications of the film, there is one other relevant fact which seems significant. Hitchcock's film, which had been withdrawn from distribution, was re-released in December 1983, by Hitchcock's estate, three years after his death. This was also the year in which Donald Spoto's tell-all biography was published. It was in the immediate aftershock of these events that *Vertigo* replaced *Rear Window* as Victor Burgin's point of reference. In 1984 came *The Bridge* and, the very same year, Burgin's essay 'Tea With Madeleine', published in a special issue of *Wedge* and designed to coincide with the opening of the show *Difference: On Representation and Sexuality* at the New Museum of Contemporary Art in New York. Madeleine, I should note, is the name of the drowning woman rescued by Scottie and then taken back by him to his apartment. It is also, of course, the name of the cake dipped in tisane in Proust's *Remembrance of Things Past*.

Tea With Madeleine is a double text, in the sense that it comprises two texts aligned in two columns side by side in parallel through six pages. The left-hand text is an essay on the psychoanalytic implications of the triad 'Desire'—'Image'—'Man' (the position, as Burgin notes, from which he himself speaks). However, the terminology that Burgin makes use of comes from Lacan rather than from Freud. The love object,

Burgin notes, 'is "chosen" (does choice ever really come into it? *"Coup de foudre"*?) because something about it allows it to represent the lost object, which is *irretrievably* absent'—and of which, he then adds, the maternal breast is invariably the prototype. The 'image' Burgin has invoked is a 'psychic image', which is not necessarily visual—it can be a memory of touch, taste, smell, hearing or bodily sensation. The desire which follows, on the part of the man, is a desire to investigate the body of the woman in the hope of re-discovering this lost image. Inevitably, it is diverted into compulsive repetition, into fetishism.

The right-hand text is a collage of citations, but it reads more like a fiction. It begins with *Brief Encounter*, the final scene at the railway station, but now given a Lacanian twist. Then Olympia and Fellini's *Casanova*. A glance back to Lacan, the right and the wrong toilet: *Gentlemen, Ladies* (Burgin's untitled photograph, accompanying this text, shows his own image—as the photographer standing outside—but reflected back in the mirror of the open-doored *Ladies*). *Vertigo*, with a synopsis and an allusion to Freud. An 'adult movie' on the hotel TV. Then, unexpectedly, the Marx Brothers. Shklovsky flees across the ice to Finland. Suddenly, we are in Warsaw: a businessman's hotel, where prostitutes lounge in the bar. Virginia Woolf is followed by Julia Kristeva, with her admonishment: 'Woman, as such, does not exist.' Wanda, from *Venus In Furs*. Kristeva on the repression of maternity. 'The image is on the side of the feminine'—Is this the pre-Oedipal? As opposed to the Law?—'Words added to an image always have an air of paternal guidance and/or reproval.' A moment's pause. But 'we must be suspicious of this appealing assimilation of image to liberty and word to prison. Patriarchy depends on its divisions.'

'As she leaves the restaurant ["Ernie's", where Scottie first saw Madeleine?] he glances at her again. She does not appear to see him. Amongst her symptoms: all the people she sees seem like wax figures; in a bunch of flowers she can only see one flower at a time [Freud's Anna O?]. She will scatter the nosegay of narcissi on the black waters of the bay [The wax figure of Madeleine in the Golden Gate tableau, the flowers scattered by Ophelia? Virginia Woolf?]. He will descend into that darkness beneath the bridge, where she floats like Ophelia [the rescue fantasy? Gluck's *Eurydice Restored*?] for love of the face he glimpses just below the surface [the fetish?], believing it to be that of someone other than himself [the disavowal of Narcissus?]. Throughout the film they will miss each other, or they will miss their trains [*fehlleistung*, the slip, Freud's very own 'bungled action'], waiting until the last possible moment, when they can't wait any longer. Then, finally, each will be lost to the other, closing their respective doors behind them [Gentlemen, Ladies? This is where the self-portrait is placed, right there on the opposite page! But the door marked "Men" is closed].'

In 1986 Victor Burgin published *Diderot, Barthes, Vertigo*, the third in a series of essays which began with Barthes's *Diderot, Brecht, Eisenstein* and continued with Burgin's own *Diderot, Barthes, Hieroglyph*. What does it mean, this substitution of '*Vertigo*' for '*Hieroglyph*'? Burgin's interest, among other things, has now shifted to a new question: what is the relationship between movie and still? The cinema, Burgin points out, is in a certain sense, 'the "negative" of the gallery'.

> In the cinema, we are in darkness; the gallery is light. In the cinema we are immobile before moving images; in the gallery it is we who must move. In the cinema we may interrupt the sequence of images only by leaving; in the gallery we may order the duration of our attention in whatever sequence we wish. The much remarked 'hypnosis of cinema' suppresses our critical attention; in the gallery the critical attention is less easily beguiled.

Yet there is also a kinship between cinema and gallery—films provoke still images in our fantasies. The film scenario is simply an expansion of a series of moments, 'condensations' which distil for us a series of recurrent fantasy moments: 'A woman is in the water', 'I am rescuing a woman', and so on.

These hieroglyphic moments carry their own associations with a series of other images—Millais's painting of *Ophelia* or Botticelli's of *The Birth of Venus*—which in turn give rise to a further chain of images, associations and memories. The multifarious ways in which images are seen, interpreted and remembered are always the product of our own fantasies, rather than the intentions of the artist, photographer or film-maker. Burgin returned to *Vertigo* in his video-work *Venise*, made in 1993, where the associations are very different indeed. Marseilles, the topic of this commission, was the city in which the writers Boileau and Narcejac set the final section of their novel, *Entre Deux Morts*, upon which Hitchcock based the screenplay of *Vertigo*. In the Boileau–Narcejac version Madeleine is saved by Flavières [Scottie] after she jumps into the Seine, but, as in *Vertigo*, she finally commits suicide by leaping, a second time, from a belfry. Years later, Flavières believes he has seen her again in Marseilles, visible in a film newsreel. He succeeds in finding her, she confesses all and, in a fury, he strangles her. Marseilles thus becomes San Francisco's own double, the site of Hitchcock's oneiric repetition of the violence of the primal scene.

Since making *Venise*, Burgin has concentrated his work mainly on a series of new city videos: featuring Lyon, San Francisco, Budapest, Weimar, San Francisco again, and then Paris. In the midst of this cascade of videos, in 1996, came his book, *Some Cities*, which explores the urban experience in literary rather than visual form. It begins as follows:

> Our relations with cities are like our relations with people. We love them, we hate them, or are indifferent toward them. On our first day in a city that is new to us, we go looking for the city. We go down this street, around this corner. We are aware of the faces of the passers-by. But the city eludes us, and we become uncertain whether we are looking for a city, or for a person.

We might wonder whether that person is alive or dead, real or imaginary. His book begins, as it should, with Sheffield, city of his birth. The photograph which illustrates it, however, is not of Sheffield at all but another image made by the great photographer Bill Brandt in the nearby factory town of Halifax. I was recently in Sheffield myself—to see an exhibition on the theme of dreams, curated by the artist Susan Hiller—and I couldn't help thinking that the Sheffield of Victor Burgin's childhood has become by now so distanced from reality that it has itself taken on the semblance of a dream.

Even Burgin's photographs of London now look like images of some alien landscape. His photographs of the King's Road in Chelsea, where most of them were taken, now seem to him like images of Melrose Avenue in Los Angeles. To me the two most striking series of photographs were those of Berlin, with its images of captivity and surveillance—the zoo with observers gazing at the caged beasts, the peepshow booth with naked women peered at by paying customers, and the Wall with East Berlin under surveillance from Western watch-towers; and then a series taken in Singapore, with its weird mixture of the new and the old, huge skyscrapers and the sedate Palm Court of the old Raffles Hotel. Best of all, there is his series of images of the Tiger Balm Gardens, one of the few monuments of the old Singapore that has remained—by the time he arrived, the Great World, 'a legendary and infamous pleasure garden of the 1930s' had been totally destroyed: there was nothing but 'manicured grass'. At least when I saw it, it was still standing, locked up and overgrown, with creepers coiled around the mountainous and rusting roller-coaster.

In a way which I would never have anticipated, Aw Boon Haw, creator of the Tiger Balm Gardens, has become a kind of Hitchcock figure, whose fantasy world has somehow meshed with that of Victor Burgin. His pleasure gardens are filled with sculptured tableaux, representing pivotal moments from morality plays or instructive scenes from Chinese novels, capturing precisely those moments which Diderot would have recommended. On the other hand, they are also like dream fantasies, at least to the Western eye. One of the tableaux which Burgin photographed shows the temptations offered by a gaudy cabaret, with men and women succumbing to the lures of wine and sexual desire. Another shows an industrious student proffering an instructive book to a lazy student. These scenes even have written texts framed and placed within the tableaux to explain their moral teaching. Yet despite the deliberate and self-evident *studium* of these tableaux, it must have been the fabulous dream-like *punctum* of each tableau which appealed to Burgin's own unconscious fantasies, as strange scenes of vice and depravity are mingled with moments of moral uplift amid the adventures of troubled visitors in Hell.

In *Love Letters*, a video installation made for exhibition in Budapest, Burgin returned again to psychoanalysis—specifically the relationship between Freud, from Vienna, and Ferenczi, a colleague from Budapest. In 1911 Ferenczi had written to Freud explaining that he had fallen in love with an analysand, Elma Pálos, daughter of his former lover, Gizella Pálos. As events developed, he reached the conclusion that he had made a mistake and that Elma required further treatment. He now asked Freud to undertake Elma's analysis, since he could no longer be responsible for it. Subsequently Freud opposed the whole idea of marriage, and eventually Elma left for America, whereupon Ferenczi fell ill. He never forgave Freud for the betrayal and eventually married Gizella. Three separate soundtracks accompanied the same video in three galleries of the museum. The first told the story of the triangle, the second was a reading of Freud's *Observations of Transference Love*, on patients who fall in love with their therapists, and the third intercut the two. The video is shot through the window of the Budapest–Vienna train, together with film by Marie Bonaparte of crowds greeting the Nazis outside Freud's Vienna home.

What do the Tiger Balm Gardens and the troubles of Ferenczi and Freud have in common? The answer is not immediately obvious, but thinking about it could lead us to something significant about Burgin's approach to photography and videography. First, of course, there is the exoticism of both, but also the invocation of two histories—the history of Chinese novels, the history of psychoanalysis. In one the secondary form taken is the tableau and the photograph, in the other it is the video and the reading of letters. Image and text, in fact. Both raise issues of morality, of ethical teaching and, in both, ethics are related to sexuality—to the cabaret, to the familial entanglement. In both also there is a disavowal of the lost object through fetishization, through the search for traces of the old days of Singapore, before the Raffles and the Cricket Club and the Anglican Cathedral, before post-modernity and the skyscrapers, as for the old days of Vienna and Budapest, the era of the Austro-Hungarian Empire, the time of Freud and Ferenczi, the time of the train running between twin capitals. We are reminded once again of *Vertigo*, which invokes the storied days of San Francisco, the gold-rush days, the time of Carlotta Valdes, days recalled in the antiquarian bookshop and the art museum, in both text and image.

In his wonderful book, *Hong Kong*, Ackbar Abbas discusses the role of 'disappearance' in our perception of history. 'Roland Barthes', he notes, 'believed that the photograph is always "a certificate of presence". Disappearance, too, is more a matter of presence rather than absence, of superimposition rather than erasure. Hence an elective affinity between the photograph and disappearance.' Burgin's video *Lichtung*, set in Goethe's Weimar, is, quite literally, about *Elective Affinities*, Goethe's novel set in the parkland of Weimar, a parkland which was also the site of the Buchenwald camp, all too present despite its 'disappearance', despite every effort to erase it from memory. There it stays, returning to haunt the German Enlightenment. There too, in Singapore, is the Great World, haunting the manicured lawn, haunting (in my own memories) the deserted dance-floor and the rusting roller-coaster. 'To look out for indices of disappearance', Ackbar Abbas continues, 'is not the same as to fetishize, or to seize on a detail as a substitute gratification faute de mieux, rather it is a matter of interrogating in detail the fetish itself.'

In my copy of Phyllis Grossfurth's *The Secret Ring*, there is a photograph of Elma Pálos, subtitled 'loved by Ferenczi but rejected by Freud as a surrogate daughter-in-law'. Grossfurth describes her entanglement with Ferenczi as 'the most bizarre soap opera' and comments that 'Freud's voyeuristic involvement in the situation is curious'. Ferenczi, she suggests, was 'Freud's Scheherazade, entertaining him with the neverending saga of his triangular love situation, whose variations and crisis seemed endless'. The triangle, we might recall, is also the central figure of Hitchcock's *Vertigo* as well as of Nietzsche's relationship with Lou Andreas Salomé, subject of Burgin's most recent video, *Nietzsche's Paris*. Goethe's *Elective Affinities* too, as Burgin notes, could be considered 'a study in the geometry of changing relationships, in the syntax of problematical arrangements within the grammar of middle-class society'. In fact, as Grossfurth points out, Freud was almost addicted to this form of geometry, playing the marriage-broker, analysing in turn the lovers of Ferenczi, Jones and (*'à distance'*, in a series of letters) Sabina Spielrein, Jung's analysand, the three lovers of his three most brilliant followers, his favourite sons.

Freud, seen in this perspective, becomes almost a kind of Gavin Elster, the murderous villain of *Vertigo*, who manipulates his old college friend Scottie by leading him into a relationship with the mysterious Madeleine, who then, of course, abandons him, as Elma, under Freud's guidance, abandoned Ferenczi. In *Vertigo*, however, Madeleine reappears as Judy, who must then be re-created as Madeleine, so that Scottie can substitute himself for Elster. Talking in 1997 about his book *In/Different Spaces: Place and Memory in Visual Culture*, Burgin insisted that 'it's all about psychical space. That's all my work was ever about. That's what that work at the Camden Arts Centre in the 1970s was about.' In other words, Freudian concepts are transposed into a visual and, therefore, spatial setting: whether Austria-Hungary or San Francisco or Paris or the office with its secretary/boss couple, re-created as a tableau by Burgin in *Office at Night*. As Rob Lapsley has observed, 'the space of the city is defined by the gaze of the Other', a space in which we are trapped, always within view of unknown others. It is to defend against this anxiety that we struggle to reverse the gaze, to seek empowerment by controlling the visual field. Freud, after all, made sure that he could not be observed by his patients.

Out of all Victor Burgin's work, the one for which I have a special fondness is *Family*. This is a tiny hardcover book, published by Lapp Princess Press in New York in 1977, modelled on a child's first alphabet book, about four inches square with a text on each left hand page and a photographic image facing it, on the right. Each of the six texts consist of just one sentence, beginning in turn with the letters F, A, M, I, L and Y. They describe how family units gradually ceased historically to be working units, consuming what they produced, as commodity production was moved completely outside the family circle, which thus became designated the site of 'personal' life, as opposed to its other, a 'dehumanizing' factory life. Personal life itself, however, became dominated by consumerism and the family gradually evolved into a support structure for the factory, 'reproducing a psychology of submission-to-authority'. Each facing page has the same six letters in the top right hand corner: Ff, Aa, Mm, etc. In the bottom left are the words, 'marry, obey, teach, hide, elide, repeat', whose initial letters spell out the word 'mother'. The six photographs show an American flag, a Marlboro ad, a TV screen, a suburban home, an EXIT sign and a silhouetted figure seen as if through a reflective glass sheet.

It is a simple piece. The photographs were taken, I imagine, during Burgin's first trip to America, in 1976–77, when he crossed the continent from Los Angeles to Cape Canaveral. It is a work which intrigues me so much partly because it is so simple, partly because of its political stance, not yet subordinated to a psychoanalytic discourse. This is not to say that politics and psychoanalysis should be kept apart. On the contrary, I agree with Victor Burgin that they are fundamentally inseparable. Throughout his career he has presented the image—and the concomitant desire to look—in unashamedly political terms, whether as surveillance or voyeurism or captivation by the spectacle. Over time, he has adjusted his own point of view, a process which took him from Barthes to Hitchcock to Freud and beyond, as I have tried to trace. In *Family* we find, in miniature, many of his insistent preoccupations: working-class childhood in a factory town, the bond between politics and psychoanalysis, the desire to travel, the power of the look, the collision or collusion of text with image, the omnipresence of the spectacle, the irrevocably social context of art.

16

FRIDAMANIA

The first retrospective of Frida Kahlo's work outside Mexico opened at the Whitechapel Gallery in London in May 1982, organized and co-curated by Laura Mulvey and myself. In fact, it was a joint exhibition of works by Kahlo and Tina Modotti, the Italian–American–Mexican photographer, who herself subsequently became the object of a minor kind of 'Tinamania'. At that time, Mulvey and I were hostile to the idea of shows limited to the work of a single artist and felt that a contrast between two related bodies of work was more revealing than a self-contained one-person event. We also wanted to display photography on an equal footing with painting. After its opening at the Whitechapel the show travelled to Germany and Stockholm, before going on to the Grey Gallery in New York and, finally, to the National Art Museum in Mexico City. The North American venues were added after the exhibition had opened, as a direct result of its impact in Europe, its word-of-mouth reputation. The effect of this was to introduce Kahlo's work to the US—more specifically to its artistic and intellectual capital, New York—in 1983, at roughly the same time that Hayden Herrera's biography of Kahlo came out. It was, I believe, the conjunction of these two events, the exhibition and the book, that sparked off an interest in the US, which later fed into or converged with the enthusiasm in Europe and Mexico to produce 'Fridamania': the elevation of Kahlo to cult status.

Since then, there has been a stream of further exhibitions, catalogues, books—and eventually postcards, calendars, wall-posters, folding screens, diaries and feature films, Paul Leduc's and now Julie Taymor's. Within a decade, Frida Kahlo had become probably one of the most instantly recognizable artists in the world. How did it happen? And why? As we shall see, these questions raise a number of issues that are central to the way we construe the history of taste, the reception of art and the generation of cultural icons.

To begin with the question of why we wanted to put on the show in the first place: this may verge on self-portraiture, but perhaps that is appropriate in writing about an artist like Kahlo. We were not art historians and had never organized an art exhibition before. We were film theorists and avant-garde film-makers. We went to Mexico together for a Christmas holiday, 1978–79, staying with a friend who taught Japanese Political History at the Colegio de México. Before that, I had seen one Kahlo painting, *Portrait of Frida and Diego*, at the historic exhibition 'Women Artists: 1550–1950', put on by Ann Sutherland Harris and Linda Nochlin in 1976. However, Kahlo did not figure at all prominently in my thinking as I planned what to see on the trip. There was scant information in the books I looked at—Rivera's wife, did some painting. I first became more conscious of her role after arriving in Mexico City, because she is portrayed—alongside Tina Modotti—as a revolutionary handing out arms to the workers and peasants in the murals Rivera painted in the courtyard of the Ministry of Education building in Mexico City. Later we went to the suburb of Coyoacán, primarily to visit Trotsky's house. The Blue House, which belonged to Kahlo, was nearby, and so we decided to visit that too. As it turned out, it was the Blue House that made the greater impact.

In fact, there was only one room of Kahlo paintings there—by no means the best ones. The impact came from the house itself. Looking back on it, I located it in my mind in a series that included the Gaudí houses in Barcelona (especially the Casa Batlló and the roof of the Pedrera) and the Watts Towers in Los Angeles. I had already, in a sense, 'exhibited' Gaudí via the script of Antonioni's film, *The Passenger*, which I co-wrote with Mark Peploe some years previously. A number of scenes in the film are set in Gaudí buildings. In general, I was interested in a certain kind of intensely personal or 'outsider' architecture. I still am. This interest derives from surrealism and it came as no surprise that it was André Breton who 'discovered' Kahlo as a painter, wrote the catalogue essay for her first New York show (1939, at the Julien Levy Gallery) and organized an exhibition of her work in Paris that same year. Breton personally instigated the reception of her work abroad and it was as a surrealist (or para-surrealist) that she was originally perceived outside Mexico—and to some extent inside as well.

The 'outsider' aspect of the Blue House had another important quality, beyond its relationship with surrealism. It stood in stark contrast to the white walls, empty spaces and techno-hygienic aspect of the typical museum of modern art. It was a cluttered, domestic space, brightly coloured and full of idiosyncratic objects. In many ways, I saw Kahlo as challenging orthodox doctrines of modernism. First, of course, she was a woman artist and, by then, it was already well established that women had been relegated to a secondary place within the history of modernism. Second, she was, in a sense, an 'outsider' artist, untrained, non-professional, painting out of her own desire without seeking to exhibit; and this too put her in a marginal position vis-à-vis the mainstream art world. Third, she was from Mexico, a country outside the European–United States bloc that was culturally hegemonic. Fourth, she had ties with surrealism which, although accepted within the history of modernism, was still somewhat suspect, both within the rationalist Bauhaus account of art history and within the Greenberg art-for-art's sake version. I was also interested in the implications of her political involvements—with Trotsky, but also with orthodox Communism.

After visiting the Blue House, I made more of a conscious effort to see Kahlo's work and the decisive moment probably came when, shortly afterwards, I saw the paintings exhibited in the Modern Art Museum in Chapultepec Park, especially *The Two Fridas*, certainly her most ambitious work available to me. On returning to London we went to the Whitechapel Gallery and suggested an exhibition—a project accepted by the director and by Mark Francis, the in-house curator responsible. I made a number of trips to Mexico, by myself and then with Mark Francis, to trace all the work and to secure the loans. During this time I met Hayden Herrera, through mutual friends; we were able to exchange information—although I learned more from her than she did from me. Her work was already more advanced than mine although the book finally appeared after the show. During this time I also wrote a piece, a hybrid of fiction and essay, called 'Mexico/Women/Art', which was published in London in 1979 in the *SaturdayNight Reader*, an anthology edited by Emma Tennant.

I recently reread this piece for the first time in many years and was intrigued to see the line I took. The first paragraph mentions Rivera and muralism, Breton and surrealism, Trotsky and revolutionary communism. But its centrepiece is 'her unrelenting struggle against injury and ill-health'. As we shall see, this was a crucial element in the construction of the Kahlo legend. I go on to stress the 'non-western' (or 'Third World') aspects of Kahlo's art and compare Mexico with Iran, a country in which I had lived for some time. I was clearly preoccupied with questions about the history of modernism and the meaning of the idea of an 'avant-garde', issues which simultaneously arose for me out of my work as a film-maker. I was also fascinated by Kahlo's use of popular art and imagery, especially the ex-voto paintings she collected, which relate directly to her own history of medical disasters. I was interested in the ways in which the avant-garde of the sixties—Fluxus, for example—picked up the threads of the twenties—women's art, political art, photography, popular imagery, environment, performance—and how these threads were also relevant to Kahlo. There is a whole section on Kahlo's use of Tehuana costume, linking it to feminism, to the tragic drama of the body, to the 'creolization' of indigenous cultures and to the psychoanalytic theory of masquerade.

In a way, I was trying, through a consideration of Kahlo, to develop a theory of what was not yet called postmodernism, through recourse to the repressed other side of modernism, while retaining the very non-postmodern concept of the avant-garde. In a way, I saw Kahlo as presaging a different kind of avant-gardism, as a proleptic art-historical mutation. The things that interested me in her work were in many ways the same things that drove the formation of the Kahlo cult. The work had an immediate relevance and a powerful impact, for me personally, back when I first encountered it; so, in a certain sense, I should not have been so surprised when, as the work became disseminated, it began to have such a powerful effect on others. This is all the more true, perhaps, in that I was not an art historian or a museum professional. I was myself a lay viewer. Yet the formation of a cult requires more than personal relevance or impact, however powerful—and I believe Fridamania is a kind of cult; seeming, at times, like the classic cult of the Virgin of Guadalupe (or the Mater Dolorosa) in its implications and its intensity. Kahlo too has her disciples, her devotees, her pilgrims and even her altars. There have to be specific features in the work that converge towards the generation of a cult, but there also has to be something else—a relationship between work and life, a certain historical context. What follows are some hypothetical suggestions about cult-formation and its preconditions.

First, there was the rise of feminism and the associated interest in women's art. Kahlo's work was originally (partially) introduced into the United States in a chicano context, on the West Coast, a few years before the Grey Gallery show. But it was as a woman painter that she seized the public imagination. In many ways she was an ideal candidate for culthood. She was dead, and therefore monumental in a way barred to any living artist, without being too remote in time. She died in 1954, still in her early forties. She was also Mexican—in a way that enabled her to appear both as a Third World artist, even a woman of colour, and as an artist who was herself able to appropriate the 'otherness' of Mexico to double the primary 'otherness' of being a woman. She was overshadowed by a more famous husband—as were Sophie Tauber, Sonia Delaunay, Varvara Stepanova, Gabriele Münter, Barbara Hepworth, Georgia O'Keefe, Lee Krasner and others. Her situation was both typical, in this crucial respect, while untypical in others. She was a deeply wounded woman, literally—if also psychologically, by aspects of her relationship with Rivera. The mystique of the suffering artist has always been powerful, but its effect was intensified in the context of feminism.

Second, the re-discovery of Kahlo coincided with the return of figuration in painting in the 1970s: Kiefer, Immendorf, Chia, Clemente, Salle, Fischl. This was linked, of course, to the decline of high modernism, the backlash against conceptualism and the rise of the idea of postmodernism. This painting, however, was almost exclusively a male affair. Women artists were on track two—photography, the medium used by Kruger, Sherman and others. Kahlo suggested an alternative pictorial tradition for women, one which was given added force by her choice of self-portraiture as a primary mode. Her art was intimate, private and personal; it was about her identity as a woman and a Mexican; it was about the body—very specifically the female body and, even more specifically, her own; it was about babies or the lack of them, clothes and their signification, the contradictory projection of both strength and weakness. It was in violent contrast to the pretentious asceticism of much late modernism, to its vatic emptiness, to its tedious aspiration to being high art, to its ultra-refined painterliness. Moreover, Kahlo's paintings, though small in size, unlike much male gallery art, were immediately striking, poignant, even violent in their attack. They prevailed, in part, because of their sheer quality. They also reproduced well—and this is meant as a compliment rather than a reproach.

More needs to be said about the cult of the 'suffering artist'—a phenomenon that underlies earlier cults such as those of Van Gogh or Modigliani, and even Judy Garland or Marilyn Monroe. The 'suffering woman artist' brought with it an extra emotional charge—personal suffering was overlaid on gender victimization in a way that facilitated intense psychological identification with the cult figure. Kahlo's art, of course, is much more complex than this formulation suggests, but cults are not themselves driven by a concern with complexity. In many ways the closest analogy to the cult of Kahlo is that of Sylvia Plath. Plath too was damaged and hospitalized—although psychologically rather than physically—and lived through a deeply ambiguous and painful relationship with a more famous husband. (Of course, degrees of fame change over time. Kahlo may well be more famous now than Rivera, Modotti than Weston. I believe that in both cases their work now sells for more than that of their male partner.) The energy driving interest in Plath plainly comes from a complex of victimization, blame, abjectness and fascination with violence, inwardly and outwardly directed. Much the same could be said about Kahlo.

In both cases the cult is sustained by the construction of a multiplicity of different types of documentation: the publication of the work, of biographies, collections of letters, private diaries, critical assessments, books of photographs, films and television programmes, as well as the related works of their husbands or other intimates. This build-up of sources makes possible a much stronger identification than would be possible simply from the work itself. Devotees can feel they know the object of their devotion in a detailed and intimate way, one that provides privileged insights into the idol's emotional life. This is not simply the accumulation of trivia: as more and more material on their private lives is made available, the sense that one can understand how Kahlo or Plath felt, that one can identify with their deepest and innermost feelings, becomes more convincing. In this sense too, the Blue House is also a site with a strong emotional charge, comparable to that provided by Charleston or Virginia Woolf's home, similarly open to the public, in the consolidation of the Bloomsbury cult. Culthood relies on this kind of identification. It becomes self-sustaining, as the growth of a cult provides its own audience for more publications that have to be filled with more information, images and commentary.

Of course, the personal material on which Kahlo drew when she painted remains important and significant, not in any way irrelevant to her art. Problems only arise because there is simultaneously a drive towards simplification. In reality, Kahlo's art is unusually complex and contradictory, as indeed is Plath's. We can see this by looking, for example, at the role played by Kahlo's costume in her self-portraits and, as we know from biographies and photographs, in her self-presentation in everyday life. In the first instance, her choice of traditional Mexican costume, particularly of long skirts, reflects the need (or desire) to conceal her injuries, sustained in a traffic accident when she was eighteen. An electric train crashed through the bus in which she was travelling. Kahlo was impaled on a broken piece of steel handrail from the lead car of the train. Her spine was broken in three places, two ribs were broken, her pelvis was broken in three places, her collar-bone was broken, her right leg had eleven fractures, her right foot was crushed and the left shoulder dislocated. Plainly, what she wore served to conceal the extent of her injuries. The particular choice of clothes, however, also served to remind viewers of the injuries by drawing attention to the studied idiosyncrasy of her dress, through a kind of 'negative display'. Kahlo made her costumes into extreme and multiple signifiers and, as time went on, they became increasingly elaborate.

First, the clothes simply signified her Mexicanness. In the 1920s, following the Mexican Revolution, this was an unproblematic choice. Kahlo, however, persisted in this emphasis throughout her life, becoming more extreme as she adopted Tehuana costume as her preferred style. It seems that originally this may have been to please Rivera, who frequently visited the Isthmus of Tehuantepec and painted the women there. After his return to Mexico from Paris shortly after the stabilization of the Revolution, Rivera was sent on a visit to Tehuantepec by his patron, José Vasconcelos, then Minister of Education. Vasconcelos wanted to de-Europeanize Rivera, to restore his sense of Mexicanness, and chose Tehuantapec as the representative site of an unspoiled, yet rich, native culture. As it happened, the region was most renowned for its women—both for their social status as 'strong women' and for their striking local costumes. (They were also famed for their unembarrassed nudity. Naked Tehuanas standing in the river were a frequent subject for folkloric photography.) Rivera learned the lesson Vasconcelos intended and painted images of Tehuana women in full costume in the Ministry of Education murals which he executed after his return. He retained his artistic interest in women of the Isthmus and, supposedly, was pleased when Kahlo adopted their style. In any case, she clearly made it her own. It combined the imagery of the strong woman, the matriarch, with that of authentic Mexicanness (at least, according to legend) as well as making a virtue out of necessity by turning defensive concealment into aggressive and extravagant display.

Rivera himself was renowned as a mythomane, a compulsive liar and inventor of amazing tales. As Kahlo noted, he was a fabulist on the grand scale, rather than a petty deceiver. He was also a fervent publicity-seeker who consciously projected a larger-than-life image. In this respect, Kahlo learned from Rivera how to create a vivid public legend of oneself. The fact that she was intent on creating her own mythic identity—of which the cripple/Tehuana complex was the central element—itself facilitated the creation of a cult many years after her death. Paradoxically perhaps, her highly semioticized self-presentation only had its full effect at a kind of meta-level, through her self-portraiture, as it appeared to a quite different audience in a context far from any she had anticipated. It is important to stress that Kahlo's self-portraiture was imbricated with selffabulation from a very early stage. The self she portrays is a constructed and carefully contrived one that finally crystallizes in the imagery of Frida-as-Tehuana, which appropriates what was for her, as for Diego, as indeed for us, an exotic image and develops it for her own purposes.

In the early 1990s, I saw an exhibition in Mexico City of representations of Tehuana women by Mexican painters, from the early nineteenth century through to the present. The imagery Kahlo used falls into a long tradition of pictorial representation of the Tehuana and celebration of tropical and feminine Mexico. This imagery changed as artistic styles did, but also as attitudes to the Isthmus and the South evolved. Different artists used the Tehuana image in very different ways. Saturnino Herrán evokes the Andalusian gypsy; Adolfo Best Maugard assimilates the Tehuana to the Indian houri; Roberto Montenegro's portrait of Rosa Rolando in the elaborate face-encircling Tehuana head-dress is severe and makes her look like a Mother Superior. Rivera stresses a haughty aloofness and self-possession, preferring images of men and women together, dancing the *sandunga*. Tina Modotti (in her photographs) shows women at menial work or with infants and small children; Miguel Covarrubias stylizes and emphasizes Indianness, and so on. More recently the photography of Graciela Iturbide and the painting of Julio Galán strike a more eccentric note, garish and even grotesque.

Kahlo uses Tehuana costume explicitly as a form of masquerade with multiple and contradictory associations: masquerade as signifier of and defence against femininity; of—and against—physical damage and trauma; masquerade as exaggerated signifier of Mexicanness, concentrated in the legend of the Isthmus. Masquerade, of course, is always necessarily, in some sense, a theatrical mode. Kahlo dramatizes herself through her costume. On one level this is the simple display of identification with the other that accompanies all exotic dress, whether hippie street-fashion or designer clothes from Zandra Rhodes. At another level, it dramatizes the trauma Frida Kahlo had undergone, with its symbolic implications of rape and castration. These implications, in turn, link the physical maiming to the symbolic maiming we can associate, in psychoanalytic terms, with femininity. At the same time the fearless exhibitionism and bravura of the costume conveys pride and self-confidence. This in turn can be associated with the folkloric association of the Tehuana woman with power and strength, with Tehuantapec as the site of a mythical matriarchy. As with Plath's symbolic universe, the central metaphors are used to convey both extreme and contradictory fantasies. In two important paintings, the costume is depicted on a hanger, detached from the body, a signifier in its own right.

Kahlo's iconography is carefully controlled and contains other significant elements beyond costume. Her hair becomes a metaphor, whether close cropped or flowing luxuriously, adorned with ribbons, combs, flowers or butterflies. Some paintings show her moustache, others eradicate it. She tends to emphasize the single strong continuous line of her eyebrows, whereas in photographs this striking feature is much less pronounced, even absent. Her self-portraits always have a powerful directed gaze, looking straight out at the viewer. 'Look at those eyes', Picasso supposedly wrote to Rivera, 'neither you nor I are capable of anything like it'. Apocryphal or not, it seems right to compare Kahlo's concern over eyes in her paintings with Picasso's. They immediately engage the viewer, piercingly, with complete self-possession. Finally, there are the accoutrements—above all, the wounds and the monkeys. The wounds speak for themselves, although where they are most blatantly and bloodily displayed—as in the series which followed her miscarriage in Detroit: *Henry Ford Hospital* and *My Birth*—or, displaced, as in *A Few Small Nips* or the ex-voto *The Suicide of Dorothy Hale*, they are related directly to the themes of birth and death as violent acts. The monkeys—mimics, grimacers, pets—are associated with infants (desired, miscarried, defunct), with Diego (as ape, as child), with Frida herself (with facial hair), with Mexico (its exuberant local fauna) and with tropical nature (contrasted with the cold industrial north). Again the apparent stylistic simplicity of Kahlo's paintings, with their vernacular sources, is belied by its metaphoric and allegorical complexity.

Kahlo's relationship with the imagery of Mexicanness has also played a part in the reception of her work abroad. Mexico has long had an appeal for artists and intellectuals, becoming a kind of semi-mythical country, a site for the projection of dreams and fantasies: Mayakovsky, Eisenstein, Lawrence, Lowry, Huston, Hart Crane, Edward Weston, Burroughs, Breton—the list goes on. Eisenstein, in particular, internalized the legends of Mexicanness—including those of Tehuantapec and the *sandunga*—and sought to re-project them outside in his film *¡Que viva México!* The cult of Kahlo draws on this historic fascination, a mythology first constructed in Mexico itself during the 'Mexican Renaissance' of the 1920s as a myth of identity, then re-fashioned elsewhere or by visitors as a myth of otherness. This mythology of Mexico is one of an alternative America, constructed in contrast and opposition to the North, to the United States. Nature versus manufacture, dream versus reality principle, magic and miracle versus science and technology, essential humanity versus mechanization, enjoyment versus work or repression, acceptance versus denial of death. These antinomies also structure Kahlo's work—as well as the utopian vision of the grafting together of the two which she and Rivera saw metaphorically realized in the agricultural experiments of Luther Burbank. The availability of this myth—and its potential attractiveness, as with all myths of otherness—also underlies the appeal of Kahlo's work outside Mexico and provides a foundation for Fridamania.

From a purist point of view, the cult of Kahlo may seem to disqualify her from being a great artist. But this is no more true of Kahlo than it is of Plath. Looking for a moment at literature rather than at visual art, it has always struck me that literary critics are deeply ambivalent about works with mythic status. Melville's Great White Whale is acceptable, even admirable, yet Mary Shelley's Frankenstein monster is less so, Bram Stoker's Dracula hardly acceptable at all. And what about J. M. Barrie's Peter Pan or Wodehouse's Jeeves? In art history these issues hardly come up at all—mythic iconic figures belong to the movies or to strip cartoons, not to art at all. Only with Pop Art, when Lichtenstein or Warhol produce work parasitic on popular art, is this popular mythology admitted and then it is assumed that, as a meta-discourse, high art somehow elevates its subject matter by appropriating it. Myth is somewhat different from cult, but the two are closely connected. Cult figures almost always draw on myths, just as cult films do: *Casablanca*, *Rebel Without A Cause*, *Blade Runner*. In the case of Kahlo the growth of Fridamania is partly dependent on her manipulation of mythic, and psychoanalytic, material; but at the same time, Kahlo's art is unthinkable without it.

Given the cultural status the art world assigns to itself, there could plainly be a tendency for Kahlo's status as an artist to fall as her status as a cult figure rises. This is not necessarily the case, as the example of

Van Gogh demonstrates—although Toulouse-Lautrec would probably be a better comparison here. I believe, however, that as the modernist paradigm disintegrates, her position as an artist will remain secure. Whether we look at Kahlo from the vantage-point of women's art, Third World art or surrealism; whether we are interested in the appropriation of vernacular forms or the crossover between outsider and fine art, we will find Kahlo's paintings staring us right in the face. As a woman artist Kahlo is certainly comparable with Tanning, Carrington, Agar or the more mainstream female surrealists, all of them underestimated; and as a surrealist *tout court* she is comparable with Miró or Matta or Lam or Masson. Mexican art is due for revaluation, as is the place of the two major women artists, Kahlo and María Izquierdo, within it. Kahlo's use of vernacular forms is complex and unique and a re-evaluation of outsider art, breaking down the artificial barriers erected around specialized forms like the art of psychotics or naive art, can only benefit her. Once we recognize that even an artist like Jackson Pollock has an outsider aspect, it will be hard to hold such status against Kahlo. Indeed it may well come to appear one of her greatest strengths.

Paradoxically, it was precisely Kahlo's success that threatened to do most damage by diverting attention from women artists of the sixties and seventies whose reputation was still not firmly secured—artists as different as Eva Hesse, Judy Chicago or Mary Kelly. Kelly, in particular, is an artist whose work is autobiographical in ways that are strangely similar to Kahlo's, though formally completely different, more intellectually demanding and lacking Kahlo's immediate eye-catching appeal. It is important to place Kahlo alongside artists like these, to recontextualize her historically, in order to reconfigure the history of women's art itself and establish its foundations more securely. In a similar way, the Mexican Renaissance also needs to be reconfigured. I began by explaining how I became interested in Kahlo's work precisely because it seemed to me to challenge what I saw as orthodox interpretations and doctrines of modernism. Since then, the reconfiguration of modernism itself has been under way in many different places, involving many different arguments. Frida Kahlo was as good a place to start as any other. But we still need to extend and expand our reconsideration of twentieth-century art, looking at every aspect of modernism that was marginalized and reconceptualizing the role of women, non-western and outsider or eccentric artists. As we do this we shall diminish the importance of Fridamania and be able to focus once again on the complexity, intensity and startling beauty of her work.

SELECT BIBLIOGRAPHY

Ackbar Abbas, *Hong Kong Place*, Minnesota: University of Minnesota Press, 1997.
Anon., *Etablissement de l'Académie royale de danse en la ville de Paris*, Paris: Bibliothèque Nationale, BN ms fr 21732, fols. 273r.–273v.
Robert C. Allen, *Horrible Prettiness, Burlesque And American Culture*, Chapel Hill: University of North Carolina Press, 1991.
Perry Anderson, *Lineages of the Absolutist State*, London: Verso, 1984.
Libero Andreotti and Xavier Costa, eds, *Theory of the Dérive and Other Situationist Writings on the City*, Barcelona: Museu d'Art Contemporani de Barcelona with ACTAR, 1996.
Jean-Marie Apostolidès, *Le Roi-machine*, Paris: Editions de Minuit, 1981.
Art & Language, Eindhoven: Van Abbe Museum, 1980.
Maurice Ashley, *Louis XIV and the Greatness of France*, London: Hodder and Stoughton, 1948.
Dan Auiler, *Vertigo: The Making of A Hitchcock Classic*, New York: St. Martin's Press, 1998.
Stefan Aust, *The Baader–Meinhof Group: The Inside Story of a Phenomenon*, London: Bodley Head, 1987.
Judith Barry, *Public Fantasy*, London: Institute of Contemporary Arts, 1991.
Roland Barthes, *Camera Lucida, Reflections on Photography*, London: Jonathan Cape, 1982.
— *Elements of Semiology*, London: Jonathan Cape, 1967.
— *The Fashion System*, London: Jonathan Cape, 1985.
— *Image-Music-Text*, London: Fontana/Collins, 1977.

— *Mythologies*, London: Jonathan Cape, 1972.
— *S/Z*, London: Jonathan Cape, 1975.
David Batchelor, *Minimalism*, London: Tate Publishing, 1997.
Gregory Battcock, ed., *Idea Art*, New York: E. P. Dutton, 1973.
Philippe Beaussant, *Versailles*, Opera, Paris: Gallimard, 1981.
Samuel Beckett, *Waiting for Godot*, Cambridge: Cambridge University Press, 1989
Jeremy Black, *The Military Revolution? Military Change and European Society, 1550–1800*, Atlantic Highlands, NJ: Humanities Press International, 1991.
Pierre Boileau and Thomas Narcejac, *Vertigo [Entre Deux Morts]*, London: Bloomsbury, 1997.
Jacques Bonnet, *Histoire de la Musique et ses Effets*, Paris: Cochart, 1715.
Eva Brabant and others, eds, *The Correspondence of Sigmund Freud and Sándor Ferenczi*, vol. 1, 1908–1914, Cambridge, MA: Belknap, 1993.
Bertolt Brecht, *The Threepenny Opera*, Astor Books, 1993.
André Breton, *Nadja*, Harmondsworth: Penguin Books, 1999.
Victor Burgin, *Between*, Oxford: Basil Blackwell, 1986.
— 'The Bridge', in *The Other Body: Cultural Debate in Contemporary British Photography*, Boston University: Photographic Resource Centre, 1987, with accompanying text by Tim Norris.
— 'Diderot, Barthes, *Vertigo*', in Victor Burgin, James Donald and Cora Kaplan, eds, *Formations of Fantasy*, London: Methuen, 1986.
— 'Diderot, Barthes, Hieroglyph', in Lauren Asher and others, eds, *Subjects/Objects*, Providence: Brown University, 1985.
— *Family*, in Amy Baker, series ed., New York: Lapp Princess Press in association with Printed Matter, 1977.
— 'Framed (image with text)', in *Aspects*, no. 7, Newcastle upon Tyne 1979.
— Hôtel Latone, Calais: Edition Musée de Calais, 1982.
— *In/Different Spaces: Place and Memory in Visual Culture*, Berkeley: University of California Press, 1996.
— 'Looking at Photographs', in *Screen Education*, no. 24, London: Society for Education in Film and Television, 1977; reprinted in part in *Hayward Annual 1979*, London: Arts Council of Great Britain, 1979.
— 'Man—Desire—Image', in *Desire*, London: Institute of Contemporary Arts, 1984.
— 'Margin Note', in Rosetta Brooks, ed., *A Survey of the Avant-Garde in Britain*, vol. 2, London: Gallery House, 1972.
— 'Office at Night', no. 4 and no. 6, in 'Thatcher's Britain', *Aperture: British Photography*, New York: Aperture Foundation Incorporated, 1988.

— 'Perverse Space', in Stephen Bann and William Allen, eds, *Interpreting Contemporary Art*, London: Reaktion Books, 1991.
— 'Photographic Practice and Art Theory', in *Studio International*, London: Studio Trust, July/August 1975.
— 'Modernism in the work of art', in *Newcastle Writings*, Newcastle upon Tyne: Robert Self Publications in association with Northern Arts, 1977.
— 'Psychical Space and Postmodernism', in *The British Edge*, Boston: The Institute of Contemporary Art, 1987.
— 'Socialist Formalism', in *Studio International*, London: Studio Trust, March/April 1976.
— *Some Cities*, London: Reaktion Books, 1996.
— 'Some Thoughts on Outsiderism and Modernism', in *Block*, no. 11, 1985/86.
— 'Tea with Madeleine', in Silvia Kolbowski, ed., *Wedge*, no. 6, New York 1984.
— 'US 77', in Peter D'Agostino and Antonio Muntadas, eds, *The Un/necessary Image*, New York: Tanam Press, 1982.
— *Venise*, London: Black Dog Press, 1997.
— video stills from 'Venise', in *Icons: Urban Images*, Edition Fotohof, Salzburg, 1998, with accompanying text by Jochen Kornelius Schutze.
— *Work and Commentary*, London: Latimer New Dimensions, 1973.
Peter Burke, *The Fabrication of Louis XIV*, New Haven and London: Yale University Press, 1992.
Ed Buscombe, 'Inventing Monument Valley, Nineteenth-Century Landscape Photography and the Western Film', in P. Petro, ed., *Fugitive Images: From Photography to Video*, Bloomington: Indiana, 1995.
Jean-Louis Calvet, *Roland Barthes, A Biography*, Bloomington: Indiana University Press, 1994.
Catherine Camboulives et al., eds, *Salomé, Dans Les Collections Françaises*, Saint Denis: Musée d'Art et d'Histoire, 1988.
Aldo Caretenuto, *A Secret Symmetry, Sabina Spielrein between Jung and Freud*, New York: Pantheon Books, 1982.
Aleksa Celebonovic, *Some Call It Kitsch*, New York: Harry Abrams, 1974.
Felix Cherniavsky, *The Salome Dancer, The Life And Times Of Maud Allan*, Toronto: McClelland & Stewart, 1991.
Agatha Christie, *The Mysterious Affair at Styles*, London: HarperCollins, 2001.
Marie-Françoise Christout, *Le Ballet de Cour de Louis XIV*, Paris: A. et J. Picard, 1967.
Barnaby Conrad III, *Absinthe, History In A Bottle*, San Francisco: Chronicle Books, 1988.

Michael de Cossart, *Ida Rubinstein*, Liverpool: Liverpool University Press, 1987.
G.A. Crapelet, *Notices sur la vie et ouvrages de Quinault*, Paris: 1824.
Jonathan Crary, *Techniques of the Observer*, Cambridge, MA: MIT Press, 1990.
Guy Debord, *The Society of the Spectacle*, Donald Nicholson-Smith, translator, New York: Zone Books, 1994.
Manuel De Landa, *War in the Age of Intelligent Machines*, Zone Books, 1992.
Bram Dijkstra, *Idols of Perversity, Fantasies of Feminine Evil In Fin-De-Siècle Culture*, Oxford: Oxford University Press, 1986.
Alfred Döblin, *Berlin Alexanderplatz*, Harmondsworth: Penguin, 1971.
Daniel Dorling & David Fairbairn, *Mapping: Ways of Representing the World*, Harlow: Addison Wesley Longman, 1997.
Michael Duffy, ed., *The Military Revolution and the State*, Exeter: University of Exeter, 1980.
Keith Douglas, *Alamein to Zemzem*, London: Faber & Faber, 1996.
Richard Ellmann, *Oscar Wilde*, London: Hamish Hamilton, 1984.
Raoul-Auger Feuillet, *Chorégraphie*, Bologna: Forni, 1970.
— *Receuil de dances*, Westmead: Gregg International Publishers, 1977.
Michel Foucault, *Discipline And Punish*, New York: Vintage, 1979.
Hollis Frampton, *Circles of Confusion*, Rochester, New York: Visual Studies Workshop Press, 1983.
A. H. Franks, *Social Dance*, London: Routledge & Kegan Paul, 1963.
Michael Fried, *Absorption and Theatricality: Painting and Beholder in the Age of Diderot*, Chicago, IL: Chicago University Press, 1988.
Sigmund Freud, *The Standard Edition of the Collected Psychological Works of Sigmund Freud*, James Strachey, ed., London: The Hogarth Press and the Institute of Psychoanalysis, 1974.
Karl Fuchs, *Seig Heil!*, Hamden, CT: Archon Book, 1987.
J. F. C. Fuller, *Fascist and Liberal Visions of War*, Oxford: Oxford University Press, 1998.
— *The Secret Order of the Qabala*, 1937.
— *The Star in the West*, Neptune Press, 1976.
Paul Fussell, *The Great War and Modern Memory*, New York: Oxford University Press, 1975.
Lynn Garafola, *Diaghilev's Ballets Russes*, New York: Oxford University Press, 1989.
Richard Gilman, *Decadence, The Strange Life Of An Epithet*, New York: Farrar, Strauss & Giroux, 1975.
Claude Gintz and others, *L'Art Conceptuel, une Perspective*, Paris: Musée d'Art Moderne de la Ville de Paris, 1995.

Anne Goldstein and Anne Rorimer, eds, *Reconsidering the Object of Art: 1965–1975*, Cambridge, MA: MIT Press, 1995.
Peter Gould and Rodney White, *Mental Maps*, Boston: Allen & Unwin, 1974, 1986.
Kenneth Graham, *Wind in the Willows*, Oxford: Oxford Paperbacks, 1999.
Martin Green, *New York 1913*, London: Simon & Schuster, 1990.
Clement Greenberg, *The Collected Essays and Criticism*, Chicago, IL: University Press, 1988.
Zane Grey, *The Heritage of the Desert*, New York: Pocket Books, 1993.
— *Tales of Lonely Trails*, Flagstaff: Northland Publishers, 1986.
Phyllis Grosskurth, *The Secret Ring*, London: Jonathan Cape, 1991.
George Grossmith, *Diary of a Nobody*, Xlibris Corporation, 2001.
John G. Hanhardt, ed., *Nam June Paik*, New York: Whitney Museum of American Art, in association with W. W. Norton, 1982.
Helen Mayer Harrison and Newton Harrison, *The Lagoon Cycle*, Ithaca: Herbert F. Johnson Museum of Art, Cornell University, 1985.
Jill Hartz, ed., *Agnes Denes*, Ithaca: Herbert F. Johnson Museum of Art, Cornell University, 1992.
Martin Heidegger, *The Question Concerning Technology and Other Essays*, Harper Torchbooks, 1977.
Stuart Hood, *On the Marble Cliffs*, Harmondsworth: Penguin, 1972.
Douglas Huebler, *"Variable", etc.*, Limoges: Fonds Régional D'Art Contemporain, 1993.
Alexis Hunter, 'Interview with Victor Burgin', in John Roberts, ed., *The Impossible Document: Photography and Conceptual Art in Britain 1966–1976*, London: Camerawords, 1997.
Robert M. Isherwood, *Music in the Service of the King*, Ithaca: Cornell University Press, 1973.
Derek Jarman, *At Your Own Risk*, Overlook Press, 1993.
— *Chroma*, London: Vintage, 1995.
Ernst Jünger, *Storms of Steel*, London, Chatto, 1922.
— *The Worker*, London, Chatto, 1932.
Julius Kaplan, *Gustave Moreau*, Los Angeles: Los Angeles County Museum Of Art, 1974.
Elizabeth Kendall, *Where She Danced*, New York: Khnopf, 1979.
Hugh Kenner, *The Mechanic Muse*, Oxford University Press USA, 1987.
Frank Kermode, *Romantic Image*, London: Routledge & Kegan Paul, 1957.
Joseph Kosuth, *Art after Philosophy and After*, Cambridge, MA: MIT Press, 1993.

Rosalind Krauss, *The Originality of the Avante-Garde*, Cambridge, MA: MIT Press, 1985.
— *Grids*, New York: Pace Wildenstein, 1980.
Thomas Kulka, *Kitsch and Art*, Penn State University Press, 1996.
Milan Kundera, *The Unbearable Lightness of Being*, Faber & Faber, 1985.
Jacques Lacan, *Ecrits*, London, Routledge, 2001.
Serge Leclair, 'Philo, or the Obsessional and his Desire', in *Démasquer le réel*, Paris: Le Seuil, 1971.
Le Corbusier, *The Decorative Art of Today*, Cambridge, MA: MIT Press, 1987.
Sol LeWitt, *Critical Texts*, Rome: Incontri Internazionale D'arte, 1994.
Wyndam Lewis, *Blasting and Bombardiering*, Calder Publications Ltd, 1970.
Lucy Lippard, *Six Years: The Dematerialization of the Art Object*, New York: Praeger, 1973.
— *Six Years*, Berkeley: University of California Press, 1997.
Jean Lognon, ed., *Louis XIV, Mémoires*, Paris: Librairie Jules Tallandier, 1978.
John Lomax, *Cowboy Songs*, Gale Group, 1986.
Jack London, *Iron Heel*, Rebel Inc, 1999.
Emile Magne, *Les Plaisirs et les Fêtes en France au XVIIe Siècle*, Geneva: Editions de la Frégate, 1944.
Curzio Malaparte, *Kaputt*, Casella a Napoli, 1944.
— *The Skin*, UK: Picador, 1952.
— *The Volga Rises in Europe*, UK: Alvin Redman, 1957.
John Anthony Maltese, *Spin Control, The White House Office of Communications and the Management of Presidential News*, Chapel Hill: The University of North Carolina, 1992.
Louis Marin, *Portrait of the King*, London: Macmillan, 1988.
Filippo Tommaso Marinetti, *Mafarka*, London: Calder Publications, 2000.
Guy de Maupassant, *Boule de Suif*, London: Penguin, 1995.
Patrick Mauriès, *Shell Shock: Conchological Curiosities*, London: Thames and Hudson, 1994.
Hermann Melville, *Moby Dick*, Konemann UK Ltd, 1996.
Mark Monmonnier, *Cartographies of Danger*, Chicago: University of Chicago Press, 1997.
Michael Morris, *Madam Valentino, The Many Lives of Natacha Rambova*, New York: Abbeville Press, 1991.
Margaret Morton, *Transitory Gardens, Uprooted Lives*, New Haven: Yale University Press, 1995.
Edgar Munhall, *Whistler And Montesquiou, The Butterfly And The Bat*, Paris: Flammarion, 1995.

Elliot Neaman, *A Dubious Past; Ernst Jünger and the Politics of Literature after Nazism*, Berkeley and Los Angeles: University of California Press, 1999.
Henry Pearson, *Creating Country Music, Fabricating Authenticity*, Chicago, IL: University of Chicago Press, 1997.
Jean-Pierre Néradau, *L'Olympe du Roi-Soleil*, Paris: Société d'Edition: "Les Belles Lettres", 1986.
Celeste Olalquiaga, *The Artificial Kingdom of the Kitsch Experience*, Pantheon Books, 1998.
Yoko Ono, *Grapefruit*, New York: Simon & Schuster, 1964, 1970.
Charles Perrault, 'Mémoires' in Peter Burke, *The Fabrication of Louis XIV*, Newhaven: Yale University Press, 1992.
Mary Elizabeth Perry, 'The Popular History of the Reign', in Paul Sonnino, ed., *The Reign of Louis XIV*, Atlantic Highlands, NJ: Humanities Press International, 1990.
Jocelyn Powell, *Restoration Theatre Production*, London: Routledge & Kegan Paul, 1984.
Mario Praz, *The Romantic Agony*, Oxford: Oxford University Press, 1933.
Astrid Proll, *Baader Meinhof/Pictures on the Run*, 67–77, Scalo, 1998.
Derrick Puffett, ed., *Richard Strauss, Salome*, Cambridge: Cambridge University Press, 1989.
Pierre Rameau, *The Dancing Master*, London: C. W. Beaumont, 1931.
G. Reitlinger, *The Economics of Taste*, London: Barrie and Rockliff, 1961.
Gerhard Richter and Robert Storr, *Gerhard Richter, October 18, 1977*, Museum of Modern Art, New York, 2002.
John Roberts, ed., *The Impossible Document: Photography and Conceptual Art in Britain 1966–1976*, London: Camerawords, 1997.
Michael Roberts, *The Military Revolution, 1560–1660*, Belfast: Queen's University, 1956.
Rollinat, *Les Neuroses*, Wisbech: Red Candle Press, 1986.
Simon Sadler, *The Situationist City*, Cambridge and London: MIT Press, 1998.
Edward W. Said, *Orientalism*, New York: Random House, 1978.
Naomi Salomon, 'Victor Burgin in conversation with Naomi Salomon', in Naomi Salomon and Ronnie Simpson, eds, *Postcards on Photography*, Cambridge: Cambridge Darkroom Gallery, 1998.
Elaine Showalter, *Sexual Anarchy, Gender And Culture At The Fin De Siècle*, New York: Viking, 1990.
Charles I. Silin, *Benserade and his Ballets de Cour*, Baltimore: The Johns Hopkins Press, 1940.

May Sinclair, *The Tree of Heaven*, New York: Macmillan, 1917.
Peter N. Skrine, *The Baroque*, London: Methuen, 1978.
A. J. Smithers, *A New Excalibur, The Development of the Tank 1909–1939*, Leo Cooper, 1986.
H. Sohm, ed., *Happening & Fluxus*, Koeln: Koelnischer Kunstverein, 1970.
Bjorn Springfeldt, ed., *On Kawara, continuity/discontinuity, 1963–79*, Stockholm: Moderna Museet, 1980.
Ernest Swinton, *Eyewitness*, Arno Press, 1933.
Fiona Templeton, *You—The City*, New York: Roof Books, 1990.
Emma Tennant, ed., *Saturday Night Reader*, London: W. H. Allen, 1979.
Jean-Louis Thireau, *Les Idées Politiques de Louis XIV*, Paris: Presses Universitaires de France, 1973.
Michael Thompson, *Rubbish Theory: The Construction and Destruction of Value*, Oxford: Oxford University Press, 1979.
Edward R. Tufte, *The Visual Display of Quantitative Information*, Cheshire, Connecticut: Graphics Press, 1983.
Ed Van Der Elsken, *Love on the Left Bank*, Stockport: Dewi Lewis Publishing, 1989.
Carl Van Vechten, *Peter Whiffle*, R. A. Kessinger Publishing, 2003.
Antoine Vallot, Antoine d'Aquin, and Guy-Crescent Fagon, *Journal de la Santé du Roi Louis XIV*, J.-A. Le Roi, ed., Paris: Auguste Durand, 1862.
Michele Wallace, *Invisibility Blues: From Pop to Theory*, London and New York: Verso, 1990, 2004.
Stanley Weintraub, *Aubrey Beardsley, Imp Of The Perverse*, University Park: Pennsylvania State University Press, 1976.
Tom Wolfe, *The Painted Word*, New York: Farrar, Straus and Giroux, 1975.
Denis Wood, *The Power of Maps*, New York and London: The Guilford Press, 1992.
Patrick Wright, *Tank: The Progress of a War Machine*, London: Faber and Faber, 2001.

ACKNOWLEDGEMENTS

'Government by Appearances' was first published in *New Left Review*, 3, May–June, 2000.

'Tanks' was first published in *London Review of Books*, 16 November 2000.

'October 18, 1977' was first published in *London Review of Books*, 4 April 2000.

'Kitsch' was first published in *London Review of Books*, 17 February 2000.

'Blue' was first published in *New Left Review*, 6, November–December, 2000.

'Magritte and the Bowler Hat' was first published in *New Left Review*, 1, January–February, 2000.

'Mappings: Situationists and/or Conceptualists' was first published in *Rewriting Conceptual Art*, edited by Michael Newman and Jon Bird, Reaktion Books, London, 1999.

'The Situationists and Architecture' was first published in *New Left Review*, 8, March–April, 2001.

'Fridamania' was first published in *New Left Review*, 22, July–August, 2003.

INDEX

Aberley, Doug 159
Acker, Kathy 213
Adorno, Theodor 95
Agar, Eileen 246
Alden, John Madison, 186
Algoud, Albert 133
Allan, Maud 108
Alma-Tadema, Lawrence 161
Alvarez Bravo, Manuel 73
Anderson, Bronco Billy 189
André, Carl 17, 20, 28, 32
Annenberg, Walter 66
Antheil, George 57–8
Apostolides, Jean-Marie 13
Asher, Michael 18, 33, 34
Asquith, H. H. 38
Astruc, Gabriel 106
Aust, Stefan 80, 83
Autry, Gene 198
Aw Boon Haw 230

Baader, Andreas 75–6, 80, 81, 82–84
Bakst 107, 162, 163, 167, 181
Baldessari, John 18, 28, 33
Baldwin, Neil 171
Balenciaga, Cristóbal 173
Ball, Hugo 56

Barbas, Raymond 169
Barr, Alfred H. 67, 70, 71
Barrell, Robert 196
Barrie, J. M. 245
Barry, Judith 12–13
Barry, Robert 17
Barthes, Roland 27, 28, 29, 131, 132, 219, 220, 221–2, 223–4, 234
Bataille, Georges 26, 69
Batchelor, David 20, 21
Battersby, Martin 170
Baudelaire, Charles 88, 106
Bausch, Pina 111
Baxter, Iain 18
Beardsley, Aubrey 105–6, 110, 111
Beauchamps, Charles 3, 7, 8
Becher, Johannes 56
Becker–Ho, Alice 203
Beckett, Samuel 134, 140–1, 142, 145
Bell, Vanessa 163
Benjamin, Walter 58, 70, 88–9
Bentham, Jeremy 1
Bernhardt, Sarah 103, 104
Best Maugard, Adolfo 243
Beuys, Joseph 78, 180
Beveridge, Karl 33
Bierstadt, Albert 186, 192

Bion, Wilfred 45
Birtwhistle, Grahame 207, 208
Blake, William 122, 127
Blume, Peter 98
Blumenschein, Ernest 185
Boas, Franz 63, 196
Boccioni, Umberto 45, 55
Bochner, Mel 17, 18, 33
Boetti, Alighiero 157
Boetticher, Budd 197
Boll, Heinrich 85
Botticelli, Sandro 138, 228
Bonaparte, Marie 231
Boni, Aida 106
Brancusi, Constantin 21, 171
Brandt, Bill 229
Braque, Georges 135, 145
Brecht, Bertolt 213
Breton, André 71, 132, 136, 163, 170, 186, 204, 205, 237, 244
Broch, Herman 89
Brummel, Beau 164
Budd, Michael 193
Burbank, Luther 245
Buren, Daniel 18
Burger, Peter 16
Burgin, Victor 22, 29, 33, 219–234
Burke, Peter 11
Burns, Robert 184
Burroughs, William 244
Busa, Peter 186, 196
Buscombe, Ed 191–3
Butler, Perpetua 24
Byron, Lord 184

Cage, John 20, 23, 27, 205
Caillebotte, Gustav 145
Cale, John 175
Cardin, Pierre 174
Carné, Marcel 216
Carra, Carlo 55
Carrington, Dora 246
Carter, Nick 132
Cartier-Bresson, Henri 223

Castelli, Leo 95
Catlin, George 186, 187
Cawelti, John 193–4
Celant, Germano 23
Cézanne, Paul 135, 145
Cha, Therese Hak Kyung 32
Chanel, Coco 167–8, 169, 170, 171, 172, 173
Chaplin, Charles 133–6, 145
Chaplin, Ralph 182
Charcot, Jean-Martin 103
Chardin, Jean-Baptiste-Siméon 94
Charles-Roux, Edmonde 168
Charlot, Jean 73
Chéret, Jules 105
Chicago, Julie 246
Chomsky, Noam 28
Chopin, Frédéric 108
Christo 178
Churchill, Winston 37, 38
Clah, Al 200
Clark, Lygia 180
Clark, T. J. 215
Cocteau, Jean 135, 166, 169, 171, 177
Cody, Buffalo Bill 187–8, 194
Coke, William 142
Coles, Robert 94
Collier, John 199–200
Condé, Carole 33
Constant 203, 204, 206, 212, 214–15
Courrèges, André 173–4
Covarrubias, Miguel 243
Crane, Hart 244
Crane, Walter 161
Crary, Jonathan 10–11, 122, 123
Crawford, Joan 216
Crowley, Aleister 41–2
Cruze, James 190

Daly, Norman 159
Dalí, Salvador 170, 171, 172
D'Annunzio, Gabriele 107
Darboven, Hanne 17
Darrow, Whitney 197

Dasburg, Andrew 184, 185
Dassin, Jules 150
Daum, Howard 196
Davis, Stuart 185
De Caux, Len 199
De Chirico 98, 210
De Landa, Manuel 43–44, 59
De Lauwe, Chombart 151, 204
de Montesquiou, Robert 111
de Osma, Guillermo 161
De Sade, Marquis 106, 225
De Saint-Phalle, Niki 205
Debord, Guy 10, 11, 13, 121–2, 147, 149–153, 155, 156, 159, 203–218
Dew, Diana 175
D'Eyncourt, Tennyson 37, 38, 39, 40
Delaunay, Robert 163
Delaunay, Sonia 163, 169, 239
Delluc, Louise 135
Denes, Agnes 32, 158, 159
Denon, Vivant 61
Diaghilev, Serge 14, 106, 107, 163, 166, 169, 170, 177
Dibbets, Jan 18
Diderot, Denis 223–4, 230
Dijkstra, Bram 110
Dior, Christian 172–4
Döblin, Alfred 56, 57
Dodge, Mabel 182, 184–5, 199, 200
Dorfles, Gillo 23, 89
Dorling, David 159
Doucet, Jacues 163
Douglas, Keith 45
Duchamp, Marcel 16, 21, 27, 28, 31–2, 93
Duncan, Isadora 14, 108, 111, 161, 168
Duncan, Raymond 168
Dürer, Albrecht 204
Durham, Jimmie 200
Dutschke, Rudi 81
Dyck, Aganetha 180

Edward VII, King 142
Eisenstein, Sergei 58, 124, 244
Eliot, T. S. 42, 58

Ellis, Clough Williams 44
Ellman, Richard 111
Eno, Brian 116
Ensslin, Gudrun 75–6, 80, 83, 84
Ernst, Max 186
Evans, Walker 90

Fairbairn, David 159
Farber, Manny 196–197
Fassbinder, Rainer Werner 85–6
Felibian 6
Fellini, Federico 227
Ferenczi, Sándor 230–2
Ficino, Marsilio 122, 127
Fini, Léonor 171
Finkelstein, Nat 175
Fischer, Joschka 82
Flaubert, Gustav 102
Flavin, Dan 20, 21
Floge, Emilie 162, 181
Flynt, Henry 31
Fokine, Michel 106, 107
Fol, Carine 139
Fontana, Lucio 126
Ford, Henry 167
Ford, John 190–1, 192, 193, 197
Fortuny, Mariano 161–2
Foucault, Michel 1, 2, 8, 10 , 14
Fragonard, John-Honoré 94
Frampton, Hollis 32, 147
Francis, Mark 237
Franzen, Ulrich 176
Freud, Sigmund 103, 224–5, 226, 227, 230–1, 232, 233, 234
Fried, Michael 94
Fuchs, Karl 46–47
Fuller, J. F. C. 40–43, 52
Fussell, Paul 53

Galán, Julio 243
Gallizio, Pinot 214, 215
Gamboa, Harry 30–1
Garafola, Lynn 106
Garland, Judy 240

Gass, William 125
Gat, Azar 42, 43
Gaudí, Antonio 205
Gill, Eric 122
Ginsburg, Carlo 131–2
Gintz, Claude 34
Godwin, E. W. 104, 162
Goethe, Johann Wolfgang von 123, 124, 232
Goleizovsky, Kasian 109
Goll, Ivan 135
Gould, Peter 158
Graham, Dan 17, 31
Graham, Kenneth 132
Grahame, Martha 111
Grass, Günter 57
Gray, Eileen 177–8
Green, George 199
Green, Martin 182, 183, 184, 185
Greenaway, Peter 119
Greenberg, Clement 19–20, 28, 29, 89, 90–3, 94, 96, 98, 220, 223
Greimas, Algirdas 219–220
Grey, Zane 192–3
Grooms, Red 198–9
Grossfurth, Phyllis 232
Guest, Haden 97
Guggenheim, Peggy 195

Haacke, Hans 18, 30, 31, 33
Haden-Guest, Anthony 96
Hamilton, Richard 77, 78
Hapgood, Hutchins 184
Harlow, Jean 170
Harris, Ann Sutherland 236
Harrison, Helen Meyer 158–9
Harrison, Newton 158–9
Hart, Liddell 40, 43, 52
Haydon, Sterling 216
Hayman, Ronald 83
Haywood, Bill 183–4
Heckert, Matt 49
Heidegger, Martin 45, 51–2, 53–55, 58–59, 60

Heim, Jacques, 169
Heindel, Max 117
Hepworth, Barbara 239
Hergé 133, 140
Hernandez, Anthony 216
Herrán, Saturnino 243
Herrera, Hayden 72, 235, 237
Herrón, Willie 30
Hesse, Eva 17, 246
Hickey, Dave 93–6, 97
Hiller, Susan 229
Hirst, Damien 98, 99
Hitchcock, Alfred, 225–6, 228, 230, 232
Hitler, Adolf 11–12, 45
Hjelmslev, Louis 220, 221
Hood, Stuart 54
Huebler, Douglas 17, 18, 152–6
Huot, Robert 32
Husserl, Edmund 221
Huysmans, J.-K. 102–3, 104, 105, 109
Ibsen, Henrik 106
Ingleby, Richard 45
Iolas, Alexandre 128
Iturbide, Graciela 243
Ivain, Gilles 149
Izquierdo, María 246

Jakobson, Roman 220, 221
James, Edward 142, 143
Jameson, Fredric 25
Jarman, Derek 113–127
Jeffers, Robinson 185
Johns, Jasper 28, 176
Johnson, Betsey 175
Johnson, Poppy 31
Jones, Robert Edmond 185
Jordan 119
Jorn, Asger 149–150, 202–4, 207–8, 217, 218
Joyce, James 58
Joyce, Mary 216
Judd, Donald 17, 20, 28, 29, 220
Jung, Carl 232
Jünger, Ernst 46, 53–5, 60

Bion, Wilfred 45
Birtwhistle, Grahame 207, 208
Blake, William 122, 127
Blume, Peter 98
Blumenschein, Ernest 185
Boas, Franz 63, 196
Boccioni, Umberto 45, 55
Bochner, Mel 17, 18, 33
Boetti, Alighiero 157
Boetticher, Budd 197
Boll, Heinrich 85
Botticelli, Sandro 138, 228
Bonaparte, Marie 231
Boni, Aida 106
Brancusi, Constantin 21, 171
Brandt, Bill 229
Braque, Georges 135, 145
Brecht, Bertolt 213
Breton, André 71, 132, 136, 163, 170, 186, 204, 205, 237, 244
Broch, Herman 89
Brummel, Beau 164
Budd, Michael 193
Burbank, Luther 245
Buren, Daniel 18
Burger, Peter 16
Burgin, Victor 22, 29, 33, 219–234
Burke, Peter 11
Burns, Robert 184
Burroughs, William 244
Busa, Peter 186, 196
Buscombe, Ed 191–3
Butler, Perpetua 24
Byron, Lord 184

Cage, John 20, 23, 27, 205
Caillebotte, Gustav 145
Cale, John 175
Cardin, Pierre 174
Carné, Marcel 216
Carra, Carlo 55
Carrington, Dora 246
Carter, Nick 132
Cartier-Bresson, Henri 223

Castelli, Leo 95
Catlin, George 186, 187
Cawelti, John 193–4
Celant, Germano 23
Cézanne, Paul 135, 145
Cha, Therese Hak Kyung 32
Chanel, Coco 167–8, 169, 170, 171, 172, 173
Chaplin, Charles 133–6, 145
Chaplin, Ralph 182
Charcot, Jean-Martin 103
Chardin, Jean-Baptiste-Siméon 94
Charles-Roux, Edmonde 168
Charlot, Jean 73
Chéret, Jules 105
Chicago, Julie 246
Chomsky, Noam 28
Chopin, Frédéric 108
Christo 178
Churchill, Winston 37, 38
Clah, Al 200
Clark, Lygia 180
Clark, T. J. 215
Cocteau, Jean 135, 166, 169, 171, 177
Cody, Buffalo Bill 187–8, 194
Coke, William 142
Coles, Robert 94
Collier, John 199–200
Condé, Carole 33
Constant 203, 204, 206, 212, 214–15
Courrèges, André 173–4
Covarrubias, Miguel 243
Crane, Hart 244
Crane, Walter 161
Crary, Jonathan 10–11, 122, 123
Crawford, Joan 216
Crowley, Aleister 41–2
Cruze, James 190

Daly, Norman 159
Dalí, Salvador 170, 171, 172
D'Annunzio, Gabriele 107
Darboven, Hanne 17
Darrow, Whitney 197

INDEX

Aberley, Doug 159
Acker, Kathy 213
Adorno, Theodor 95
Agar, Eileen 246
Alden, John Madison 186
Algoud, Albert 133
Allan, Maud 108
Alma-Tadema, Lawrence 161
Alvarez Bravo, Manuel 73
Anderson, Bronco Billy 189
André, Carl 17, 20, 28, 32
Annenberg, Walter 66
Antheil, George 57–8
Apostolides, Jean-Marie 13
Asher, Michael 18, 33, 34
Asquith, H. H. 38
Astruc, Gabriel 106
Aust, Stefan 80, 83
Autry, Gene 198
Aw Boon Haw 230

Baader, Andreas 75–6, 80, 81, 82–84
Bakst 107, 162, 163, 167, 181
Baldessari, John 18, 28, 33
Baldwin, Neil 171
Balenciaga, Cristóbal 173
Ball, Hugo 56

Barbas, Raymond 169
Barr, Alfred H. 67, 70, 71
Barrell, Robert 196
Barrie, J. M. 245
Barry, Judith 12–13
Barry, Robert 17
Barthes, Roland 27, 28, 29, 131, 132, 219, 220, 221–2, 223–4, 234
Bataille, Georges 26, 69
Batchelor, David 20, 21
Battersby, Martin 170
Baudelaire, Charles 88, 106
Bausch, Pina 111
Baxter, Iain 18
Beardsley, Aubrey 105–6, 110, 111
Beauchamps, Charles 3, 7, 8
Becher, Johannes 56
Becker–Ho, Alice 203
Beckett, Samuel 134, 140–1, 142, 145
Bell, Vanessa 163
Benjamin, Walter 58, 70, 88–9
Bentham, Jeremy 1
Bernhardt, Sarah 103, 104
Best Maugard, Adolfo 243
Beuys, Joseph 78, 180
Beveridge, Karl 33
Bierstadt, Albert 186, 192

Dasburg, Andrew 184, 185
Dassin, Jules 150
Daum, Howard 196
Davis, Stuart 185
De Caux, Len 199
De Chirico 98, 210
De Landa, Manuel 43–44, 59
De Lauwe, Chombart 151, 204
de Montesquiou, Robert 111
de Osma, Guillermo 161
De Sade, Marquis 106, 225
De Saint-Phalle, Niki 205
Debord, Guy 10, 11, 13, 121–2, 147,
    149–153, 155, 156, 159, 203–218
Dew, Diana 175
D'Eyncourt, Tennyson 37, 38, 39, 40
Delaunay, Robert 163
Delaunay, Sonia 163, 169, 239
Delluc, Louise 135
Denes, Agnes 32, 158, 159
Denon, Vivant 61
Diaghilev, Serge 14, 106, 107, 163,
    166, 169, 170, 177
Dibbets, Jan 18
Diderot, Denis 223–4, 230
Dijkstra, Bram 110
Dior, Christian 172–4
Döblin, Alfred 56, 57
Dodge, Mabel 182, 184–5, 199, 200
Dorfles, Gillo 23, 89
Dorling, David 159
Doucet, Jacues 163
Douglas, Keith 45
Duchamp, Marcel 16, 21, 27, 28, 31–2, 93
Duncan, Isadora 14, 108, 111, 161, 168
Duncan, Raymond 168
Dürer, Albrecht 204
Durham, Jimmie 200
Dutschke, Rudi 81
Dyck, Agaietha 180

Edward VII, King 142
Eisenstein, Sergei 58, 124, 244
Eliot, T. S. 42, 58

Ellis, Clough Williams 44
Ellman, Richard 111
Eno, Brian 116
Ensslin, Gudrun 75–6, 80, 83, 84
Ernst, Max 186
Evans, Walker 90

Fairbairn, David 159
Farber, Manny 196–197
Fassbinder, Rainer Werner 85–6
Felibian 6
Fellini, Federico 227
Ferenczi, Sándor 230–2
Ficino, Marsilio 122, 127
Fini, Léonor 171
Finkelstein, Nat 175
Fischer, Joschka 82
Flaubert, Gustav 102
Flavin, Dan 20, 21
Floge, Emilie 162, 181
Flynt, Henry 31
Fokine, Michel 106, 107
Fol, Carine 139
Fontana, Lucio 126
Ford, Henry 167
Ford, John 190–1, 192, 193, 197
Fortuny, Mariano 161–2
Foucault, Michel 1, 2, 8, 10 , 14
Fragonard, John-Honoré 94
Frampton, Hollis 32, 147
Francis, Mark 237
Franzen, Ulrich 176
Freud, Sigmund 103, 224–5, 226,
    227, 230–1, 232, 233, 234
Fried, Michael 94
Fuchs, Karl 46–47
Fuller, J. F. C. 40–43, 52
Fussell, Paul 53

Galán, Julio 243
Gallizio, Pinot 214, 215
Gamboa, Harry 30–1
Garafola, Lynn 106
Garland, Judy 240

Gass, William 125
Gat, Azar 42, 43
Gaudí, Antonio 205
Gill, Eric 122
Ginsburg, Carlo 131–2
Gintz, Claude 34
Godwin, E. W. 104, 162
Goethe, Johann Wolfgang von 123, 124, 232
Goleizovsky, Kasian 109
Goll, Ivan 135
Gould, Peter 158
Graham, Dan 17, 31
Graham, Kenneth 132
Grahame, Martha 111
Grass, Günter 57
Gray, Eileen 177–8
Green, George 199
Green, Martin 182, 183, 184, 185
Greenaway, Peter 119
Greenberg, Clement 19–20, 28, 29, 89, 90–3, 94, 96, 98, 220, 223
Greimas, Algirdas 219–220
Grey, Zane 192–3
Grooms, Red 198–9
Grossfurth, Phyllis 232
Guest, Haden 97
Guggenheim, Peggy 195

Haacke, Hans 18, 30, 31, 33
Haden-Guest, Anthony 96
Hamilton, Richard 77, 78
Hapgood, Hutchins 184
Harlow, Jean 170
Harris, Ann Sutherland 236
Harrison, Helen Meyer 158–9
Harrison, Newton 158–9
Hart, Liddell 40, 43, 52
Haydon, Sterling 216
Hayman, Ronald 83
Haywood, Bill 183–4
Heckert, Matt 49
Heidegger, Martin 45, 51–2, 53–55, 58–59, 60

Heim, Jacques, 169
Heindel, Max 117
Hepworth, Barbara 239
Hergé 133, 140
Hernandez, Anthony 216
Herrán, Saturnino 243
Herrera, Hayden 72, 235, 237
Herrón, Willie 30
Hesse, Eva 17, 246
Hickey, Dave 93–6, 97
Hiller, Susan 229
Hirst, Damien 98, 99
Hitchcock, Alfred, 225–6, 228, 230, 232
Hitler, Adolf 11–12, 45
Hjelmslev, Louis 220, 221
Hood, Stuart 54
Huebler, Douglas 17, 18, 152–6
Huot, Robert 32
Husserl, Edmund 221
Huysmans, J.-K. 102–3, 104, 105, 109
Ibsen, Henrik 106
Ingleby, Richard 45
Iolas, Alexandre 128
Iturbide, Graciela 243
Ivain, Gilles 149
Izquierdo, María 246

Jakobson, Roman 220, 221
James, Edward 142, 143
Jameson, Fredric 25
Jarman, Derek 113–127
Jeffers, Robinson 185
Johns, Jasper 28, 176
Johnson, Betsey 175
Johnson, Poppy 31
Jones, Robert Edmond 185
Jordan 119
Jorn, Asger 149–150, 202–4, 207–8, 217, 218
Joyce, James 58
Joyce, Mary 216
Judd, Donald 17, 20, 28, 29, 220
Jung, Carl 232
Jünger, Ernst 46, 53–5, 60

Kaes, Anton 86
Kahlo, Frida 71–2, 235–247
Kahn, Albert 58
Kahn, Moritz 58
Kandinsky, Wassily 73
Karno, Fred 133, 135
Kawakubo, Rei 177–8
Kawara, On 18, 30, 152–153
Keifer, Otto 239
Kelly, Ellsworth 95, 121
Kelly, Mary 27, 246
Kelley, Mike 93
Kendall, Elizabeth 109
Kenner, Hugh 57–58
Kerouac, Jack 199
Kinkade, Thomas 95, 96
Kitaj, Ronald 197
Kitchener, Lord 36, 40
Kimmelman, Michael 94
Klaus, Alfred 84
Klee, Paul 202
Klein, Hans-Joachim 82
Klein, Yves 113–19, 120–1, 124, 126
Klimt, Gustav 162, 181
Koch, Gertrud 81
Koons, Jeff 95–7
Korngold, Julius 108
Kosloff, Theodor 110
Kosuth, Joseph 17, 18–19, 21–3, 24–7, 29, 33
Kozlov, Christine 17, 18, 21, 30
Krasner, Lee 239
Krauss, Rosalind 26
Kristeva, Julia 224, 227
Kuhn, Thomas 69
Kulge, Alexander 85
Kulka, Thomas 89–90
Kundera, Milan 144–5

Lacan, Jacques 28, 224, 226, 227
Lacquer, Thomas 110
Lapsley, Rob 233
Lautrec, Toulouse 145
Lawrence, D. H. 185, 244

Le Bon, Gustav 42
Le Corbusier 55, 136–8, 145, 165– 6, 178, 207, 208
Le Va, Barry 18
Le Vau 1
Leduc, Paul 236
Leighton, Frederick 161
Léger, Fernand 58, 135, 136, 163, 172, 207
Lenglen, Suzanne 168–9
Lenin, Vladimir 59, 142
Levine, Les 32
Levinson, André 107
Lewis, Wyndham 45, 57
LeWitt, Sol 17, 18–19, 20, 21, 23, 26–7, 32, 33
Lincoln, President 192
Lippard, Lucy 26, 29, 31, 32
Litell, Deanna 175, 176
Lloyd George, David 38, 39, 40
Lobenthal, Joel 176
Locke, John 124
Lomax, John 197
London, Jack 183
Loos, Adolf 164–5
Lorrain, Claude 206, 210
Losurdo, Domenico 59
Louis XIV, King 1–14
Lowry, L. S. 135–6, 140, 145, 244
Lozano, Lee 17, 30
Ludwig, King of Bavaria 205–6
Luhan, Tony 199
Lully, Jean-Baptiste 6, 14
Lundberg, Erik 203
Lundquist, Erik 207

Magritte, René 19, 128–45
Mahler, Gustav 108
Malaparte, Curzio 45–6, 47
Malevich, Gustav 117, 126, 170
Mallarmé, Stéphane 104, 111
Malone, Bill 198
Malraux, André 74
Manet, Edouard 225
Man Ray 71, 163, 171

Mann, Anthony 192, 197
Marble, Alice 169
Marc, Franz 56
Marcuse, Herbert 25, 33
Marden, Brice 125
Margiela, Martin 180
Marin, John 185
Marinetti, Filippo Tomasso 45, 55, 56
Marioni, Tom 18
Marlowe, Christopher 115
Marx, Karl 58, 122, 183
Matisse, Henri 107, 162, 163, 167, 170, 181
Maugham, Syrie 170
Maupassant, Guy de 190
Mazarin, Jules 4, 6
Mayakovsky, Vladimir 244
Meinhof, Ulrike 76, 81, 82, 84, 85
Meins, Holger 76, 82
Melly, George 143
Melville, Herman 80, 245
Mendelssohn, Felix 108
Mendes, Leopoldo 73
Menton, Seymour 98
Mesens, E. L. T. 139, 143
Messel, Oliver 170
Miller, Alfred Jacob 186
Millet, Catherine 24
Milton, John 184
Miro, Joan 246
Mix, Tom 188–190
Miyake, Isse 178, 179
Modigliani 240
Modotti, Tina 71, 235, 236, 240, 243
Moholy-Nagy 16, 27
Möller, Irmgard 75–6
Molyneux, William 124
Monroe, Marilyn 240
Montenegro, Roberto 243
Moore, Albert 161
Mordkin, Mikhail 109
Moreau, Gustave 101–2, 108, 109, 111
Morris, Robert 17, 20, 31, 220
Morton, Margaret 216
Mosley, Sir Oswald 41

Mulvey, Laura 71, 235
Münter, Gabriele 239

Naifeh, Steven 194, 195
Nazimova, Alla 109
Neaman, Elliot 53
Nevinson, Christopher 45
Newman, Barnett 21
Nietzche, Friedrich 59, 232, 233
Nijinska, Bronislava 169
Noguchi, Isamu 178
Nougé, Paul 139

O'Keefe, Georgia, 185, 186, 239
Olalquiaga, Celeste 87–91, 92, 98–100
Ono, Yoko 30, 157
Oppenhaim, Meret 171
O'Pray, Michael 115
Ozenfant, Amédée 136, 166

Paalen, Wolfgang 186
Paik, Nam June 157
Palermo, Blinky 126
Pálos, Elma 230–1, 232
Pálos, Gizella 230–1
Patou, Jean 168–9, 170
Pauline, Mark 50, 60
Pearson, Richard 198
Peckinpah, Sam 197
Philips, Bert 185
Picabia, Francis 163, 171
Picasso, Pablo 64, 77, 135, 145, 163, 166
Pinkerton, Nat 132
Pinot Gallizio, Giuseppe 203
Piper, Adrian 18, 30
Pfemfert, Franz 56
Plath, Sylvia 72, 240–1, 244
Poiret, Paul 107, 162–3, 166–7, 169, 170, 171, 172, 177, 181
Pollock, Jackson 99, 172, 186, 194–7, 199, 200, 214, 246
Pollock, Sande 195
Posada, José Guadalupe 72–3
Pound, Ezra 58

Poussin, Nicolas 119
Praz, Mario 110
Prina, Stephen 126
Proll, Astrid 80–1
Proust, Marcel 88, 167–8

Rainer, Yvonne 85, 111
Rambova, Natasha 110
Raspe, Jan-Carl 75–6, 80, 83, 84
Rauschenberg, Robert 77, 125, 126, 198–199
Ray, Nicholas 216
Reddin, Paul 186, 187, 188
Rémy, Marcel 108
Regnault, Henri 102, 104
Reich, Wilhelm 45
Reid, Jamie 147
Reinhardt, Ad 125, 220
Reitlinger, G. 66
Reitz, Edgar 85
Remington, Frederic 186
Renshaw, Patrick 183
Rhodes, Zandra 243
Richter, Gerhard 75, 76–9, 81, 86, 126, 135
Rinaldi, Michael 21
Ringgold, Faith 31
Rita, Saint 114, 119
Ritter, Tex 197
Rivera, Diego 71–2, 73, 240, 242, 244, 245
Robert, Hubert 90
Roberts, John 22
Robinson, Fred Miller 142
Robinson, Heath 214
Rockwell, Norman 74, 93–4, 95, 97
Rodchenko 16, 27, 28, 126
Rodin, Auguste 222
Rogers, Will 198
Rogers, Roy 198
Rollinat, Maurice 103–4
Roosevelt, Edward 189
Rosler, Martha 31, 33
Rossie, Ernest 21
Rothko, Mark 21, 99
Rubens, Peter Paul 104
Rubinstein, Ida 106–7, 108

Ruppersberg, Allen 18
Ruscha, Ed 95
Ruskin, John 122, 123, 124
Russell, Charles 186
Ryman, Robert, 17, 121, 126

Sadler, Simon 149, 150–1
Saint-Laurent, Yves 174
Sakata, Eiichiro 178
Salome 101–112
Sargent, John Singer 45
Sartre, Jean-Paul 82–3
Saussure, Ferdinand de 132, 220, 221
Schiaparelli, Elsa 170–2, 177
Schubert, Franz 104
Schleyer, Hanns Martin 85
Schlondorff, Volker 85
Schwitters, Kurt 71, 206–7, 208
Sedgwick, Edie 174–5
Sekula, Allan 31, 33
Semmes, Beverly 180
Serrano, Andrew 121
Servrancks, Victor 136
Seurat, Georges 145
Severini, Gino 45, 55
Shaw, Jim 99
Shelley, Mary 245
Shepard, Ernest 132
Shomi, Chieko 157–8
Showalter, Elaine 110
Siegelaub, Seth 17, 18, 146
Sinclair, May 45
Sischy, Ingrid 178
Sloan, John 185
Smith, Donald Nicholson 215
Smith, Gregory White 194, 195
Smith, Tony 197
Smithson, Robert 17
Snow, Michael 32, 147
Solomon, Solomon 45
Sontag, Susan 99
Spencer, Diana 72
Spielrein, Sabina 232
Stalin, Joseph 11–12

Stein, Gertrude 184
Stella, Frank 17, 21, 32
Stepanova, Varvara 239
Sterbak, Jana 180
Stern, Albert 37, 39
Sterne, Maurice 185
Sterry, Mrs 168
Stevens, Henry James 68
Stevens, Thomas 67–8
Stoker, Bram 245
Stone, Elisa 175–6
Storey, Helen 180
Stramm, August 56
Strand, Paul 185
Strauss, Richard 106, 107–8, 109
Swinton, Ernest 35–40, 59
Swinton, Tilda, 116
Szeeman, Harald 24

Tal, Israel 44
Tanning, Dorothea 246
Tatlin, Vladimir 16
Tauber, Sophie 239
Tavel, Ronald 174–5
Taymor, Julie 236
Templeton, Fiona 152, 153, 156
Tenant, Emma 238
Thompson, Fred 183
Thompson, Michael 65–6, 67–9
Thoré, E.-J.-T. 67
Torellli, Gioacomo 6
Toulouse-Lautrec, Henri 105, 246
Trauberg, Leonid 214
Tretchikoff, Vladimir 99
Trotsky, Leon 236
Trouhanova, Natalia 106
Turk, Gavin 141
Turner, Frederick Jackson 183
Turner, Simon 114, 116

Van Gogh, Vincent 92, 240, 246
Van Hecke, Paul-Gustave 139, 140
Van Hecke, Norine 139

Van Vechten, Carl 184
Vanegas Arroyo, Antonio 73
Vermeer, Jan 66, 67
Victoria, Queen 194
Vostell, Wolf 156

Wagner, Richard 102
Walden, Herwarth 56
Walker, James 186
Walsh, Raoul 190
Warhol, Andy 21, 31–2, 77, 95, 174–6
Waugh, Evelyn 143
Wayne, John 190–1, 197, 198, 200, 201
Weber, Max 184
Weiner, Lawrence 17, 18
Wells, H. G. 39
Wendler, John W. 17
Wendler, Robert 146
Weston, Edward 244
Wheeler, Steve 186, 196
Whistler, James McNeil 104, 111, 125, 162
White, John 197
White, Rodney 158
Wieland, Joyce 32
Wigman, Mary 111
Wilde, Oscar 103–5, 106, 108, 109, 111
Wills, E. W. 104
Wills, Garry 190, 193, 200
Wills, Helen 169
Wilson, Ian 18
Wilson, Walter Gordon 38, 39
Wimmer-Wisgrill, Eduard 162
Wittgenstein, Ludwig 28, 118, 124, 127, 221
Wodehouse, P. G. 245
Wolman, Gil 213–14
Wood, Denis 147
Wood, Grant 98
Wright, Patrick 35, 40, 41, 44–5, 47–9, 52
Wyeth, Andrew 98

Zhukov, Georgi 43
Zola, Emile 106

www.ingramcontent.com/pod-product-compliance
Lightning Source LLC
Chambersburg PA
CBHW031612210526
45464CB00004B/1535